4/89

WALTER BENJAMIN

Walter Benjamin, Paris, 1926

WALTER BENJAMIN

The Story of a Friendship

GERSHOM SCHOLEM

Translated From the German by Harry Zohn

SCHOCKEN BOOKS · NEW YORK

Acknowledgment is gratefully extended to
Karen Ready and Gary Smith for editorial research
in the preparation of this volume.

◩

All rights reserved under International and Pan-American Copyright
Conventions. Published in the United States by Schocken Books
Inc., New York. Distributed by Pantheon Books, a division of Ran-
dom House, Inc., New York. Originally published in Germany as
Walter Benjamin—die Geschichte einer Freundschaft by Suhrkamp
Verlag, Frankfurt am Main. Copyright © 1975 by Suhrkamp Verlag,
Frankfurt am Main. This translation first published in the United
States by The Jewish Publication Society of America in 1981.

Library of Congress Cataloging-in-Publication Data

Scholem, Gershom Gerhard, 1897–
Walter Benjamin : the story of a friendship.

Reprint. Previously published: Philadelphia :
Jewish Publication Society of America. 1981.
Translation of: Walter Benjamin.
Includes index.
1. Benjamin, Walter, 1892–1940—Friends and associates.
2. Authors, German—20th century—Biography.   3. Scholem,
Gershom Gerhard, 1897–   .   4. Scholars, Jewish—
Germany—Biography.   5. Scholars, Jewish—Israel—
Biography.   6. Jews—Germany—Intellectual life.
I. Title.
PT2603.E455Z8913   1988   838'.91209   [B]   88-42734
ISBN 0-8052-0870-4

Manufactured in the United States of America

CONTENTS

PREFACE

Not many people are still alive who remember Walter Benjamin with any clarity and detail. Benjamin had superficial relations with many people, but to only a few did he ever offer an insight into his person. It is greatly to be regretted that those who were close to him have written next to no memoirs. Six months after his death, I tried to induce Dora, his former wife, who probably knew him best over a period of fifteen years, to write down what she knew and had witnessed of his life and his real self, but my efforts were unfortunately not successful. Asja Lacis, who was close to Benjamin between 1924 and 1930, published some reminiscences of him in her book *Revolutionär im Beruf* [Revolutionary by profession, 1971]. To the extent that I am able to verify these, they are not exactly distinguished by reliability as far as either substance or chronology are concerned. Some of the events became disarranged greatly in the recollection of the author, who spent many years in detention camps under Stalin and thus lost all her papers.

What I am able to offer here is the story of our friendship and my testimony of Walter Benjamin as I knew him. Now and then I shall also have to talk about myself—particularly in the early pages and in some of the recorded notes and letters—whenever necessary for the understanding of this friendship.

Anyone who writes a memoir, particularly when his associate has been dead for thirty-five years, must take to heart the unmistakable warning presented to our generation by the publication of Gustav Janouch's *Conversations with Kafka*—a work of highly dubious authenticity that nevertheless was swallowed uncritically by a hungry world, a book the author published (or fabricated), along with an unverifiable explanation of the delay, only when Kafka became world famous after the Second World War. Such a memoirist must expect to be asked—particularly in a case as rife with polemics as that of Walter Benjamin—what right one has to report, paraphrase, and interpret facts that are not always supported by firsthand documentation. To be sure, much of what is reported here is based on diary entries, other notes, and numerous letters that I was able to use directly or for purposes of verification. But it is in the nature of things that for many items the memoirist cannot claim credibility except what he must believe to be his proven personal reliability and integrity. To anyone who wishes to contest that claim, these recollections will remain mute—even though (or perhaps precisely because) they are based on years of a very close association, which means that, in today's parlance, they involve the kind of "bias" of which those who interpret away without qualms are of course completely free.

Important aspects of our relationship are preserved in Benjamin's letters to me, published in the two-volume edition of his correspondence.* Many of those aspects are amplified in the present memoir, which also contains a great deal that is not mentioned or is only hinted at in the correspondence. In a considerable number of instances I have reproduced pertinent unpublished letters

*Walter Benjamin, *Briefe,* edited and annotated by Gershom Scholem and Theodor W. Adorno, 2 vols. (Frankfurt/M.: Suhrkamp Verlag, 1966). Subsequent quotations from these volumes are cited as *Briefe* 1 and *Briefe* 2. A selection of Walter Benjamin's essays is available in *Illuminations,* edited and with an introduction by Hannah Arendt, translated by Harry Zohn (New York: Harcourt, Brace & World, 1968), and in *Reflections: Essays, Aphorisms, Autobiographical Writings,* edited and with an introduction by Peter Demetz, translated by Edmund Jephcott (New York: Harcourt Brace Jovanovich, 1978). Subsequent references to these collections are cited as *Illuminations* and *Reflections*. There are also references to Gershom Scholem's collection *On Jews and Judaism in Crisis: Selected Essays*, edited by Werner J. Dannhauser (New York: Schocken, 1976).—TRANS.

from or to Benjamin in their entirety or in part. With very few exceptions, then, the excerpts from letters presented here have been drawn from the hitherto unpublished correspondence;* what exceptions there are have been unavoidable in context. Of Benjamin's approximately 300 letters to me, only 130 appeared completely or partially in the above-mentioned collection.

The present volume thus is intended to facilitate in large measure the writing of Walter Benjamin's biography, even though under present conditions this is an impossible task.

In the eight years of our personal association we naturally carried on a great many conversations whose substance I have forgotten; owing to the importance of the subject, however, or through some special concomitant circumstances, judgments, and formulations, many things became indelibly engraved in my memory. The picture of Benjamin offered here is undoubtedly very personal, shaped by the experiences and decisions of my own life. I hope it is nevertheless authentic.

Jerusalem, February 1975

*A portion of this correspondence has since been published. See note, p. 195.—Trans.

WALTER BENJAMIN

First Encounters (1915)

Before I made Walter Benjamin's personal acquaintance, I saw him in the autumn of 1913 at a meeting that took place in a hall above the Café Tiergarten in Berlin. The meeting was held jointly by Jung Juda, the Zionist youth organization to which I belonged, and the "Sprechsaal der Jugend" [Youth Forum], a discussion group composed of members of the "Jugendbewegung" [Youth Movement] founded by Gustav Wyneken. Both organizations recruited their members from the upper terms of the *Gymnasien* in Berlin, and most of Wyneken's followers also were Jews (a point that is consistently suppressed in references to this period, at least in the published accounts known to me)—although they were Jews for whom that fact was of little or no practical significance. At that meeting about eighty young people had gathered to discuss their relationship to their Jewish and German heritages. Each side presented two or three speakers; the main spokesman of the Wyneken people was Walter Benjamin, who was rumored to be their most gifted intellect. He made a very tortuous speech in which he did not reject Zionism outright but somehow relegated it to a secondary position. I cannot recall the details of the talk, but I shall never forget his manner of presentation. Without looking at the audience, he delivered his absolutely letter-perfect speech with great intensity to an upper corner of the ceiling, at which he stared the whole time. I do not recall the rejoinder made by the Zionists.

The Youth Forum was a meeting place for secondary-school and university students who were particularly disappointed by the institutions of "higher learning" and who actually aimed for much more profound intellectual revolutions. Georg Strauss, one of my fellow students who later embraced Zionism himself, vainly sought to induce me to join this group in the spring of 1914.

If one considers Benjamin's bitter rejection of his school as expressed in his *Berliner Chronik* ["A Berlin Chronicle," in *Reflections,* pp. 3–60], it is surprising to learn (as schoolmates of his have told me) that the Kaiser Friedrich School in Berlin was a decidedly progressive institution. It was a blend of *Gymnasium* and *Realschule* in which French was taught from the first year on, Latin from the fourth or fifth year, and Greek not until the sixth or seventh—the last not on the basis of grammars but directly from the text of the *Iliad.* The director of that school, Professor Zernickel, was an educational reformer. Benjamin's schoolmates included, among others, Ernst Schoen, Alfred Cohn, Herbert Blumenthal (who later changed his name to Belmore), Franz Sachs, Fritz Strauss, Alfred Steinfeld, and Willy Wolfradt (later a writer on art). These students formed a circle that met regularly to read and discuss works of literature. Fritz Strauss told me that this group regarded Benjamin as its leader and that his intellectual superiority was evident to all.

The Youth Forum not only espoused the ideas of radical educational reform but also stood for an autonomous youth culture, with Gustav Wyneken's recently published *Jugendkultur* [Youth culture] as its classic text. These ideas were propounded with much passion by the periodical *Der Anfang* [The beginning], which was edited by Georges Barbizon (a pseudonym for Georg Gretor) and Siegfried Bernfeld. It was generally known, however, that the most important essays were written by students like Benjamin, who wrote under the name Ardor. The Zionists, with their keen historical consciousness, had little use for the radically ahistorical stance of *Der Anfang.* The sociological orientation prevalent today in related undertakings of revolutionary youth was lacking in the

groups around *Der Anfang;* "youth" as such seemed to constitute
for them the guarantee of a new dawning of creation.

I did not know it when I first heard him speak, but Benjamin
by that time already had participated in several intensive discussions about Zionism, both orally and in writing, in 1912 and 1913.
Those with Kurt Tuchler have not been preserved, but the letters
he wrote to Ludwig Strauss (in 1913) have. Strauss was a schoolmate of Fritz Heinle, who played a central role in Benjamin's life
from April 1913, when he came to Freiburg from Göttingen, until
the outbreak of the war in 1914. Both Strauss and Heinle came
from Aachen, did creative writing, and were active to a greater or
lesser extent in the Freie Studentenschaft [Free Students' Associa-
tion] during their studies in Freiburg and Berlin.

When I met Benjamin, all this was past history. The First
World War had put an end to the activities of the Youth Movement.
I was then in my first semester as a university student, taking
courses in mathematics and philosophy, while outside the university I studied Hebrew and the sources of Jewish literature with at
least as much intensity. At the end of June 1915 I heard a lecture
by Kurt Hiller, whose book *Die Weisheit der Langeweile* [The wisdom of boredom] I had read. Following in Nietzsche's footsteps, so
to speak, Hiller in his lecture vehemently denounced history as a
force that was inimical to life and spirit alike. His argument seemed
totally inadequate and wrongheaded to me. History? Nonsense! We
live without history; what has all the rubbish of the millennia to
do with us? We live with the generation that was born with us! Thus
did I summarize the substance of Hiller's talk in my diary. At the
end of the lecture it was announced that there would be a discussion
of Hiller's remarks the following week somewhere in Charlotten-
burg, at the settlement house of the Freie Studentenschaft. I went
there, along with many other participants, and stood up to protest
—albeit rather clumsily—against Hiller's concept of history, thus
incurring the displeasure of the chairman, Rudolf Kayser, a friend
of Hiller's. When I faltered at one point, he simply cut me off.
Benjamin also made some remarks, and again I was struck by his
characteristic way of speaking. In fact, those mannerisms probably
arose because of his pronounced myopia, which made it difficult for
him to focus on moving groups.

A few days later I entered the catalogue room of the university library and found myself face to face with Benjamin, who looked at me intently, as though trying to remember who I might be. He left the room then but came back a short while later, made a perfect bow before me, and asked whether I was the gentleman who had spoken at the Hiller discussion. I said I was. Well, he wanted to speak with me about the things I had said, and asked me for my address. On July 19, I received the following invitation: "Dear Sir —I should like to ask you to visit me this Thursday around 5:30." Later I received a phone call changing the invitation to Wednesday.

Thus I visited Benjamin for the first time on July 21, 1915. He lived with his parents in the Grunewald section of Berlin, at Delbrückstrasse 23, on the corner of Jagowstrasse (today Richard-Strauss-Strasse). He had a large, very respectable room with many books, which struck me as a philosopher's den. At once he proceeded in medias res. He told me that he occupied himself a great deal with the nature of the historical process and had also been reflecting on the philosophy of history; that is why my remarks had interested him. He asked me to explain to him what I had meant by my statements in opposition to Hiller. Thus we were soon discussing the things that especially concerned me in those years —namely, socialism and Zionism. At that time I had already been in the Zionist camp for four years, having been led there by my recognition of the self-deception practiced by my family and the circles in which they moved, as well as by my reading of several works on Jewish history, particularly Heinrich Graetz's *History of the Jews.* At the outbreak of the war, which I rejected so completely from the beginning that I was completely untouched by the waves of emotion that were sweeping over the nation, I unexpectedly found myself in the same political camp as my brother Werner, my elder by a few years, who had already joined the Social Democratic Party but was a member of its resolute pacifist minority. In those days I read a great deal about socialism, historical materialism, and above all anarchism, with which I was most in sympathy. Nettlau's biography of Bakunin and the writings of Kropotkin and Elisé Reclus had made a profound impression upon me. In 1915, I began to read the works of Gustav Landauer, especially his *Aufruf zum Sozialismus* [Call to socialism]. I had undertaken to unite the two paths of socialism and Zionism in my own life and presented this quest to Benjamin, who admitted that both paths were viable. Of course, like every Zionist in those days, I also was influenced by Martin Buber, whose *Drei Reden über das Judentum* [Three addresses on Judaism, 1911] played a large part in the intellectual world of Zionist youth—something I hardly can understand sixty years later. Even in our first conversation Benjamin expressed strong reservations about Buber, and so struck a very responsive chord in me, because I had been particularly outraged over the positive stance Buber and his main disciples had taken toward the war (the so-called "experience" of the war). Thus Benjamin and I inevitably came to discuss our attitudes toward the war. I told him I shared the viewpoint of Karl Liebknecht, who had voted in the Reichstag against war credits since the end of 1914. When Benjamin said that he fully shared this standpoint, I told him my own story. In February 1915, I had joined a group of like-minded members of Jung Juda in writing a letter of protest against the inclusion of militant articles in the *Jüdische Rundschau* [Jewish review], the organ of the Zionists in Germany. In our letter to the editor we had outlined our own position in regard to the war, but of course under the prevailing military censorship there was no chance that this attitude would be given public expression. Copies of this letter did circulate, however, and one came to the attention of several of my fellow students at the Luisenstädtisches Realgymnasium. They informed the administration, and I was forced to leave school a year before graduation. As it turned out, I was able to enter the university on the basis of the so-called "Kleine Matrikel," which permitted young people who had completed all but a year or two of secondary school to enroll for four semesters as regular, full-time students. This regulation, devised for the benefit of the younger sons of Prussian Junkers, was not known widely, but it happened to come to my attention after my expulsion and enabled me to study at the university. Since the beginning of that year I had joined my brother in attending the clandestine meetings that the Social Democratic pacifists held in a Neukölln restaurant; at these meetings, as I recall, the major leaders of the opposition reported on the domestic situation every two weeks. Benjamin was extraordinarily taken with all this, and my reports interested him

greatly. He was eager to be active at once in this opposition group
in some way. I invited him to come to see me on the following day
and said I would show him some of their publications, particularly
the first (and only) issue of *Die Internationale,* the periodical edited
by Rosa Luxemburg and August Thalheimer; my brother and I had
participated in its illegal dissemination. All in all, our first conversation that evening lasted more than three hours.

The first thing that struck me about Benjamin—indeed it was
characteristic of him all his life—was that he never could remain
seated quietly during a conversation but immediately began to pace
up and down in the room as he formulated his sentences. At some
point, he would stop before me and in the most intense voice
deliver his opinion on the matter. Or he might offer several view-
points in turn, as if he were conducting an experiment. If the two
of us were alone, he would look me full in the face as he spoke.
At other times, when he fixed his eyes on the most remote corner
of the ceiling (which he often did, particularly when addressing a
larger audience), he assumed a virtually magical appearance. This
rigid stare contrasted sharply with his usual lively gestures.

I already have mentioned his appearance. No one would have
called Benjamin handsome, but there was something impressive
about him, with his unusually clear, high forehead. Over his forehead he had rather full, dark brown hair, which was slightly wavy
and hard to manage; later it turned grey, but he kept it to the end.
Benjamin had a beautiful voice, melodious and easily remembered.
He was an excellent reader and read very effectively when his voice
was calm. He was of medium height, very slender then and for
some years to come, dressed with studied unobtrusiveness, and was
usually bent slightly forward. I don't think I ever saw him walk
erect with his head held high. There was something unmistakable,
deliberate, and groping about his walk, probably due at least in part
to his nearsightedness. He did not like to walk fast, and it was not
easy for me, who was much taller, had long legs, and took big,
quick steps, to adapt to his gait when we were walking together.
Very often he would stop and go on talking. He was easy to
recognize from behind by his peculiar gait, which became even
more pronounced over the years. Under his forehead one immediately noticed his strong eyeglasses, which he frequently would

remove during a conversation, revealing a pair of striking, dark blue eyes. His nose was well proportioned, the lower part of his face still very gentle at that time, the mouth full and sensuous. In its as yet incomplete development the lower half of his face contrasted with the upper, which was severe and expressive. When he spoke, his face assumed a strangely reserved, somewhat inward expression. Except for the rather full mustache Benjamin invariably wore, his face was always clean shaven and slightly pink in color; otherwise his skin was absolutely white. His hands were beautiful, slender, and expressive. Taken as a whole, his physiognomy was definitely Jewish, but in a quiet, unobtrusive way, as it were. The best photos we have of him are those by Germaine Krull (1926) and Gisèle Freund (of about ten years later), all taken in Paris.

From the first, Benjamin's markedly courteous manner created a natural sense of distance and seemed to exact reciprocal behavior. This was especially difficult in my case, since by nature I tended to be anything but polite; I had been somewhat notorious since my youth because of my provocative deportment. Benjamin had nothing of the rough, flippant manner affected by most Berliners, which I had experienced often enough in my relations with childhood friends. He was probably the only person toward whom I was almost invariably polite. To be sure, in one sense I was his equal in my conversations with him. Benjamin chose his words carefully, but his speech was unpretentious and unostentatious; now and then he would lapse into the Berlin dialect with which he was not completely comfortable—not very convincingly and more by way of mimicry. He had been born and raised in the old western section of Berlin where the dialect had undergone corruption, whereas I came from Old Berlin, which meant that the dialect and mannerisms of Friedrichsgracht and the Märkisches Viertel were natural to me. When we were not discussing philosophy or theology, I liked to slip into pure *Berlinisch*, which I knew better than he. To my surprise, Benjamin would listen attentively and with good humor. When it came to speaking High German, however, I was distinctly inferior. In the course of time his speech greatly influenced me, and I adopted a good number of his mannerisms. His highest praise in those years was the word *ausserordentlich*, "extraordinary," which he always pronounced with particular intonation. A favorite critical

term was *objektive Verlogenheit*, "objective mendacity." At that
time he never used Jewish expressions; only later, under his wife
Dora's influence and mine, did he begin to employ them. To my
shame I must confess that in editing his letters I let myself be
persuaded to omit one such expression in one of his letters (*Briefe*
1, p. 381) and to insert an ellipsis in its place.

When I met Benjamin he had just turned twenty-three; I was
seventeen and a half. His "profile" thus was naturally more developed than mine. I was pursuing a definite direction, whereas he had
abandoned his path after the collapse of the Youth Movement,
which had meant so much to him, and had not yet struck out on
a new one. Neither of us knew clearly what our future would be.
Despite all we shared in common, our social backgrounds were
quite different. He came from an upper-middle-class family that had
known periods of real wealth; I came from the Jewish petty bourgeoisie, which was then on the rise and was well off but never
wealthy. Though we may not have been fully conscious of it, our
lives had taken an almost dramatically different course. It was
normal enough that the sons of assimilated families should dedicate
themselves to the German Free Students' Association, the Youth
Movement, and literary ambitions. But that such a son should
devote himself passionately to the study of the Talmud even though
he did not come from an Orthodox family, and should seek a way
to Jewish substance and its historical development, was very
unusual even among the Zionists, whose numbers in those years
were anything but small. When Benjamin was devoting himself to
the Youth Movement, I already had begun these studies. The first
time I visited him, I had decided that week to edit a journal called
Die blauweisse Brille [The blue-white spectacles] together with my
childhood friend Erich Brauer, who was a graphic artist at the time.
This journal, of which three issues appeared, was to represent the
opposition of radical Zionist youth to the war and to the Zionist
circles that had fallen prey to the psychosis of war. On my first visit
Benjamin had given me the first nine issues of *Der Anfang*. I had
seen some of them in 1914 at a fellow student's place; now I read
them through carefully, but I was not impressed. Nor did Benjamin's own essays from those years appeal to me.

One afternoon several days later Benjamin visited me for a

long conversation that brought us much closer together. When I presented my objections to *Der Anfang,* he said he had left that world that had collapsed with the outbreak of the war—especially since the most important person in it, his friend Fritz Heinle (whom he later always referred to simply as "my friend"), had committed suicide with his girlfriend a few days after the beginning of the war. I told him about the two opposition groups with which I was concerned in those days, the Zionist Jung Juda and the extreme left of the Social Democrats. Benjamin offered to attend one of the Jung Juda discussions at which I was to speak. Judaism occupied him greatly, he said, although he really did not know anything about it. I had the feeling, however, that he would not be very comfortable in that circle, so I did not pursue his suggestion further. Even in those days I was seized by bibliomania and owned a considerable library, in which he found a number of titles of great interest to him. He was interested especially in Gustav Landauer's monograph *Die Revolution,* about which I was very enthusiastic at that time. I presented Benjamin with a copy of the first issue of *Die Internationale* and lent him my copies of *Lichtstrahlen* [Light beams], edited by Julian Borchardt, the only organ of the "Zimmerwald" Socialists, which had committed itself to a strictly antiwar policy. We then had a lengthy discussion about Kant. I had been reading his *Critique of Pure Reason* in Max Dessoir's course. Benjamin said he had to confess in all honesty that he never had got past the Transcendental Deduction, which he said he did not understand. We spoke about Kant's theory of synthetic a priori judgments in relation to mathematics. To my surprise, Benjamin (who was not well grounded in mathematics) turned out to be generally familiar with Henri Poincaré's critique of that particular theory. I had been very impressed by Poincaré's discussion, but Benjamin was not convinced and introduced me instead to Schelling's solution of the problem.

Later I accompanied him to an appointment he had on Unter den Linden. He told me how he had managed late in 1914 to get himself exempted from military service as a victim of palsy. I made a note of this in my diary without mentioning any details—which, understandably, I never did in such matters, not even where my own experiences with the military were concerned. Benjamin did not tell me until a little later (when he reported this in his "Berlin Chronicle") that together with several friends from the Youth Movement he had volunteered for military service in early August of 1914 in Berlin—not out of enthusiasm for the war but to anticipate the ineluctable conscription in a way that would have permitted him to remain among friends and like-minded people. He was rejected by the recruiting board, however, and then Heinle's death changed everything for him. At the next regular call-up of his age group, which must have taken place in September or October of 1914, Benjamin presented himself (having rehearsed beforehand) as a palsy victim. He consequently was granted a year's deferment. Many years later he offered to acquaintances an embellished version of these events, but at the time of which I speak he gave me an unvarnished account of their true content.

That afternoon on Unter den Linden, Benjamin introduced me to his fiancée, Grete Radt. I could not help noticing that during our next encounters he repeatedly referred to her as "my wife." I already had noticed that he was wearing an engagement ring. Right after my introduction to his fiancée I took my leave, and I never saw Grete Radt again during Benjamin's lifetime. Fifty years later, however, she told me in Paris that this engagement had come about originally through a curious misunderstanding. She had been close to Benjamin since 1913, and in July 1914 she spent some time with him in the Bavarian Alps. Toward the end of that month his father sent him a telegram with the terse warning "Sapienti sat" [A word to the wise], presumably to induce him to leave the country for some neutral territory such as Switzerland. But Benjamin misinterpreted the message and replied by formally announcing that he was engaged to Grete Radt.

Ten days after that second conversation we again met for a few hours. The first issue had appeared of *Der Aufbruch* [The awakening], a periodical edited by Ernst Joël that soon would be prohibited because of its antiwar orientation. Joël subsequently was expelled from the university; because of the unfair procedure, this created some stir. Benjamin told me that when he had been elected president of the Freie Studentenschaft in Berlin, Joël was among those who had led the opposition against him. Joël was the head of a group whose program called for social reform, while Benjamin regarded that kind of orientation as a false solution. As evidenced by his essay "Das Leben der Studenten" [The life of students], which is based in part on his inaugural address as president, he himself advocated an intellectual "renewal." Benjamin related that he had been invited by Joël to contribute to the journal, but he had declined with a detailed explanation. He did not tell me, however, what this explanation consisted of. The first issue of *Der Aufbruch* contained articles by Gustav Landauer and Kurt Hiller, men who were ill suited to each other by nature but who had banded together in this periodical, which, so we thought, suffered from general feebleness and despite its antiwar stance lacked a definite aim. Benjamin made a very good analysis of Landauer's essay, which I defended to some extent. He praised highly the issue of *Die Internationale,* being particularly impressed by the strict objectivity of its articles. Thus the conversation turned to socialism, Marxism, the philosophy of history, and the question of what a historical work would look like if it actually were based on history. Benjamin conceded that no laws could be observed in history, but he insisted on upholding his definition of history as "the objective element in time, something *perceptibly* objective." In this he found the possibility of demonstrating such an objective factor scientifically. He admitted that he had not yet succeeded in doing so; for my part, I undertook to demonstrate the impossibility of such an enterprise. At length each of us said, Well, when you have come to the end you will admit I am right.

When I brought up Karl Lamprecht's psychological historiography, Benjamin dismissed Lamprecht and began to talk reproachingly about what he called Buber's schematized psychological philosophy of history. I thought more highly of Buber's philosophy in those days, and disagreed. Benjamin thought little of Buber's *Daniel* (1913). He told me he had had a long discussion about that book with Buber at a meeting of the Freie Studentenschaft. I had been impressed by the book and even more so by Buber's afterword to *Reden und Gleichnisse des Tschuang-Tse* [Speeches and parables of Chuang-tzu], a marvelous book with which Benjamin was not familiar; I promised to lend it to him. He told me he was working on translations from Baudelaire. As a matter of fact, on the massive desk, where I sat facing him before we began to pace up and down in the room during our arguments, lay Rowohlt's edition of *Les Fleurs du mal,* published in Paris in 1909 or 1910, an especially beautifully printed volume, as well as several volumes of the Insel Verlag edition of Hölderlin—not the version edited by Norbert von Hellingrath for the Piper publishing house, which Benjamin later used exclusively—and Crépieux-Jamin's *Graphology,* a volume that indicated Benjamin's intensive interest in this field. Next to these books lay several notepads in various formats, one of them strikingly minuscule.

On Friday evening, August 15, Benjamin invited me for supper. He introduced me to his parents and his sister Dora, who was fifteen or sixteen years old at the time. Earlier he had told me that the relationship with his family was not a happy one. On a later occasion he introduced me to his brother Georg, who later became a physician and a very active Communist. I never exchanged more than a few polite phrases with him, however. Benjamin read to me four poems from *Fleurs du mal* in his translation and in Stefan George's. He read very beautifully but not in the style of George's disciples. In all four cases I thought his translations were George's work; in two instances I was certain that Benjamin's translation was better. I told him about my translation of the Song of Songs, the first version of which I was then preparing. He called his own work child's play in comparison, saying mine was the more difficult undertaking by far. The conversation then turned to the Bible. He showed me a translation from the 1830s, edited by Leopold Zunz; he thought very highly of its style and said he often dipped into it. I told him that before visiting him I had attended the Friday evening service at the Alte Synagoge, whose strictly Orthodox liturgy greatly attracted me. I related how I had learned Hebrew and was, in fact, still absorbed in its study. When he asked how many hours I had devoted to it, I replied that I had been studying ten to fifteen hours a week—there was no other way to do it. I told him that I was studying Talmud for two or three evening hours twice a week, and this interested him very much. He wanted to know how I was going about it; I tried to explain what I found so fascinating about the reading of talmudic discussions. At that particular time a group of six or eight of us were studying the tractate about the drafting of bills of divorcement. I explained to him what form such a halakhic discussion takes: the teachers of the Scriptures approach a subject from all sides, often on the basis of variously interpreted Bible passages. To my surprise Benjamin said, "It must be something like Simmel's classes, then." At that time I knew hardly any of Georg Simmel's writings (Simmel himself already had left Berlin), and Benjamin's remark stimulated me to read some of them; I did not like them nearly as well as the Talmud, to whose mode of thought they really were closely akin. I commended to Benjamin my teacher Isaak Bleichrode, the very pious, modest, and reclusive rabbi of a small private synagogue association in our neighborhood. This great-grandson of one of the last great Talmudists of Germany at the beginning of the nineteenth century had a great gift for interpreting a page of Talmud and teaching the Jewish tradition generally. Benjamin sighed and said, "If only there were something like that in philosophy." I said, "But you studied with Rickert." (Heinrich Rickert was regarded then as one of the most sharp-witted, successful teachers of philosophy.) Benjamin said he had been disappointed in Rickert, who was indeed very sharp but lacked depth. He then showed me valuable items he had acquired for his library: Gerstenberg's *Ugolino*— Benjamin spoke of this drama in the highest terms, and lent me a copy in a later edition—and the first edition of Klopstock's *Odes,* from which in a very beautiful voice he read me a short poem, "An Cidli," declaring it to be one of the most beautiful poems in the German language ("Cidli, du weinest, und ich schlummre sicher" [Cidli, you weep and I slumber securely]). I thereupon bought myself the Reclam edition of the *Odes,* and in memory of that hour I have preserved the volume to this day. Benjamin was very fond of reading aloud; I remember hearing him read not only Baudelaire but also Pindar, Hölderlin, and Mörike. Later, in Switzerland, he read on a number of evenings from his cycle of sonnets on the death of Heinle and said he was going to write fifty such sonnets. I told him about the "fifty gates of insight," which according to the Talmud were opened to Moses, with the exception of the last; strangely enough, Benjamin was greatly taken with this.

One evening the conversation turned again to Ernst Joël's periodical *Der Aufbruch*—it had been banned in the meantime— and Benjamin rather angrily showed me a postcard from Kurt

Hiller, the "activist," with a postscript on the address side that I can visualize even now. "I've just heard that Joël has been baptized. Have you perhaps been baptized also? I have found that baptism goes hand in hand with an uncheerful cast of mind." Benjamin said, "And this on an open postcard!" When I asked him why he associated with such a tactless person, he replied that he had known Hiller for some years, since the days of the Expressionist "Neopathetisches Kabarett" [Neopathetic cabaret], which Hiller had founded in 1910, and considered him as basically a very decent person. The evaluation was hardly reciprocal, for Hiller hated Benjamin with a vengeance and expressed himself in very bitter terms on this subject in 1944, when he learned about Benjamin's death, in a letter I have before me to Erwin Löwensohn. At the time of our conversation, Hiller's anthology *Das Ziel* [The goal] was in preparation, and Benjamin already had agreed to contribute his essay on student life. When the book appeared in February 1916, I was carried away by its overt opposition to the war; I wrote a rather enthusiastic letter about it, in which I wondered how this call to revolution had got past the censor. My enthusiasm was dampened when in a letter dated March 2, 1916, Benjamin wrote: "My opinion of *Das Ziel* is completely different from yours. At most I approve of my article and Werfel's, not any of the others. I hope to be able to present my reasons for this when I see you in Berlin." Werfel's essay, ironically titled "Gespräch mit einem Staatsmann" [Conversation with a statesman], was an attack on Kurt Hiller's political philosophy, activism. Later Benjamin told me how he profoundly disliked the rationalism expressed in most of the anthology's articles, particularly those by Hiller, Ludwig Rubiner (at that time an out-and-out anarchist), and Alfred Wolfenstein. Without reaching any conclusion, we argued about Heinrich Mann's essay on Zola, which I considered very beautiful and which Benjamin rejected for reasons not comprehensible to me.

All this was yet to come, however. When we first spoke of Hiller it was August 1915, and Benjamin was planning to leave Berlin shortly for two weeks in Bad Arendsee. He promised that during his stay there he would read the book I had lent him, Buber's Chuang-tzu. The trip did not materialize until later, from September 8 to 22, 1915, because Benjamin was detained by other things that kept him busy. After his return I had three more lengthy conversations with him before his departure for Munich, where he planned to study during the following semesters. On October 1 he spoke about Hölderlin and gave me a typewritten copy of his essay "Zwei Gedichte von Friedrich Hölderlin" [Two poems of Friedrich Hölderlin], which contained a profoundly metaphysical analysis, written in the first winter of the war, 1914–15, of the two poems "Dichtermut" [Poet's courage] and "Blödigkeit" [Timidity]. Only later did I realize that this gift was a sign of his great trust in me. Hölderlin, who had been rediscovered by Stefan George and his group, was regarded by the circles in which Benjamin moved between 1911 and 1914 as one of the supreme figures in poetry. Benjamin perceived his deceased friend Heinle, whom Ludwig Strauss later described to me as "a wholly pure lyric poet," as a figure akin to Hölderlin. As was evident from Benjamin's every reference to Heinle, death had moved his friend to the realm of the sacrosanct. Yet Benjamin's notes in *Berliner Chronik* clearly reveal that there had been no dearth of major tensions between the two friends in Heinle's lifetime, even during the period immediately preceding Heinle's death. In the course of the above-mentioned conversation about Hölderlin I first heard Benjamin refer to Norbert von Hellingrath's edition of Hölderlin as well as to von Hellingrath's study of Hölderlin's Pindar translations, which had made a great impression upon Benjamin. But at the time I knew very little about such things.

On another evening we began to play chess, having discovered that we both enjoyed the game, though neither of us had much theoretical training. Over the subsequent years we played often, especially in Switzerland.

I vividly remember the night from October 20 to 21, preceding Benjamin's reexamination for military service. At his request I kept him company until morning—first conversing for hours at the Neue Café des Westens on Kurfürstendamm and then playing chess and cards ("66 to 1000," a variant of Sixty-Six, a game very popular at the time) in his room on Delbrückstrasse, while Benjamin consumed vast quantities of black coffee, a practice then followed by many young men prior to their military physicals. We were together from 9:00 P.M. to 6:00 A.M. In the Café des Westens he spoke a bit about himself and his period in the Youth Movement, a subject he normally discussed very little. That evening I heard for the first time the name of Simon Guttmann, who played a major part in the Neopathetisches Kabarett and in the circle around *Der Anfang,* to whom Benjamin after their parting made obscure references as a demonic figure. Early in 1914 Guttmann played a definite role in the rows that broke out among members of the Youth Forum, when in a sort of putsch he tried to replace the magazine's editors, Georges Barbizon and Siegfried Bernfeld, with Benjamin and Heinle. Benjamin also told me that his paternal grandmother, Brunella Meyer, then still alive, was a descendant of the van Gelderns, the family of Heinrich Heine's mother. Later I learned that the first name Brunella, which in Jewish families frequently was substituted for the Jewish name Braine or Bräunle (at least for official purposes), had been traditional in the van Geldern family since the beginning of the eighteenth century. At the time of our conversation, Benjamin still had relatives from this family in the Rhineland —in Mühlheim near Cologne, I believe. He also told me that his mother was a sister of Arthur Schönflies, then a very well-known mathematician who later became a full professor at the University of Frankfurt. Benjamin spoke about the circle of the Youth Movement only in very general terms, however, and only hinted at crises and tensions without going into detail about them. (I own some documents relating to the subject, given me mainly by Barbizon.) Benjamin only spoke about a "genius cult," which he said was practiced in that circle.

After the night described above, Benjamin was deferred for one year. I, who had just passed my final secondary-school examination as a special student before a special committee, expected to be called up for military service. As he had planned, Benjamin went to Munich—where Grete Radt also was studying—at the end of October. For a long time I did not hear from him. He did not write me again until I had been declared unfit for service by a doctor at Verden an der Aller shortly after my call-up; I had written him early in December about my release and the resumption of my studies. But Benjamin was very worried that the censors might open the mail and was afraid that I might be rash enough to make incriminating political statements. "There is no c[ensorship] between Berlin and Munich," he wrote me, "yet *every* [underlined twice] bit of *prudentia* is indicated. I beg you to bear this in mind."

Growing Friendship
(1916–1917)

At the beginning of March, Benjamin informed me that he would return around the fifteenth of the month and that we then could discuss in greater detail the questions I had raised in my letters about Plato (several of whose writings I was reading at the time) as well as the critical reflections on mathematics that I had made.

I anticipated great things to come from these discussions and wrote in my diary: "When one has been reflecting about certain matters for a long time, one cannot help but be uplifted by the prospect of such inspiring and reverent company. I cannot talk about these things with [Erich] Brauer or anyone else, for that matter; nor can I discuss my Zionist interests with the Zionists— a truly depressing fact for both parties. . . . Instead I have to go to the non-Zionist and nonmathematician Benjamin, who has sensibility where most of the others no longer respond." I have only few memories, however, of the several conversations we had when he was in Berlin from April 9 to the end of the month.

When Benjamin went to Munich, intending to work there in seclusion, he hoped to find Ludwig Klages, whose writings on graphology, as he mentioned in passing, had attracted him greatly. Benjamin learned that Klages was not there; as we now know, he had left for Switzerland two months earlier because he too was in complete opposition to the war. The almost fourteen months that Benjamin spent in Munich had a decisive influence on the next years of his life. Spring brought the dissolution of his engagement to Grete Radt and the beginning of his liaison with Dora Pollak, who lived at Seeshaupt on Lake Starnberg, in the villa of her (very rich) husband, from whom she separated in the course of that year. Dora, originally from Vienna, was the daughter of the well-known Anglicist and Shakespeare specialist Professor Leon Kellner, a pioneer Zionist who acted as editor and literary executor for the Zionist writings and diaries of his close friend Theodor Herzl. She thus had grown up in a Zionist environment; later she strayed far from it and, after her marriage to Max Pollak, joined the Youth Movement in Berlin. In the Berlin Youth Forum she played a major role, though her participation was primarily social in nature. As a child Dora had attended school in England for a year and had an excellent command of English; she was very musical and played the piano, but her greatest talent lay in her ability to absorb, appropriate, and keenly respond to anything she deemed important. Her speech was very animated, with strong Viennese inflections; she had a knack for stimulating conversations or steering them around to different subjects. A member of the Youth Forum who had lived near the Pollaks told me that he and many others in their circle were greatly impressed by Dora and a little in love with her. Some of Benjamin's published letters from that period (1914) testify to her concern for Benjamin and what was then an amicable relationship with him. In April 1915, when she was living at Seeshaupt, she took a trip to Geneva with Benjamin in order to visit his childhood friend and schoolmate Herbert Blumenthal, who was a close friend of both for a long time and had taken an active part in the Youth Movement. Blumenthal was a British subject; a few months before the outbreak of the war he had gone to England, presumably for further training as a graphic artist, and after the beginning of the war he had moved to Switzerland and married Carla Seligson, with whom Benjamin had been friendly in 1913 and 1914. From time to time the two men were drawn to each other. There are letters from Dora to Blumenthal that give detailed accounts of the tensions in the Youth Movement in the spring of

1914 and prove that even then she had recognized Benjamin as the outstanding mind of the movement. In the middle of May 1915, however, she parted company with Benjamin—in order to "save her life," as she put it in one letter. They did not resume their association until early in 1916.

When I reflect on what it was we had in common after these first encounters, I can cite a few things that are not to be overlooked easily. I can describe them only in general terms as a resoluteness in pursuing our intellectual goals, rejection of our environment—which was basically the German-Jewish assimilated middle class—and a positive attitude toward metaphysics. We were proponents of radical demands. Actually, at the universities the two of us did not have any teachers in the real sense of the word, so we educated ourselves, each in a very different way. I cannot recall either of us ever speaking of our university teachers with enthusiasm, either then or later; if we had praise for any of them, they were eccentrics and outsiders—for example, one of Benjamin's teachers, the philologist Ernst Lewy, and Gottlob Frege, whose course I took in Munich. We did not take the philosophy teachers very seriously; perhaps we were too presumptuous in this. I was very disappointed in Ernst Cassirer's course on Greek philosophy before Plato, which I took in the winter semester of 1916–17; Benjamin, who did not think highly of Alois Riehl, induced me not to enroll in his seminar on Kant's *Prolegomena,* which I had intended to take. He quoted a pun that was then making the rounds about Riehl and another full professor, Carl Stumpf: "In Berlin ist die Philosophie mit Stumpf und Riehl ausgerottet worden" [In Berlin philosophy has been destroyed root and branch, *Stumpf und Stiehl*]. In those years he spoke of Heinrich Rickert without any respect, though he did concede that he was a man of considerable acuity. On the basis of this judgment alone I studied one of the later editions of Rickert's *Der Gegenstand der Erkenntnis* [The object of knowledge]. We followed our stars without academic guides. During a discussion of Franz von Baader's writings, which we had in Switzerland—if I remember correctly, the only collected philosophical works in Benjamin's library at that time, aside from Plato, were those of Baader —we tried to imagine what must have been the level of the students who were able to follow lectures of such flights of the imagination and such profundity. At that time I had just read Baader's *Vorlesungen über die Theorie des Opfers nach Jacob Böhme* [Lectures on the theory of sacrifice according to Jacob Böhme] and mentioned this work. Benjamin found Baader more impressive than Schelling; he told me that in his Freie Studentenschaft period the only thing he had read by Schelling, aside from Schelling's arguments with Kant, was the collected *Vorlesungen über die Methode des akademischen Studiums* [Lectures on the methodology of university studies].

Ernst Lewy came up in our conversations on April 16 when I told Benjamin that I had acquired a secondhand copy of Steinthal's edition of Wilhelm von Humboldt's *Sprachphilosophische Schriften* [Writings on the philosophy of language]. My attention had been drawn to this book by my reading of Fritz Mauthner's *Beiträge zu einer Kritik der Sprache* [Contributions to a critique of language], on which I was trying my skill at the time. Benjamin was very surprised; he told me that in an earlier semester he had participated in Ernst Lewy's course on Humboldt's philosophy of language and had been particularly impressed by the introductory lecture. Ernst Lewy had asked one of the relatively numerous students present to read a long passage from an edition of these writings—it may have been Steinthal's—and then asked, "Do you understand that? I don't." With this and similar remarks he managed to irritate and drive off most of the class, so only a small number returned for the second lecture, Benjamin among them. Then Lewy said, "All right, we've gotten rid of the plebeians. Now we can begin." The rest of the course was very interesting. Benjamin told me the story of the rather extraordinary scandal at Lewy's *Habilitation* [qualification for teaching at a university] at the University of Göttingen. He had fulfilled all other requirements but was denied his appointment, the *venia legendi*, on the basis of his public "trial lecture" (normally a pure formality) on the subject "Zur Sprache des alten Goethe" [The language of the old Goethe]. In that lecture Lewy had undertaken to substantiate his thesis that in Goethe's later writings there was a shift in linguistic character from Indo-European to Finno-Ugric, the latter being the subject of Lewy's special research. The Göttingen professors regarded this as sacrilege as far as Goethe was concerned, and Lewy was not granted *Habilitation* until some time later, when he offered a more innocuous subject at the University of Berlin. Benjamin pulled out the pamphlet containing that inaugural lecture and lent it to me. (I later bought a copy for fifty pfennigs.) In his preface the author alludes to the Göttingen incident only in an altogether veiled, noble-minded sentence.

Associating with Benjamin was fraught with considerable difficulties, though on the surface these seemed insignificant in view of his consummate courtesy and willingness to listen. He always was surrounded by a wall of reserve, which could be recognized intuitively and was evident to another person even without Benjamin's not infrequent efforts to make that area noticeable. These efforts consisted above all in a secretiveness bordering on eccentricity, a mystery-mongering that generally prevailed in everything relating to him personally, though it sometimes was breached unexpectedly by personal and confidential revelations. There were primarily three difficult requirements. The first was respect for his solitude; this was easy to observe, for it was dictated by a natural sense of limits. I soon realized that he appreciated this respect, a sine qua non for associating with him, and that it heightened his trust. The observance of the second requirement was particularly easy for me: his utter aversion to discussing the political events of the day and occurrences of the war. Some reviewers of the *Briefe* expressed astonishment at the fact that the published letters contain no reference to the events of the First World War (which, after all, so decisively influenced our generation) and blamed the editors (I was the one responsible for this period) for an incomprehensible omission or, worse, censorship. The fact of the matter is that in those years anyone who wished to have a closer association with Benjamin either had to share this attitude (as I did) or respect it. As I have stated, we did discuss our basic attitude toward the war, but concrete events were never mentioned. Particularly between 1916 and 1918 the subject was tacitly excluded without any prior discussion; Benjamin's letters from those years authentically reflect this state of affairs. The third requirement, that of overlooking his secretiveness, often demanded a real effort, because there was something surprising, even ludicrous, about such secretiveness in someone as sober, as melancholy as Benjamin. He did not like to give the names of friends and acquaintances if he could avoid it. When circumstances of his life were mentioned, there frequently was attached an urgent request for absolute secrecy; more often than not this made very little sense. Gradually, but even then only partially, this secretiveness (which by that time others had noticed as well) began to dissipate, and Benjamin began to speak of people without the accompanying stamp of anonymity, at least when he had initiated the discussion. It was in keeping with this aversion that he tried to keep his acquaintances separate; for a time this was more effective with me, who came from another environment—Zionist youth—than it was with those from the same sphere as he, namely members of the German-Jewish intelligentsia. Only occasionally did it turn out that we had mutual acquaintances, such as the poet Ludwig Strauss or the philosopher David Baumgardt. Other friends and acquaintances of his I did not meet until years later, from 1918 on, some of them only after 1945. In short, then, to associate with Benjamin took a great deal of patience and consideration—qualities that were by no means natural to my temperament and that, to my own surprise, I was able to muster only in my association with him.

Added to this was the immediate impression of genius: the lucidity that often emerged from his obscure thinking; the vigor and acuity with which he experimented in conversation; and the unexpectedly serious manner, spiced with witty formulations, in which he would consider the things that were seething within me, as alien as my main concerns—the urgency of my Zionist convictions and the problems arising from my mathematical-philosophical studies—must have been to him. He was nevertheless a very good listener, though he himself liked to talk often and at length. He assumed that the person he was conversing with had a much higher level of education than was actually the case. Whenever I said that I was not acquainted with something, Benjamin went wide-eyed with astonishment. He asked very good and usually surprising questions. In 1915 he could not learn enough about Germany's share in the outbreak of the war, so I obtained for him a few pamphlets that were being disseminated illegally by left-wing Social Democrats and that contained evidence of the warmongering attitude of Austria and Germany. Benjamin was by no means a "pacifist by conviction," as he has been called elsewhere. His refusal to have anything to do with this particular war did not stem from any pacifist ideology; that simply was not his style. Later we hardly discussed those things. Another thing that was striking about him was his extraordinary sensitivity to noise, which he often referred to as his "noise psychosis." It really could disturb him. Once he wrote me: "Do other people manage to have peace and quiet? I'd like to know the answer to that."

I visited Benjamin only twice while he was in Munich. In the summer of 1916, on the advice of a physician, I did not study at the university but instead spent a considerable period of time in Heidelberg. From there I went via Munich to the Allgäu region, hiking part of the way to Oberstdorf, where I stayed until the end of August. From June 16 to 18 I was together with Benjamin in Munich and Seeshaupt, although I did not meet Dora at that time. He lived in a relatively small room near the English Garden in Munich, at 4 Königinstrasse. From there I accompanied him to Seeshaupt, where he was going to see his friends—he did not name them; I stayed there overnight at a hotel. In the meantime, the first issue of Buber's periodical *Der Jude* [The Jew] had appeared; we both strongly disliked the leading essays, although I thought the second issue was quite good. We had a long discussion on Jewish affairs, for Benjamin had been invited to become a contributor to *Der Jude* and wished to discuss his response with me. He had written me to Heidelberg as follows: "I had planned—and this is intended only for you personally—to address an open letter to Buber concerning *Der Jude*. Now I am not sure whether I shall postpone this until I have spoken with you." The letter evidently was meant to be polemical in nature, but the one he actually wrote was greatly toned down. During our conversation I received the impression that he "has found his way to Judaism, and it probably won't be long before he realizes that it is necessary for him to study Hebrew." I told him a great deal about my continuing Jewish studies. According to notes I made at the time, "Naturally, he cannot and will not contribute to *Der Jude,* because, as I surmised correctly in a conversation with Buber [on a visit to Heppenheim in May, when Buber told me about his invitation to Benjamin], his present position really precludes any literary activity. At the moment he is bound to damn the very founding of such journals, quite apart from his objections to this particular periodical [i.e., its lack of objectivity and its wordiness]." Benjamin was especially angered by Buber's own essay and one written by Hugo Bergmann. On the other hand, he regarded as excellent a long essay that had been translated from the Hebrew. It was by A. D. Gordon, an agricultural worker in the *kvutzah* Dagania and a central figure in the early *kibbutz* movement.* Gordon was a Tolstoyan who sought to put the master's teachings into practice; at the same time, however, he was a man deeply committed to traditional Judaism, and between 1910 and 1922 his essays exerted a great influence on the early socialist settlements in Eretz Yisrael.

As a result of our conversation, early in July 1916 Benjamin wrote the memorable letter to Buber, which appears on pp. 125–28 of the first volume of the *Briefe*.

At Oberstdorf I received Benjamin's invitation, in the name of his friends, to visit Seeshaupt for three days. There I was put up in the Pollak villa and given the fictitious explanation that Max Pollak happened to be out of town; in reality the Pollaks were in the process of getting divorced. I was enjoined not to tell a soul about the location of my visit. Benjamin and I met in Munich. He told me that on account of his impending military reexamination he was not taking the trip he had written me about earlier. He expected to go to Berlin for that examination the following week and suggested that I stay at Seeshaupt until then, if possible. He told me that long ago he had given up reading newspapers and was kept posted from Berlin on matters concerning him. That morning at the library he once again had looked through periodicals—the *Weisse Blätter*, the *Zeit-Echo*, the *Neue Merkur*, and the like—and it had struck him that while their contributors were no longer writing as they had on August 1, 1914, the gulf between them and the events was the same as it had been on the first day of the war. To put it another way, the difference between those "radicals" and newspapers like the *Lokalanzeiger*, the *Berliner Tageblatt*, and "Tante Voss" [the *Vossische Zeitung*] had remained utterly constant. On Sunday evening we set out for Seeshaupt in a pouring rain that did not let up until the eve of my departure. With the exception

---

*A *kvutzah* is a smallish communal settlement erected on socialist principles; a *kibbutz* is one consisting of a larger number of people.

of a single half-hour's walk, I spent the whole visit in the Pollak house. On the way Benjamin told me that he was very pleased with the long letter I had written him about his essay on student life, which had been published in *Das Ziel*. We spoke about the necessity of studying Kant, something he deeply cared about, and in a curious shift of topic we discussed the new journal *Das Reich*, which was published by Rudolf Steiner's followers. (He had lent me the first issue during my previous visit in June.) Several of the very esoteric essays in that magazine had impressed him. He told me that earlier in the year he had met Max Pulver, with whom he shared an interest in Franz von Baader and in graphology. Then we trudged through the rain for another half hour to the house, where I inhabited a luxurious, beautifully appointed room on the first floor; Benjamin and the lady of the house, who was waiting for us in the music room, slept in far less luxurious rooms on the second floor. Dora was a decidedly beautiful, elegant woman; she had dark blonde hair and was somewhat taller than Benjamin. Her attitude toward me was amicable and sympathetic from the start. She participated in most of our conversations with much verve and obvious empathy. In short, she made an excellent impression upon me. I understood the situation at once: the two of them openly displayed their affection for each other and treated me as a kind of co-conspirator, although not a word was said about the circumstances that had arisen in their lives. Benjamin's engagement ring, however, had disappeared from his hand. Dora told me about the Zionist atmosphere in her parents' home, mentioning that her siblings were Zionists and she was the only one who kept aloof. That evening we had a long conversation about Zionism until one in the morning. Benjamin read me the letter he had written to Buber; it was, incidentally, never answered, although Buber made an angry remark about it when we met once in the winter of 1916. Later Buber supported Benjamin whenever he could—in the Jerusalem matter, for example—but the two men were simply of different temperaments. Benjamin told me that a few weeks after writing his letter to Buber, in which he furnished a detailed exposition of the functions of language and silence, he had found a passage on language in Friedrich Schlegel's *Philosophie der Geschichte* [Philosophy of history] that said, albeit in different terminology, exactly what he had intended to express in his letter.

The next morning Benjamin showed me the very beautiful library, which contained Schwab's 1846 edition of the works of Hölderlin, Bothe's Pindar translation of 1808, Voss's translation of Horace, and all sorts of other things, including much philosophy. On the floor lay Ernst Mach's *Erkenntnis und Irrtum* [Cognition and error], which Dora was going to sell because, she said, it really didn't amount to anything. When I urgently appealed to her to sell it to me, she said she would present it to me as a gift to the guest of the house on the occasion of my visit, as long as her husband had no objection (an absolutely fictitious condition). And in fact later she did just that. Benjamin pitied me for my poor taste; in those days he despised pragmatism for its antimetaphysical position, whereas I, who had read William James's book in German translation, saw it as important. Benjamin read aloud an ode by Pindar in Hölderlin's translation and in the original Greek. Then I read my essay "Jüdische Jugendbewegung" ["Jewish Youth Movement," in *Jews and Judaism in Crisis*, pp. 49–53], which I had written in Oberstdorf for Buber's *Der Jude*—a sharp polemic attacking the lack of radicalism among Zionist youth. "I think it is very good," said Benjamin after a long pause. Then he and Dora reproached me severely for demanding too modest an honorarium, saying that I should not behave so childishly. "To be in the possession of truth is sufficient justification for one's claim to a living," said Benjamin. Actually, I did not even know whether *Der Jude* paid for contributions at all, and I did not care. In the second issue of *Der Jude* an essay by Hillel Zeitlin, who really came from the center of the Hebrew world, met with Benjamin's approval. But in general his objection was that the journal did not deal with the substance of Judaism—the Torah, the Talmud, and the Prophets —but simply took all this for granted. Besides, he felt, every article it published somehow presupposed Zionism and desired to improve and develop it. This is why he so liked my article, which opposed the prevailing tendencies and demanded that substance be accorded primary importance among us.

During our entire stay together we spoke a great deal about Judaism, and for the first time the question arose whether it was one's duty to go to Palestine. Benjamin criticized the "agricultural

Zionism" that I championed, saying that Zionism would have to wean itself of three things: "the agricultural orientation, the racial ideology, and Buber's 'blood and experience' arguments." I agreed with him that not only agricultural workers or farmers should be permitted to go to Palestine, rather that it might be all right to have an entirely different occupation. At that time, and for the next seven years, I myself considered going there as a schoolteacher. In the face of Benjamin's critique of Buber I praised the writings of Ahad Ha'am (whom he had never heard of) and some of Ahad Ha'am's essays on the nature of Judaism, which I lent him in a German-language selection toward the end of 1916. Most of all we discussed Buber, whom Benjamin criticized in sharp terms. He was not entirely unjustified when he told me in parting that if I should run into Buber I should hand him a barrel of tears in our names. He said that Buber personally had struck him as a man who lived in a permanent trance, somewhere very much removed from his own self, a "dual ego"; this state was shown most profoundly in an essay entitled "Das Gleichzeitige" [The simultaneous], which had appeared in the *Zeit-Echo*. Benjamin was especially harsh in his rejection of the cult of "experience," which was glorified in Buber's writings of the time (particularly from 1910 to 1917). He said derisively that if Buber had his way, first of all one would have to ask every Jew, "Have you experienced Jewishness yet?" Benjamin tried to induce me to work into my article a definite rejection of experience and Buber's "experiencing" attitude. I actually did so in a later essay, as Benjamin had greatly impressed me in this matter. What I told him about Ahad Ha'am, on the other hand, especially his view of the role of righteousness in Judaism, made a great deal of sense to him. In this connection he defined righteousness as "the will to make the world the greatest good." We argued about Buber from various points of view. Benjamin said that Buber represented feminine thinking. In contrast to Gustav Landauer, who once said the same thing about Buber in an essay by way of praise, Benjamin meant it as a condemnation. We also discussed the question of whether Zion was a metaphor; at that time I answered in the affirmative, for only God was not a metaphor, but Benjamin denied it, asserting—and thus leading us into a conversation about the prophets in the Bible—that if one recognized the authority of the Bible one must not use the prophets metaphorically. Finally we read together the speech of Socrates in Plato's *Symposium,* and Benjamin discussed the peculiar doubling of the Greek gods and the curious fact that so many ancient Greek deities (such as Ananke=Necessity) apparently can be transformed directly into an idea. Benjamin read us some excerpts from a few pages he had written about Socrates (I made a copy for myself later), in which he propounded the thesis that Socrates was "Plato's argument and shield against myth."

On the next day the conversation turned to Hegel—our first discussion of Hegel that I can recall. Evidently Benjamin had read only a few things superficially and was no great admirer of Hegel at that time. As much as a year later he wrote me: "What I have read of Hegel thus far has definitely repelled me." He called Hegel's "mental physiognomy . . . that of an intellectual brute, a mystic of violence, the worst kind there is: but a mystic for all that" (*Briefe* 1, p. 171). Yet he came to Hegel's defense when, during the same conversation, I made some presumptuous remarks about the speculative philosophy of nature, which greatly offended my mathematical soul even as it impressed my mystical soul. Benjamin was totally unmoved by this and regarded the courage shown by Hegel and Schelling rather as admirable, precisely in terms of the risk of the *deductio ad absurdum* that they took. (For the same reason, he later had the highest praise for J. W. Ritter's *Fragmente aus dem Nachlass eines jungen Physikers* [Fragments from the estate of a young physicist.]) He turned to Pollak's shelves, took down the *Phenomenology of Mind,* and read a few sentences at random, including this one: "The nervous system is the immediate stability of the organism in its process of movement." I laughed. Benjamin gave me a severe look and said that he could not regard the statement as all that meaningless. Extemporaneously, without any preparation and with no knowledge of the context in which Hegel had used these concepts, he presented a lengthy, vigorous interpretation and defense of the sentence he had read. I have forgotten the tenor of his words, but Benjamin's stance as a defender of Hegel made a great impression upon me. I also remember a definition of action and a passage from G. C. Lichtenberg cited by Hegel, according to which it is folly to separate a man from his actions.

During a discussion of whether Hegel had wished to deduce the world we turned to mathematics, philosophy, and myth. Benjamin accepted myth alone as "the world." He said he was still not sure what the purpose of philosophy was, as there was no need to discover "the meaning of the world": it was already present in myth. Myth was everything; all else, including mathematics and philosophy, was only an obscuration, a glimmer that had arisen within it. I responded that in addition to myth there was mathematics—until the great differential equation had been found that would express the world, or, more probably, until it was proved that there could be no such equation. Then myth would be justified. Philosophy, I said, was nothing independent, and only religion broke through this world of myth. I denied that mathematics could be part of myth. Benjamin's decided turn to the philosophic penetration of myth, which occupied him for so many years, beginning with his study of Hölderlin and probably for the rest of his life, was manifested here for the first time and left its mark on many of our conversations. In this connection, at this early date Benjamin spoke of the difference between law and justice, calling law an order that could be established only in the world of myth. Four years later he elaborated on this idea in his essay "Zur Kritik der Gewalt" ["Critique of Violence," in *Reflections*, pp. 277–300]. Benjamin must have been familiar around this time with the writings of Johann Jakob Bachofen and also must have read the works of the ethnologist Karl Theodor Preuss on animism and preanimism; he repeatedly referred to the latter's statements on preanimism. This brought us to the subject of ghosts and their role in the preanimistic age. Here Benjamin spoke at length about certain of his own dreams in which ghosts had played a major role— for example, the motif of the large, empty house in which ghosts would float and dance around, particularly at the window.

Later I made a detailed, critical study of these conversations, since, as I wrote at the time, "if I really want to go along with Benjamin, I shall have to make enormous revisions. My Zionism is too deeply anchored in me to be shaken by anything." I also made this notation: "The word *irgendwie* [somehow] is the stamp of a point of view in the making. I never have heard anyone use this word more frequently than Benjamin." Of course, everything we had been speaking about was closely bound up with his interest in the philosophy of history. We discussed that subject for a whole afternoon, in connection with a difficult remark of his to the effect that the succession of the years could be counted but not numbered. This led us to the significance of sequence, number, series, direction. Did time, which surely was a sequence, have direction as well? I said that we had no way of knowing that time does not behave like certain curves that demonstrate a steady sequence at every point but have at no single point a tangent, that is, a determinable direction. We discussed the question whether years, like numbers, are interchangeable, just as they are numerable. I still possess a record of that part of the conversation, having written in my diary: "Benjamin's mind revolves, and will long continue to revolve, around the phenomenon of myth, which he approaches from the most diverse angles: from history, with Romanticism as his point of departure; from literature, with Hölderlin as the point of departure; from religion, with Judaism as that point; and from law. If I ever have a philosophy of my own, he said to me, it somehow will be a philosophy of Judaism."

Benjamin had just received a present from Dora: a marvelous edition of Balzac's *Contes drolatiques* with the magnificent fantastic illustrations by Gustave Doré. I spent an evening leafing through that book. In his room there was also a very fine French edition of Flaubert's *Bouvard et Pécuchet*. Benjamin praised the *Catalogue des opinions chics* and said Flaubert was utterly untranslatable.

During my visit we played chess several times. Benjamin played blindly and took forever to make a move; as I was a much faster player, it was virtually always his turn. I lost one game, in which Dora and he joined forces against me.

I might also mention here that even in those days Benjamin was very fond of reading mystery novels, particularly the German translations brought out by a Stuttgart publisher, of American and French detective classics like those of Maurice A. K. Green, Emile Gaboriau *(Monsieur Lecoq),* and—when he was in Munich—Maurice Leblanc's stories about Arsène Lupin, the gentleman burglar. Later he read a great deal by the Swedish author Frank Heller, and in the thirties he added the books of Georges Simenon, which he highly recommended to me in his letters, although with the reservation that they had to be read in French to be appreciated. Strangely enough, he never seems to have said the same about Proust, perhaps because he thought that the translations he and Franz Hessel had made did full justice to the original, or possibly because my French was not good enough for such reading. He told me about the rather careful list he was keeping of books he had read; his literary estate includes that list, from 1915 on, and it teems with titles of detective novels.

I have no doubt that the breakthrough and change in our relationship from acquaintance to friendship beginning in the summer of 1916 had much to do with Dora, to whom he had spoken about me. I originally had invited him to come see me in Oberstdorf. Dora later confided in me that the counter-invitation to come instead to Seeshaupt, which brought us together completely contrary to Benjamin's habit, had been accomplished at her initiative. She said that his report about my passion for Judaica had primarily aroused her interest.

Benjamin stayed in Munich until about December 20, 1916. There, under the Americanist Walter Lehmann, he had already started his studies of Mexican culture and religion of the Mayas and Aztecs in the summer semester—studies closely connected with his mythological interests. In these lectures, which were attended by few people and by hardly any regular university students, Benjamin became acquainted with the memorable figure of the Spanish priest Bernardo Sahagún, to whom we owe so much of the preservation of the Maya and Aztec traditions. Benjamin had a brief encounter with Rilke in Munich between the middle of November and December. He was full of admiration as he told me about Rilke's politeness—he whose Mandarin courtesy constituted the utmost that I could imagine. Some time later, in Berlin, I saw Molino's big Aztec-Spanish dictionary on Benjamin's desk; he had bought it in order to learn the Aztec language, but he never carried out this project. Remembering Benjamin's accounts of the atmosphere in the lectures, I was impelled to attend Lehmann's course when I went to Munich in 1919. Under his direction I read Aztec religious hymns, and I can still recite many of them in the original.

In Munich, Benjamin could have met Franz Kafka, who gave a reading of his story "In the Penal Colony" there on November

10, 1916. Unfortunately Benjamin missed that opportunity, and I sometimes have speculated on what an encounter between these two men might have meant.

In our conversations at Seeshaupt, Benjamin said that he saw his future in a lectureship in philosophy. Under the impression of our conversations I made this notation: "If some day Benjamin lectures on philosophy in a substantial way, not a soul will understand him, but his course could be tremendous if there were true *questioning* instead of label-sticking." (This last remark was aimed at Cassirer's lectures.) Around that time I wrote a rather long letter to Benjamin about the relationship between mathematics and language, and submitted a number of questions on the subject. His long reply to me, which he broke off in the middle, was later reworked into his essay "Über Sprache überhaupt und über die Sprache des Menschen" ["On Language As Such and the Language of Man," in *Reflections*, pp. 314–22]. He handed me a copy in December 1916 upon his return to Berlin, designating it as the first part, to be followed by two more. He had been ordered to take another military physical and had returned about a week ahead of time. On the evening of December 23 I spent a long time with him, and he told me about Erich Gutkind (1877–1965), the author of the mystical book *Siderische Geburt* [Sidereal birth, 1912], whom he had met a few months earlier. Gutkind, an extremely zealous but highly educated man from a totally assimilated family, had begun to take an enthusiastic interest in Judaism. Benjamin had told him about me and now he extended an invitation in Gutkind's name. He said to me, "You're just what this man needs." I told Benjamin that I would want him to be present, and thus on one of the following days the three of us had a conversation in a café and again discussed Jewish matters. For a long time Benjamin took a very sympathetic interest in Gutkind; in the early twenties he had close contact with him and his wife. I, too, frequently visited the Gutkinds at their house in the Berlin suburb of Nowawes, and in 1917 I gave them Hebrew lessons for a while. (Gutkind later almost became an Orthodox Jew.)

I again spent the entire evening and the greater part of the night with Benjamin before his physical examination. We ate with his family, and later I slept on the chaise longue in the living room, where a large Christmas tree stood, following the tradition observed in many liberal Jewish families. I knew that custom from my own childhood and complained to Benjamin about what I regarded as outright bad taste on the part of the milieu from which we came. He gave me the same excuse I had heard from my father when I had attacked him once for the same reason: that even his grandparents celebrated Christmas as a "national festivity." That same evening Benjamin told me about his studies in Munich, where he had written two long seminar papers for philosophy lecturers, one of them for the phenomenologist Moritz Geiger, with whom I took a course on the philosophy of mathematics in 1919–20. Benjamin hoped to return to Munich after his examination. On December 28, however, he was classified as *feldarbeitsverwendungsfähig* [fit for light field duty]. Although this did not involve the bearing of arms, Benjamin was very agitated by the news, as he told me on the telephone the next day; because I was about to leave for Halle, where my brother Werner was on military duty, I could not join him right away. Upon my return I learned that Dora meanwhile had arrived from Seeshaupt and that Benjamin had received an order to report for duty on January 8, 1917. He fell ill, supposedly with sciatica, and did not report as ordered. The Gutkinds and I wrote to him, offering our company. Then Dora told me by phone that he had received another order to report for duty on January 16. On January 12 he sent me the following note, written on a single sheet of paper that was folded three times and crammed into a tiny envelope, like a conspiratorial message being smuggled out of jail:

I thank you and the Gutkinds for your kind offer. I am still laid up with a severe attack of my sciatica, but I have received another order to report for duty (this time for Tuesday). Unfortunately, due to severe neuralgic spasms my current state is such that to my great regret I cannot receive any visitors at all. So I must decline with many thanks your kind offer of availability. You will be kept informed without fail about my condition. P.S. Please pardon the envelope!

I met with Dora, and she revealed to me in the strictest confidence that she was using hypnosis—to which Benjamin was very susceptible—to produce sciaticalike symptoms, thus making it possible for the doctor to give him a certificate for the military authorities. A medical committee came to Delbrückstrasse for an investigation, and Benjamin was actually given a few months' deferment. The sciatica story was kept up, and Benjamin remained incommunicado to everyone but Dora. I did not see him again until February. He remained in Berlin until April 17, and I visited him on a number of occasions.

At that time he read the *Neunzehn Briefe über Judentum* [Nineteen letters on Judaism] by Samson Raphael Hirsch, a basic text of Jewish Orthodox theology in the German language; *Rome and Jerusalem* by Moses Hess, one of the classical texts of Zionism; and several essays by Ahad Ha'am. In those days I was no great admirer of the writings of Theodor Herzl, so I gave him these books, which had made a deeper impression on me. We also had a long discussion about the identity problem, on which he had produced written theses in 1916.* Because of these and other conversations, he never gained me as a partner for the Japanese board game Go, as he had proposed. He evidently had begun to play this game with Dora, who was a bad chess partner and was easily offended when she lost. Benjamin claimed that Go was the oldest known game. At that time he also explained to me that his books were divided into a "first" and "second" library, with the former containing only writings that he deemed of primary importance. I remember that this section contained not a single work by Schiller, though it did include the volume called *Schillers Gespräche* [Conversations of Schiller], edited by Julius Petersen and published by the Insel Verlag. Benjamin called this volume "extraordinary" and "the only means of access to Schiller." Only from that book, he said, could one learn that Schiller was really a human being of the highest order. In fact, it was true that the road to Schiller was almost impassable for many of our generation. Even later, when we were together in Bern, Benjamin would read to Dora and me the Romanticists' derisive remarks about Schiller, having picked them out like raisins from their writings, which he was reading during the preliminary studies for his dissertation. In this way I became acquainted

*My earlier reference to these papers (in *Briefe* 1, p. 139, n. 3) stands corrected here.

with an item that Benjamin presented with much enjoyment: Karoline Schlegel's letter describing the reading of Schiller's poem "Die Glocke" [Song of the bell] in the Romanticists' circle at Jena, a reading that drew tears of laughter from all those present.

Benjamin's deep, inner relationship to things he owned—books, works of art, or handcrafted items, often of rustic construction—was evident. For as long as I knew him, even during my last visit with him in Paris, he loved to display such objects, to put them into his visitors' hands, as he mused over them aloud like a pianist improvising at the keyboard. During the months I am writing about I noticed on his desk a Bavarian blue glazed tile, depicting a three-headed Christ; he told me that its enigmatic design fascinated him. In time he gradually added to his collection various small figurines and pictures, mostly reproductions. Even then a print of Mathias Grünewald's Isenheim Altarpiece hung on the wall of his study, where it would remain for many years to come. In 1913 as a student he had made a special trip to Colmar to see the original. His notes from those years often refer to the Isenheim panels; he was overwhelmed by what he called *das Ausdruckslose*, their quality of expressionlessness. In the twenties he was apt to offer philosophical reflections as he brought forth a toy for his son. Once he brought along from Moscow a silver dagger over which he launched forth with reflections on terror that were only half ironic. In his room in Paris hung a tattoo artist's large pattern sheet that he had acquired in Copenhagen. He was particularly proud of this item and regarded it on the same plane as children's drawings and primitive art.

In those three months I did not see as much of Benjamin as would have been possible under normal circumstances. From early February on I had major family problems of my own, with the result that on March 1, 1917, I left my parents' home for six months, found lodging with a Russian-Jewish friend in a boarding house on Uhlandstrasse that was inhabited almost exclusively by Russian Jews, and sought to earn a living by giving Hebrew lessons and translating a rather large book from Yiddish and Hebrew. In the meantime Benjamin and Dora informed me that they were going to be married, and they invited me—the only nonrelative, as I recall—to the family celebration on Delbrückstrasse following the ceremony on April 16. On that occasion I met Dora's parents. I was then a great admirer and collector of the writings of Paul Scheerbart, and as a wedding present I gave them my favorite book, Scheerbart's utopian novel *Lesabéndio,* which is set on the planetoid Pallas and, with Alfred Kubin's drawings, presents a world in which the "essential" human qualities have undergone complete transformation. This was the beginning of Benjamin's conversion to Scheerbart; three years later he made this book the subject of a major essay, "Der wahre Politiker" [The true politician], which unfortunately has not been preserved.

In the months preceding Benjamin's marriage I occupied myself for some time with the attempt to translate into Hebrew portions of his study of language, which was very close to my heart; this included motifs from our conversations in Seeshaupt. Benjamin insisted that I read the first pages of my translation to him and Dora so that he might hear how his sentences sounded in the *Ursprache,* as he put it half-jokingly. That period marked the beginning of his interest in Franz von Baader, to whom Max Pulver had drawn his attention in Munich, and in Franz Joseph Molitor, who was a pupil of Schelling and Baader and the only serious German-language philosopher to study the Kabbalah, having devoted forty-five years to it. Between 1827 and 1857 Molitor published anonymously, as an introduction to a projected presentation of the Kabbalah, four volumes under the memorable title *Philosophie der Geschichte oder Über die Tradition* [Philosophy of history, or on tradition]. Although this work quite groundlessly sought to give the Kabbalah a Christological orientation—its author belonged to the liberal wing of the German Catholics—the book is still worthy of attention. I had begun to read it early in 1915, and in our conversations I repeatedly alluded to it; I also told Benjamin that three volumes of the work still were available from the publisher. These were our first conversations on the Kabbalah; at that time I was still far from a study of its sources, but I already felt an obscure attraction to that world. Shortly before his wedding Benjamin ordered the works of Baader and Molitor's book, although these did not arrive until after the wedding. By that time he and Dora had left Berlin and gone to a sanatorium in Dachau that specialized in sciatica; there Benjamin, aided by Dora, finally managed to obtain a medical certificate that enabled him to leave for Switzerland.

In mid-June 1917 I had been inducted into the infantry stationed at Allenstein, where I took energetic measures to get out of the army so that I would not have to participate in a war that I completely opposed. In May and June, Benjamin and I exchanged several more letters, some before and some after my induction. I also sent him a new translation of the Song of Songs that I had done and informed him about my situation in the army. Two of Benjamin's letters to me are contained in the published selection from his correspondence; I shall add here two more. The first was written not long before his departure for Switzerland, the second a few days after his arrival in Zurich.

On June 30 he wrote me from Dachau, of course without putting the full truth on paper:

Dear Herr Scholem

You will expect a critique of your new translation in this letter, but unfortunately I cannot supply it at this time because the turmoil of packing fills the room. Finally something decisive is to be done for the paralysis and the pain that have sapped my strength completely in recent days. The doctor insisted on a month's stay at a spa in Switzerland; despite the difficulties this entails at present, we received our passports yesterday. If one can demonstrate a need, people are considerate and friendly—probably more so toward invalids—and the strict border control that I now have glimpsed for the first time is clearly necessary.

Rumors are busily circulating here that there will be peace in September. I should like to ask a favor of you. Herr Werner Kraft, a medical orderly at the Reserve Hospital, Ilten near Hannover (that is the complete address), is greatly interested in my study of language. My own copy is one of the few manuscripts I shall probably be permitted to take along to Switzerland—i.e., I have submitted only a small number for clearance (since one is permitted to take only a small number) and hope those will be approved. Please be good enough to send your copy of my study to Herr Kraft on loan.

About the Song of Songs in my next letter, which I hope to write you from Switzerland if no difficulties arise. My first stop there shall be Zurich, since I cannot possibly make the trip without a break. My address there will be the Savoy Hotel; after receipt of this letter, please use that address until further notice. By the same mail I am sending you the notebook with the identity theses; please take good care of it until you receive further instructions.

Kindest regards from my wife and myself. We think of you and hope the best for you. I cannot write to the Gutkinds before our departure and so ask you to give them our most cordial regards.

Yours,
Walter Benjamin

This morning I received your letter from Allenstein. I am terribly sorry that Mr. Gutkind's language teacher is in such bad shape. In his condition one cannot do much more for him than harbor hope, try to forget the serious and very sad aspects, and think of him. Please be assured that we are doing so. In a few days you will receive a postal money order for 30 marks, and if you have his address, please forward the money to him. If his malady ever involves extraordinary expenses, please ask him to contact us.

How are you? I am sending the notebook with the identity theses to Allenstein; if you are unable to keep it there please send it to Herr Werner Kraft by registered mail. I doubt whether you will be able to send him the study of language under these circumstances, but please do so if it is possible. / Today I can't write you about my studies but hope to be able to do so soon.

Again, kindest regards from my wife and me.

From Munich I received the key to a secret code for any delicate communications to be sent to Switzerland, along with a cover letter from Werner Kraft, expressing his surprise at the incomprehensible text of the letter that was addressed to him but evidently was meant for me. Dora had written as follows:

Dear Herr Kraft:

I just finished the Geschichte des 30. j. Krieges [*History of the Thirty Years War*]*, which you so warmly recommended to me. I find the book very good and shall write you more about it shortly. I am also familiar with Ricarda Huch's detective novel, but I think the "old-fashioned" ones by Green are better, although you criticize them* *for containing "unwieldy" cryptograms. You are mistaken if you think that the cryptogram is a recent device, for there is a cryptogram in* The Count of Monte Cristo, *and in the Middle Ages entire systems existed—putting numbers in place of words according to a key, for example, or letters instead of words, or numbers instead of letters. In fact, I recently read about systems so ingenious they do not look like secret writing but appear harmless to the uninitiated. For instance, every third word is meaningful; the others are simply fillers but so intelligently arranged that the sequence as a whole also seems to make sense. The kind my husband and I find most* brilliant *is based on a change in the key number: for example, 42345, which means first the fourth word, then the second, then the third, then the fourth, then the fifth, then the fourth again; then some other number, e.g., 4684, etc. The new key number, of course, always would be indicated unobtrusively. You have no idea how inexhaustible people were in such matters. Madame de Staël, for instance, wrote in this manner to her gentleman friend in Provence.*

My husband sends his best regards and soon will write in greater detail. He asks you to keep his letters, especially those of special *importance; he will make a* special *request regarding their preservation. (He may publish them in another form at a later date.)**

He will send you the publication date of Schiffer's *work tomorrow.*

        Best regards,
        Dora Walter

This letter marked the beginning of my friendship with Werner Kraft, to whom I later wrote letters from the military hospital on the meaning of Benjamin's study of language.

About a week later Benjamin and Dora went to Switzerland. They met Herbert Blumenthal and Carla Seligson in Zurich, with whom on July 9 and 10 they permanently broke off relations. This was partly because of tensions between Dora and Carla, but primarily because Benjamin laid claim to unconditional intellectual leadership, to which Blumenthal henceforth would have to subject himself. Blumenthal refused, and this meant the end of a friend-

---

*This paragraph actually was addressed to Kraft, to whom Benjamin was writing long letters on literature at the time. Unfortunately these have been lost.

ship of long standing. A despotic trait in Benjamin was evidenced here, which according to the accounts of a number of his acquaintances from the Youth Movement erupted not infrequently in those years, sharply contrasting to his usual civil conduct. I myself witnessed this trait on only two or three occasions, and even then in greatly attenuated form. In the Zurich incident there must have been a wish on Benjamin's part to cut off as far as possible his relations with friends from the Youth Movement, which for him were passé. The radical side of his nature, which seemed to conflict so sharply with the courtesy and patience he showed in interpersonal relationships, did not shrink from thoughtless and unthinkable breaches. Shortly after his birthday and the aforementioned incidents he wrote me at Allenstein:

Dear Herr Scholem:

We are very grateful to you for keeping us posted on how you are getting along and beg you to keep on doing so. We hope that you will continue to make the best of everything. I gratefully accept your good wishes on my [twenty-fifth] birthday. From my wife I received a number of beautiful books that do my library proud: for instance, an old edition of Andreas Gryphius, an edition of Catullus Tibullus Propertius from the Richardi Press in London that my wife was able to obtain in Germany, and very good French books: Balzac, Flaubert, Verlaine, Gide. And then there are many other things here with which one can decorate a birthday table.

Regarding the philosophical notebook in your hands, you must bear in mind that all other entries antedate the identity theses by at least a year, most of them probably by three or four years. There will be some childish things among them—for example, the scheme whereby K in the margin means Kunst [art] and R, Religion. One thing important to me, though it may require a different form and some elaboration, is the note in which I tried to clarify for myself the concept of original sin. About the shekhinah [divine presence] I cannot copy out anything for you at this time; the Baader is still in Germany, along with the major part of my library; little more than the "first library," almost complete, is here with me and will look even better because of the new gifts. . . . What do you hear about Mr. Schlechtmann's [Gutkind's] language teacher? Do you ever see him? If you do, tell him that the year of publication of Schiffer's book that he asked me about in connection with my letter concerning Ricarda Huch is 1526. Perhaps he can write me sometime./ As regards your family situation, it is probably impossible to counsel you from this distance. . . .

We shall go on to the Engadine very soon. Until you receive a new address, write us here, soon and often. We often think of you and are with you in our most heartfelt wishes.

On July 31 he wrote me from St. Moritz when I was already in the psychiatric section of the military hospital, where I had been sent for observation of my "mental condition," and where I was in the process of successfully trying to prove my unfitness for military service. I had asked Benjamin to contact Dr. Charles Meyer, a Swiss physician whom I knew and who was favorably disposed toward me, discreetly outline my situation, and perhaps obtain a certificate from him. I had given him Dr. Meyer's name as that of a physician who had treated me on an earlier occasion.

Dear Herr Scholem—

It has been a long time since we heard from you and you from us. We arrived here a week ago and have spent our time in this beautiful countryside in marvelous weather. Now the weather seems to be worsening, and the lake outside my window—a wonderful mountain lake—is of a garish green color, as before a storm. To the extent that my malady permits, we take walks and are having a good rest. For my birthday I received Regis's Rabelais translation, and I am familiarizing myself with it a bit before I tackle the French text. / My wife wrote to Herr Meyer yesterday. . . . Even if I am not able to work here for the time being, I do quite a bit of thinking, about which you will soon hear something. In the meantime we hope you are all right. Write us very soon and accept my wife's and my cordial regards every morning.

P.S. How is your father doing?

On August 18, when I was still at the hospital in Allenstein, reading in his notebook and writing him frequently—among other things a protest against his note on original sin—he and Dora wrote me as follows:

Dear Herr Scholem

Some external reasons kept me from writing earlier, but if I had had any news about myself to report, they would not have stopped me. The immediate motivation of this letter is my receipt of yours of July 31 as well as the two succeeding cards; despite the sad news about your health their contents have pleased my wife and me like little else. Our life here is devoted entirely to rest and the restoration of our strength. I shall not start my real work until the fall; by then I hope to have received the most important books. It is still uncertain at which university I shall enroll. I am reading a few things here. Thus I have begun to concern myself with Calderón's dramas. I have read Maurice de Guérin and Rimbaud. There is also an aesthetic question that occupies me at present: I am trying to trace back to its source the difference between painting and the graphic arts. This leads to very fundamental relationships, and, incidentally, in this connection the identity problem arises anew. Unfortunately the weather is very changeable, and when the sun is not shining, it is cold. We have had a few splendid excursions however; in particular we went as far as the Swiss-Italian border at the Val Bregaglia, in the southern Alps, where we breathed wonderful air and saw an absolutely pure sky. Up here in the Engadine there are the most beautiful flowers, and at high altitudes they have a wonderfully delicate scent.

I am sorry that I cannot go into your critical remarks about my notes on original sin, for I no longer clearly remember them. I wrote them down five years ago, and it is certain that in places they would no longer conform with my present views.

We may stay here for a while longer; then I shall go to Bern and Zurich. Where we are going to spend the winter will be determined from there.

As my wife will have something to add to this letter I shall close with heartfelt wishes for the future, including the flourishing of your domestic affairs. Please write me soon how you are getting along and what you are thinking.

Yours
Walter Benjamin

Below, in Dora's handwriting, was this addition:

Dear Herr Scholem,
I, too, send you my best regards and many wishes for your well-being. I suppose you also have heard about Mr. Gutkind's language teacher; we are indescribably happy for and with him. Give him our regards when you write him. We have not received any logarithms. The publication date of Schiffer's book is 1526. Herr Meyer answered our letter most charmingly—a man of honorable character.

As ever yours,
Dora Benjamin

Benjamin's reference to the difference between painting and the graphic arts, which he planned to trace to its source, evidently indicates the seed of the reflections, then still grounded entirely in metaphysics, that Benjamin in 1935 presented in his celebrated essay "Das Kunstwerk im Zeitalter seiner technischen Reproduzierbarkeit" ["The Work of Art in the Age of Mechanical Reproduction," in *Illuminations,* pp. 219–44] in a more fully developed way and in a form that had undergone Marxist metamorphoses.

Although the military doctors had diagnosed my case as dementia praecox, I was sent back to Berlin in the last week of August as "temporarily unfit for duty" and "on leave until discharged" but with the permission to wear civilian clothes again. I informed Benjamin; he wrote expressing his great joy, suggesting that we be on a first-name basis, and inviting me to join him and Dora in Bern. Our respective experiences with the military contributed greatly to the intensification of our friendship, as may be clearly discerned from Benjamin's letters to me between September 1917 and April 1918. Thus during the period from summer 1916 to May 1918, our friendship was cemented steadily and without any setbacks reached its zenith after my arrival in Switzerland. The published letters give rather detailed information about the matters that occupied us at that time. It was then that Benjamin's tendency toward microscopic handwriting began to unfold fully, abetted by the restrictions imposed by censorship on the length of letters. After examining and rejecting all other possibilities, particularly that of taking a doctor-

ate under the direction of Karl Joël in Basel, he had decided to
work toward his degree under Richard Herbertz in Bern, who was
a rather colorless man and for that very reason suited Benjamin.
In the meantime I was studying mathematics and philosophy at
Jena, where I worked very intensively, spent much time in reflection, and not only wrote Benjamin detailed reports about all that
but also plied him with numerous questions. We urged our favorite
books on each other. Benjamin not only wrote about such books
but also repeatedly sent me lists of books; I tried to obtain them
for him at a reduced rate through my father's printing firm, which
included a publishing house. For example, I induced him to read
a few books by Anatole France that I thought highly of; of these,
Thaïs and *La révolte des anges* made a great impression upon him.
Among the things I owe to Benjamin is my acquaintance with the
grotesque tales (a literary form that became impossible after Hitler
and is virtually inaccessible today) of Mynona, particularly the
volume entitled *Rosa die schöne Schutzmannsfrau* [Rosa the beautiful policeman's wife], an unsurpassed work in this genre that
almost knocked me off my chair with laughter at the time; unfortunately, I can read it today only with utter indifference. The philosophical background of these tales engaged Benjamin's attention
and then led him to a great appreciation of Mynona's magnum
opus, *Schöpferische Indifferenz* [Creative indifference], published
under the author's real name, Salomo Friedländer. Friedländer was
an orthodox Kantian as well as a strict logician and moral philosopher in theory, but in practice he was, if anything, the prototype
of a cynic, or at least he wore that mask. Since the days of the
Neopathetisches Kabarett he had been acquainted with Benjamin,
who frequently spoke of him in rather positive terms. Friedländer
was one of the most prominent personalities in the Expressionist
circle, which he himself tended to regard with amusement. Another, similar work that Benjamin recommended to me—one that
is completely forgotten today—was Louis Lewy's strange book *Die
Menschenzwiebel Krzadok und der frühlingsfrische Methusalem*
[Krzadok the human onion and spring-fresh Methuselah], a "detective story" without any point, a hidden metaphysics of doubt. Quite
differently motivated was Benjamin's great appreciation of Alfred
Kubin's *Die andere Seite* [The other side], a novel that delved deep

into the occult (with illustrations by the author), about which Benjamin once whispered to me, "I have experienced similar things in
my dreams." When I was in Jena, he asked me to procure for him
a volume published in the series of the Bavarian Academy of
Sciences, Max Grube's *Chinesische Schattenspiele* [Chinese shadow-
plays], one of the least known and yet most magnificent achieve-
ments of sinology. Benjamin grew wide-eyed when he spoke of this
book, but strangely enough he seems never to have written anything about it. I sometimes wondered whether Benjamin might
have acquainted Brecht with this wonderful volume, for Grube's
dramas, which range from a waiter's monologue to mystery plays
deeply rooted in the Buddhist tradition, are closely related to
Brecht's artistic philosophy.

In those days I wrote Benjamin a great deal about the "mathematical theory of truth," which I was speculating about. A letter
from Dora dated November 12 had to do with this theory and their
desire that I join them in their new living situation:

Dear Herr Scholem,

*I have wanted to write you for a long time and describe to you
the external aspects of our situation, but this is the first chance I have
to do so. (Walter is attending a course on Baudelaire; I have stolen
his desk lamp and made myself comfortable.) Walter always has
faithfully described to you the inner side or the coordinates of the point
relevant to us of that famous curve that is to represent the mathematical
theory of truth. I can only assure you that said curve passes quite close
to Bern and often is glimpsed briefly on clear days. All the more urgent
is the necessity to come to poor Walter's aid with suitable, i.e., male,
eyes. Or, to put it quite plainly: Come as soon as possible, or you will
incur the undying hatred of a cheated posterity. Living conditions, or
the high cost of living (probably the only thing that may seriously keep
you away), are not nearly as bad as you may think. The 64 centimes
that one now gets for a mark have a buying power of one and a half
or two marks. Then, too, you must not forget that our household,
modest though it may be, would indeed be a source of conveniences
and savings for you.*

*We are doing splendidly. The only thing we lack is company (at
this point may one suggest that you reread this letter from the begin-*

ning). But we do have a very nice acquaintance, a musician. Books we expect in the near future. Walter already has started his regular work; mine will have to wait awhile (a detective novel). Theater has been unpalatable so far, concerts very fine. I must close. Come very soon, then; we live quite close to the railway station, and if you write us in advance, we shall even pick you up! With many cordial regards,

Yours,

Dora Benjamin

Philosophy in Jena was rather annoying to me. I despised Rudolf Eucken, who looked unbelievably formal and spoke that way as well. After one sixty-minute lecture by him I stopped attending the course. Bruno Bauch's lectures, on the other hand, were mandatory and, to the extent that they dealt with Kant, of interest to me, for I read a great deal on Kant during that half-year. Bauch's great monograph on Kant had just appeared; it betokened the author's alienation from Hermann Cohen, which soon thereafter assumed such bitter form. I was greatly moved by Kant's *Prolegomena,* and I remember writing a long letter to Benjamin about my impression of this book. In a tutorial with Bauch I also read part of *The Critique of Judgment,* especially the introduction, "On Philosophy As Such," which made a lasting impression on me. Then, too, in the course of the semester I became acquainted with the polemic against Cohen, initiated by a lady, in the journal *Kant-Studien,* which betokened a nationalistic and mild but unmistakable anti-Semitic orientation on the part of certain neo-Kantians. On the positive side, I was drawn to two very dissimilar teachers. One of these was Paul F. Linke, an unorthodox pupil of Husserl, who induced me to study a major portion of Husserl's *Logische Untersuchungen* [Logical investigations], about which Benjamin had only an indistinct impression from his Munich period. The other was Gottlob Frege, whose *Grundlagen der Arithmetik* [Foundations of arithmetic] I was reading along with related writings by Bachmann and Louis Couturat (*Die philosophischen Prinzipien der Mathematik*). I attended Frege's one-hour lectures on "Begriffsschrift" [interpreted logical calculus]. At that time I was greatly interested in mathematical logic—ever since I had discovered Schroeder's *Vorlesungen über die Algebra der Logik* [Lectures on algebraic logic] in a secondhand bookshop in Berlin. These and similar attempts to attain a pure language of thought greatly fired my imagination. The logic of Hermann Lotze, which we read in Bauch's major seminar, left me cold. For my seminar paper I wrote a defense of mathematical logic against Lotze and Bauch; the latter listened to it in silence. The linguistic-philosophical element of a conceptual language wholly purged of mysticism, as well as the limits of the latter, seemed clear to me. I reported to Benjamin about this, and he asked me to send him my seminar paper. In those days I fluctuated between the two poles of mathematical and mystical symbolism—much more so than Benjamin, whose mathematical talent was slight; he was then and for a long time to come an adherent of mystical views of language.

As for Frege, who was almost as old as Eucken and like him wore a white beard, I enjoyed his utterly unpompous manner, which so agreeably contrasted with Eucken's. But in Jena hardly anyone took Frege seriously.

In November 1917, Benjamin sent me a copy of his notes on Dostoevski's *The Idiot,* written that summer, which moved me as much as my response moved him. I had written him that behind his view of the novel and the figure of Prince Myshkin I saw the figure of his dead friend. On my twentieth birthday I received a short letter from Benjamin, in which he wrote as follows: "Since receiving your letter I often have found myself in a festive mood. It is as though I have entered a holiday season, and I must celebrate with reverence the revelation in that which has made itself known to you. For it simply is the case that what has reached you and you alone must have been addressed to you and has entered our life again for a moment" (*Briefe* 1, p. 157). These lines, and my reaction to them in a lengthy diary entry, bear witness to a strongly emotional moment in our relationship, a relationship that presented itself to us in greatly heightened fashion. Owing, among other things, to his complete seclusion and the tenor of his utterances, Benjamin's figure had assumed a prophetic proportion in my eyes; this was given expression in letters I wrote at the time to contemporaries in my Zionist circle of friends, as well as in some notes I made. In March 1918, I wrote him a letter in which I compared the six years of his life from 1912 to 1918 with mine, whose focus I found in "learning"—in the specific sense that the word *lernen* has in Yiddish rather than in German linguistic usage. At the same time I sent him the new translation of the biblical Lamentations that I had made, in addition to writing a treatise entitled "Über Klage und Klagelied" [On laments and lamentations]. For my birthday Walter and Dora gave me two photos of them made in Dachau, in which he looked very serious and she beautiful. I conducted imaginary dialogues with these pictures in Jena, where they stood on my desk. A letter from Dora to me on December 7 revealed that Benjamin wrote his study "Über das Programm der kommenden Philosophie" [The program of the philosophy of the future] in November 1917, in elaboration of ideas contained in a (printed) letter to me of October 22 (*Briefe* 1, pp. 149–51). The copy of this essay in Dora's handwriting that Benjamin handed me on my arrival in Bern had originally been intended as a birthday present for December 5. Dora wrote: "For many days I worked from early to late copying a study by Walter, in order to give you some pleasure; now the tyrant won't permit me to send it off because there is supposed to be a sequel." This sequel did not materialize, however, until March 1918.

I also recall a strange coincidence. At some earlier date Benjamin had told me about the mathematician Robert Jentzsch, of the circle around Georg Heym, who also published poems in Expressionist journals; Benjamin described him to me as the only example he had ever encountered of a perfect dandy. I thereupon attended Jentzsch's *Habilitation* in 1916 in order to see what a perfect dandy looked like, although this was complicated by the fact that Jentzsch appeared in an officer's uniform. One day early in April 1918, in the reading room of the Jena Volkshaus, I read the death notices of Hermann Cohen and Jentzsch, the latter having fallen in action. The next day I received a letter from Benjamin asking whether I had heard anything of Jentzsch, in whom he said he took a great interest.

On January 14, 1918, I was reexamined in Weimar and discharged from the army as "permanently unfit for duty; not to be examined further." This made it possible seriously to consider steps that would lead to my departure for Switzerland, something that was particularly difficult to arrange at that time. The arrangements could not be completed until mid-April, and in the meantime I received a letter from Benjamin notifying me of the birth of his son Stefan. When I sent my congratulations, I wrote, somewhat rapturously: "Your marriage is the most beautiful miracle taking place before my eyes."

At that time Benjamin also arranged for Werner Kraft, with whom I meanwhile had become good friends, to send me for safe-keeping the papers he had been unable to take along to Switzerland. I had them for only a short time. I read some of those notes, which have since been lost, among them a diary of the trip to Paris that Benjamin took at Pentecost 1913 with Kurt Tuchler, as well as detailed notes about a celebration of the Freie Studentenschaft in spring 1914, which seemed to me very characteristic of the atmosphere in that circle.

At the beginning of April, Linke suggested that I take my doctorate under his direction with a dissertation on the philosophical foundations of mathematical logic. At that time it was possible to take a doctorate of philosophy after six semesters. But these and other plans came to naught when toward the end of April I received a passport for Switzerland on the strength of a certificate from the district medical officer.

Switzerland (1918–1919)

I arrived in Bern on the evening of May 4, 1918. Benjamin met me at the station, and we spent a few hours nearby in his apartment on Hallerstrasse. Thus began a long period of intensive companionship and joint studies as well as disturbances, reservations, and arguments. Now that we had resumed our personal association, our relationship could not remain as idyllic and harmonious as it so rapidly had become during the preceding year. For example, a letter that Benjamin wrote me from Locarno on February 23 contained a particularly cordial passage about our relationship, which so impressed me that a short time later I was capable of speaking of a "prestabilized harmony in which our lives are coordinated with each other" as the fundamental factor that regulates my life. I soon had to recognize that this was not so, and I was to pay for my youthful extravagance. But the calm tone of our letters provided reason enough for such errors. Our letters reflected neither the passions that were agitating me nor my conflicts with my brother Werner, who saw his ideal in political demagogy, nor, on Benjamin's part, the problems of his existence.

A few weeks after my arrival, our relationship was subjected to heavy strains for the first time, and not for the only time that

year. The expectations each of us had set up for this period, each
from his own point of view, were excessive. I expected something
prophetic of him, a figure that would be absolutely outstanding not
only intellectually but morally as well. As it soon turned out,
following my military experiences and the ensuing correspondence
between us, Walter and Dora harbored very great expectations for
my understanding of his world—yet I could not meet these all that
uncritically (I almost said: undialectically). Above all, however, the
basic reason for these tensions was not so much a conflict of ideas
(as in our later conversations and letters about Benjamin's turn to
Marxism—which Benjamin was later to remember as "fiery arguments") as it was our different characters. This expressed itself in
our attitudes toward pragmatic questions concerning the conduct of
one's life and our attitudes toward the bourgeois world (money
matters, attitudes toward our parental homes, relations with people,
and the like). On a number of occasions there were stormy scenes
that easily might have ended catastrophically without Dora's loving
intercession. The conflict in which I found myself was a moral one.
For me Benjamin's ideas had a radiant moral aura about them; to
the extent that I could intellectually empathize with them, they had
a morality of their own, which was bound up with their relationship
to the religious sphere that at that time was quite clearly and openly
at the vanishing point of his thought. Juxtaposed with this, however, in Benjamin's relationship to things of daily life there existed
a strictly amoral element that I could not come to terms with,
although he attempted to justify it by his contempt for the bourgeois world. Many of his and Dora's reflections on such matters
elicited my protest. Thus violent arguments were precipitated on
a number of occasions, sometimes quite abruptly, in which we
clashed because we made different moral decisions. There was
about him an element of purity and absoluteness, a devotion to the
spiritual like that of a scribe cast out into another world, who has
set off in search of his "scripture." It was a crisis for me when in
close contact with him I had to recognize the limitations of this
element. Benjamin's life did not have that enormous measure of
purity that distinguished his thought. I was too young, and it did
not help to tell myself—as I often did—that the same thing could
be said of all of us who were unable to extricate ourselves from

entanglements in external circumstances and had to pay a price for the fact that, in the confusion of those years, we sought to leave inviolate for ourselves a realm that these circumstances could not penetrate. It began to be apparent to me that although Benjamin and Dora recognized the supremacy of the religious sphere of revelation (and for me this was still tantamount to the acceptance of the Ten Commandments as an absolute value in the moral world), they did not feel bound by it; rather, they undermined it dialectically, where their concrete relationship to the circumstances of their lives was concerned. This was first revealed during a long conversation about the question to what extent we had a right to exploit our parents financially. Benjamin's attitude toward the bourgeois world was so unscrupulous and had such nihilistic features that I was outraged. He recognized moral categories only in the sphere of living that he had fashioned about himself and in the intellectual world. Both of them reproached me for my naiveté, telling me that I let myself be dominated by my gestures and that I offended with an "outrageous wholesomeness" that I did not have but that had me. Benjamin declared that people like us had obligations only to our own kind and not to the rules of a society we repudiated. He said that my ideas of honesty—for example, where our parents' demands were involved—should be rejected totally. Often I was utterly surprised to find a liberal dash of Nietzsche in his speeches. What was strange about all this was that such arguments, no matter how vehemently they were conducted, often ended with particular cordiality on Benjamin's part. After one such tempest, both he and Dora were of an "almost heavenly kindness," and when Benjamin saw me out, he clasped my hand for a long time and looked deep into my eyes. Did he feel that he had carried his heated formulations too far? Was it a desire not to lose the only human being other than Dora who was spiritually and physically close to him in those days?

In this connection I should like to say that Benjamin was at bottom anything but a cynical person, and this probably had something to do with his deep-rooted messianic faith. To be sure, he regarded the bourgeois world with considerable cynicism, but even this did not come easily to him. Beyond this realm the cynical element was lacking completely. When matters of substance were involved—in religion, philosophy, and literature—there was no trace of cynicism in Benjamin. His anarchism had nothing to do with cynicism, and in the years of our closest relationship "intellectual orders" was to him a concept that completely excluded this sort of thing. Yet he was not lacking in admiration for the rare authentic utterances in which cynicism and profoundly serious intellectuality were combined. I observed this in him particularly in three instances: his admiration for Flaubert's *Bouvard et Pécuchet,* though there it was probably the author's contempt for bourgeois mendacity that he found to his liking; his admiration for Mynona; and perhaps also his admiration for Ferdinand Hardekopf. In the case of Mynona I found it easy to go along with him, but I lacked the requisite feeling for Hardekopf.

When there was fair weather between Walter and Dora—soon after my arrival, while waiting in an adjoining room, I became an involuntary witness to noisy scenes—they were incomparably tender toward each other and unabashedly affectionate in my presence. There were many words in a private language that I did not understand—pet names and the like. A particular favorite was the word *Ekul,* which in contrast to *Ekel* [disgust, disgusting person] was used in a highly positive sense. In Dora's parlance Walter was "loving Ekul," while I, in the summer of 1918, managed to attain "pious Ekul." Dora was at that time full-bosomed and tending toward the Junoesque, very passionate in nature with a quick temper that produced hysterical outbursts, although she also could be irresistibly charming and affectionate. In my many conversations with them we seldom discussed erotic or sexual matters. This was all the more striking in those years in Switzerland because Dora certainly did not shun such subjects and often broached them, although Benjamin did not participate particularly much. For years, however, he stubbornly expounded the strange thesis, to me and to others, that there was no such thing as an unhappy love— a thesis that was so decisively refuted by the course of his own life.

In those years—between 1915 and at least 1927—the religious sphere assumed a central importance for Benjamin that was utterly removed from fundamental doubt. At its center was the concept of *Lehre* [teaching], which for him included the philosophical realm but definitely transcended it. In his early writings he reverted repeatedly to this concept, which he interpreted in the sense of the original meaning of the Hebrew *torah* as "instruction," instruction not only about the true condition and way of man in the world but also about the transcausal connection of things and their rootedness in God. This had a great deal to do with his conception of tradition, which increasingly assumed a mystic note. Many of our conversations—more than may be perceived from his written notes —revolved about the connections between these two concepts. Religion, which is by no means limited to theology (as, for example, Hannah Arendt believed in writing about his later years), constituted a supreme order for him. (The terms *Ordnung* [order] or *geistige Ordnung* [intellectual order] were among his most frequently used in those years. In the presentation of his own thought it usually took the place of "category.") In his conversations of the time he had no compunctions about speaking undisguisedly of God. Since we both believed in God, we never discussed His "existence." God was real for Benjamin—from his earliest notes on philosophy to letters written in the heyday of the Youth Movement to his notes for his first projected *Habilitation* thesis on the philosophy of language. I am acquainted with an unpublished letter on this subject to Carla Seligson, dated June 1914. But in these notes, too, God is the unattainable center of a system of symbols intended to remove Him from everything concrete and everything symbolic as well. Although in his Swiss period Benjamin spoke of philosophy mostly as the doctrine of intellectual orders, his definition, which I took down at the time, extends into the religious sphere: "Philosophy is absolute experience, deduced in the systematic-symbolic context as language." Thus it is a part of the "teaching." The fact that he later abandoned this specifically religious terminology, although the theological sphere remained very close and alive to him, is not in contradiction to this.

Before I came to Switzerland he had read, in addition to works by Stifter and France, the entire three fat volumes of Harnack's *Dogmengeschichte* [History of dogmas] straight through. This work had an enduring and not entirely favorable effect on his view of Christian theology; it had at least as much influence on his decided aversion to Catholicism in particular as his many conversations with me had on his inclination toward the world of Judaism, abstract though the latter remained.

Shortly after my arrival Benjamin and Dora took me along to
a piano recital by Ferruccio Busoni, who played Debussy in a small
hall. It was a "social" event by Bernese standards. It was the only
time I saw the Benjamins at that sort of function, both very ele-
gantly dressed and bowing in all directions. Dora's father had
recommended Benjamin to his close friend Samuel Singer, professor of Middle High German at the University of Bern, and from
time to time they were invited to his house along with a few
professors. The summer term had just started, and even before
formally registering I immediately started to attend a few courses
together with Benjamin. We went to Richard Herbertz's "Introduction to Critical Realism," and Benjamin remarked that its real
content was the insight that wooden iron was an impossibility.
These lectures, as well as others by Paul Häberlin and Harry
Maync's course on Romanticism (in which, according to Benjamin,
"falseness was covered up by kitsch"), were very dreary. But
because he needed these three courses for his doctorate in philosophy, psychology, and the history of German literature, and was in
particular required to participate in the seminars, he asked me to
keep him company at least in the lectures. Out of boredom we often
played a game involving the compilation of lists of famous men
according to a letter of the alphabet. Benjamin attended Paul
Häberlin's seminar on Freud and produced a detailed paper on
Freud's libido theory, arriving at a negative judgment. Among the
books he read in connection with this seminar was Daniel Paul
Schreber's *Denkwürdigkeiten eines Nervenkranken* [Memoirs of a
neuropath], which appealed to him far more than Freud's essay on
it. He also induced me to read Schreber's book, which contained
very impressive and pregnant formulations. From a salient passage
in this book Benjamin derived the designation *"flüchtig hin-
gemachte Männer"* [hastily put-up men]. Schreber, who at the
height of his paranoia believed for a time that the world had been
destroyed by "rays" hostile to him, gave this as an answer when
it was pointed out to him that the doctors, patients, and employees
of the insane asylum obviously existed. In Herbertz's seminar we
read Aristotle's *Metaphysics.* Benjamin was the uncontested favorite and, as he used to put it, earned "seminar laurels, *laurea
communis minor* [laurels of the small state]." Herbertz, who used
to talk in the tone of a philosophical barker and would proclaim

Aristotle's τό τι ἦν εἶναι the way a sideshow barker announces
the lady without an abdomen, had great respect for Benjamin and
treated him like a younger colleague. His utterly unenvious admiration for Benjamin's genius, which was in such contrast to his own
then still rather philistine mind, bespoke a great nobility of spirit,
which he demonstrated on several other occasions, including the
Second World War.

Some weeks we were together every day, at other times at least
thrice weekly. Immediately after my arrival Benjamin and Dora
suggested that because of housing conditions in the city I move to
the little village of Muri, about a half-hour's walk from the Kirchen-
feld Bridge on the road to Thun, where they were about to take an
apartment. We then lived out there until early August; my room
was only two minutes from theirs, and so an extraordinarily active
companionship developed. A week after my arrival Benjamin
proposed the joint study of a philosophical work. After some
give-and-take we agreed, in view of his special interest in Kant, to
read the fundamental work of the Marburg School, Hermann
Cohen's *Kants Theorie der Erfahrung* [Kant's theory of experience].
We spent many hours analyzing and discussing this work. Since so
little was to be learned at the university, we formed "our own
academy" (as Benjamin put it in our first conversations). Thus we
proceeded to found, half in earnest and half in jest, the "University
of Muri" and its "institutes": a library and an academy. In the
catalogue of this university, the statutes of the academy, and the
imaginary list of new library accessions, for which Benjamin supplied reviews sparkling with wit, our high spirits and ridicule of
academic activities found an appropriate outlet during the next
three or four years. Benjamin played the role of the rector and
repeatedly gave me written and oral reports about the latest goings-
on at our fantasy university. I was heard from as "Warder of the
School of the Philosophy of Religion" and sometimes also as a
member of the faculty.

My first days passed very intensively and festively. My arrival
was celebrated by a festive meal two days later, at which Benjamin
informed me that he would study Hebrew once he had passed his
examination. Conversations in the field of Judaism, philosophy,
and literature were of primary importance to us, and added to these

were the reading of poems, the playing of games, or conversations between Dora and me in which she told me about her and Benjamin's life before I had met them. Dora often went to bed early, and then Benjamin and I continued the conversation by ourselves. When we parted on May 10 he gave me the incomplete manuscript of his *Metaphysik der Jugend* [Metaphysics of youth, written 1913–14], which I copied out in longhand.

Right from the start we spoke a great deal about his "Programm der kommenden Philosophie." Benjamin discussed the scope of the concept of experience that was meant here; according to him, it encompassed man's intellectual and psychological connection with the world, which takes place in the realms not yet penetrated by cognition. When I mentioned that consequently it was legitimate to include the mantic disciplines in this conception of experience, Benjamin responded with an extreme formulation: "A philosophy that does not include the possibility of soothsaying from *coffee grounds* and cannot explicate it cannot be a true philosophy." Such prophesying may be reprehensible, as in Judaism, but it must be recognized as possible from the connection of things. As a matter of fact, even his very late notes on occult experiences do not exclude such possibilities, though more implicitly. Benjamin's sometimes lively interest in experiences with hashish is explainable from this perspective and definitely not from any supposed addiction to drugs, which was quite alien to him and has been imputed to him only in recent years. When the aforementioned study was discussed in Switzerland, Benjamin, on whose table I later saw Baudelaire's *Les paradis artificiels*, spoke of the expansion of human experience in hallucinations, some of which still managed to contain something that could not be expressed with words like *illusion*. Of Kant he said that he had "motivated an inferior experience."

This thesis played a major role in the great disappointment that Hermann Cohen's work was to us. We each at different times had attended courses or individual lectures given by Cohen in Berlin during his advanced years, and we were full of respect and indeed reverence for this figure; thus we approached our reading with great expectations and a readiness for critical discussion. But Cohen's deductions and interpretations seemed highly questionable to us; we dissected them with great severity. I still possess the notes I made after a few such sessions on the critique of Kant's syllogisms in the "transcendental aesthetics" and on the proof of their untenability. Benjamin expressed himself on the attitude of Cohen the rationalist toward interpretation: "He said that for a rationalist not only texts of absolute dignity like the Bible [and, according to Benjamin, Hölderlin as well] were capable of multilayered interpretation, but everything that was a subject was put in absolute terms by a rationalist, thus justifying violence in interpretation, like Aristotle, Descartes, Kant." In Kant's critique Benjamin also found justification for the phenomenologists in their reference to Hume. Benjamin had no use for the rationalistic positivism that occupied us during this reading, because he was seeking "absolute experience." Our complaints about Cohen's interpretation of Kant finally grew so heavy that after reading for two hours a day in July we discontinued it when the summer vacation began in August. Benjamin complained about the "transcendental confusion" of his presentation: "I might as well become a Catholic." To me the divergence between this work on Kant and Cohen's own *Logik der reinen Erkenntnis* [Logic of pure cognition], of which I had just finished the first half, was very surprising, though the two works seemed to be connected. Of some statements in the book Benjamin said they were "negative masterpieces of ponderous tomes in smallest format." He termed the book "a philosophical vespiary."

In those days he also talked a lot about Nietzsche in his final period. Not long before my arrival he had read C. Bernouilli's *Nietzsche und Overbeck,* a book he called the most irresistible example of scholarly sensationalism. This book evidently had stimulated Benjamin to do some thinking about Nietzsche. According to him, Nietzsche was the only person who had seen historical experience in the nineteenth century, a time when people "experienced" only nature. Even Burckhardt skirted the historical ethic; his ethic was not the ethic of history but that of historiography, of humanism. At that time Benjamin's statements on philosophy displayed a very clear tendency toward the systematic. Shortly after my arrival I made this notation: "He is sailing full speed into the system." Sometimes he used the terms *system* and *teaching* almost interchangeably. His critical examination of the world of myth continued to belong in this realm and, in connection with his study of Bachofen, so did his speculations on cosmogony and the prehistoric world of man. I frequently presented to him my ideas about Judaism and its fight against myth, something I had reflected on a great deal in the preceding eight months. Between mid-June and mid-August in particular we often spoke about these subjects. I suppose it was in those days that we especially influenced each other. Benjamin read to me a lengthy note on dreams and clairvoyance, in which he tried to formulate the laws governing the world of premythical spectral phenomena. He distinguished between two historical ages of the spectral and the demonic that preceded the age of revelation (which I proposed calling the messianic age instead). Benjamin said the real content of myth was the enormous revolution that polemicized against the spectral and brought its age to an end. Even then he occupied himself with ideas about perception as a reading in the configurations of the surface, which is the way prehistoric man perceived the world around him, particularly the sky. This was the genesis of the reflections he made many years later in his notes "Lehre vom Ähnlichen" [Doctrine of similar things]. The origin of the constellations as configurations on the sky surface was, so he asserted, the beginning of reading and writing, and this coincided with the development of the mythic age. The constellations were for the mythic world what the revelation of Holy Writ was to be later.

In such endeavors the spectrum of the states between dreaming and waking fascinated him as much as the world of dreams itself. He once explained to me the law governing the interpretation of dreams he thought he had found, but rereading my notes on it shows me that I did not understand it. Although, as far as my experience goes, he later refrained from interpreting dreams, at least explicitly, he continued to relate his dreams on frequent occasions and enjoyed broaching the subject of dream interpretation. I do not remember his ever contradicting my expression of profound disappointment at Freud's *Interpretation of Dreams,* contained in a letter I wrote him a few years later. In Muri he told of a dream he had had at Seeshaupt in the spring of 1916, three days before the suicide of his favorite aunt Friderike Josephy. He said this dream had greatly excited him, and he had spent hours in a futile quest to interpret it. "I was lying in a bed; my aunt and another person also lay there, but we did not mingle. People walking by outside were looking in through a window." He said he did not realize until later that this had been a symbolic announcement of his aunt's death. I do not recall whether he explicitly stated that one of the persons who looked in through the window was his aunt herself; that would have made his story plausible. Another time, following a playfully heated conversation about a Flaubert-inspired "Encyclopedia of Nonsense," he recounted a dream he had had the night before: "There were twenty people there, and in accordance with given subjects they had to line up by twos in order to act out the specific situation. In a magic way the intention made the appropriate garments materialize. Whoever was ready first set the tone for his partner, and whoever portrayed the subject best won the prize." Benjamin said he really ought to have received the prize for "Rejection"; there he had been a little rotund Chinese in blue garments, and his obtrusive partner, who wanted something from him, had crawled up his back. Another couple had performed just as well, however, and so the prize was held over for the next subject, "Jealousy": "I was the woman and lay stretched out on the floor. The man embraced me; I looked at him jealously from below and stuck my tongue out all the way."

Benjamin also indulged in comparisons between the philosophical style of our generation and that of Kant. In opposition to prevailing opinion, he regarded Kant's style as sublime and invoked Heinrich Kleist as a witness. I expected him to adduce as evidence passages from Kant's short writings or from *The Critique of Judgment,* but instead he read to me a letter from Kant to Ludwig Kosegarten. Right after that he read, slowly and in a raised voice, Samuel Collenbusch's two letters to Kant, which have been preserved in Kant's correspondence—letters from a pious Christian who protested against "religion within the limits of pure reason" ("I am sorry that I. Kant expects nothing good from God"). Benjamin then paused for a rather long time and only looked at me with wide eyes, as though he were trying to say that this prose surely could hold its own next to the Bible. He then read three letters from the correspondence between Goethe and Zelter, including Goethe's letter about the death of his son. For years to come Benjamin alluded to those letters, especially the ones that provided him with the impetus for his collection *Deutsche Menschen* [German people].*

We subsequently had quite a number of conversations about Goethe; since I had read little of Goethe at the time, they were monologues on Benjamin's part, or at best monologues interrupted by questions. Among other things, he discussed Goethe's "autobiographical life, which is founded on concealment." When he said that his own experience had enabled him to deduce the truth about Goethe from Goethe's marriage, he quite spontaneously began to discuss his first engagement, to Grete Radt. He saw a parallel between these two relationships, although I no longer recall his reasons. Benjamin's altogether ingenious view of Goethe was expressed even in his Swiss period in his only half-ironic high opinion of the three-volume Goethe biography by the Jesuit Alexander Baumgartner. He indulged in panegyrics on the "disclosures" of this polemic, whose author's hatred often was the source of his perspicacity: "A genuine Jesuit on Goethe—that is worthy of note." Or: "If I had to choose between Baumgartner and Gundolf, the choice would be easy." He was completely indifferent to Baumgartner's judgments, of course; what interested him was the detective and inquisitorial element of the book, in which Goethe is presented as a criminal to be convicted. In those days I was far more attracted to Jean Paul, who, Benjamin said, was the only great writer who could endure life in Germany; this was not meant as a reproach, for Benjamin called him the inhabitant of a tremendous historical sphere. But in the case of Schiller—so he said—this was a reproach, and there was "no greater fraud than Schiller's historical innocence." Schiller's failure in his relationship with Hölderlin was bound up with these conditions and Schiller's "demonic morality." On another occasion Benjamin read Jakob Michael Reinhold Lenz's poem about Kant: "A true homage: there is no end to it."

In those first weeks we had many more conversations lasting for hours, sometimes until after midnight. Among the things we

*The collection first appeared pseudonymously under the title *Deutsche Menschen. Eine Folge von Briefen. Auswahl und Einleitung von Detlef Holz* (Lucerne: Vita Nova Verlag, 1936). A second edition appeared in 1937. In 1977, a new edition was issued with an afterword by Theodor Adorno (Frankfurt/M.: Suhrkamp Verlag).—TRANS.

read was the draft of a new ethics that Ludwig Strauss had sent to Benjamin and me in the form of handwritten copies, which we critically dissected. On a number of occasions Benjamin presented poems of his own, but he primarily read poems by Fritz Heinle, August Wilhelm Schlegel, and August Graf von Platen; about the last-named Benjamin said that he felt a kinship with him. Like a considerable number of Jews of our generation before Hitler, we did not feel close to Heinrich Heine, and I cannot remember ever discussing Heine's writings with him. Benjamin had read Heine's *Romantische Schule* [The romantic school] while preparing his dissertation on the idea of art criticism in early Romanticism, and he made deprecatory remarks about this work. In 1916, when I first heard of Karl Kraus, I had read his *Heine und die Folgen* [Heine and the consequences]; Benjamin was as yet unacquainted with this work. At that time he was studying the prose writings of Friedrich Schlegel, who had always attracted him, in his poetic production as well; in the process he had encountered J. G. Fichte. Fichte, Kierkegaard, and Freud he numbered among the "Socratic people." Much later, in a letter of January 1936 to our mutual friend Kitty Steinschneider, he wrote that in Fichte "the revolutionary spirit of the German bourgeoisie had transformed itself into the chrysalis from which the death's-head moth of National Socialism later crawled."

Although Benjamin often spoke about Stefan George and the "circle" around him (though about the latter only with great reserve or polemical intent), he only seldom discussed the work of Rilke—in contrast to the high esteem he had had for Rilke at the time of the Youth Movement, which some of his friends from that period told me about (though I did not know it at the time). In May 1918 we had a long conversation, in which Benjamin quite unpolemically sought to define the sphere of Rilke's poetry. I remember only one detail. My friend Erich Brauer, who had begun his studies at the University of Freiburg the preceding semester, wrote me about the profound impression that a lecture by Ernst Buschor, the classical archaeologist, had made upon him. Buschor had spoken about the archaic torso of Apollo in the museum at Naples and at the end of his lecture had recited Rilke's poem by that title, whereupon he burst into tears—not an everyday occurrence in an

academic lecture on archaeology. I told Benjamin about this, and
he said, Yes, it really is an extraordinary poem. Years later he sent
me a copy of his rejoinder (which for mysterious reasons remained
unpublished) to Franz Blei's malicious obituary on Rilke in the
periodical *Die literarische Welt* [The literary world], an article that
had outraged Benjamin. Benjamin's response betokened a greatly
altered attitude toward Rilke, but he still placed that sonnet from
the *Neue Gedichte* [New poems] among the unforgettable poems.
When I mentioned three texts in a letter about lamentations—the
biblical lament of David for Jonathan and the two poems on the
same subject by Rilke and Else Lasker-Schüler—he replied that
Rilke's poem was simply a bad one. During a conversation about
lamentations—a subject I occupied myself with intensively at that
time in connection with my Hebrew studies—he told me that there
was a wonderful lament in Rilke's *Notebooks of Malte Laurids
Brigge.* I looked it up, and the passage contained, as a quotation
but without any reference to the source, the thirtieth chapter of the
Book of Job! Despite Benjamin's subsequent severe criticism of
Rilke as the classic example of "all the weaknesses of the *Jugendstil,*" he never stooped to the kind of "sociocritical" idiocy, later
so popular, that could deride a stanza in Rilke's poem about St.
Francis of Assisi as a snobbish-reactionary elegy to poverty.

Benjamin never developed a positive relationship to literary
Expressionism as a movement, though the movement did originate
in the prewar years in a circle to which Benjamin was personally
quite close. He had great admiration, however, for certain phases
of the Expressionistic painting of Vasily Kandinsky, Marc Chagall,
and Paul Klee. While still in Jena I had obtained for him Kandinsky's *Über das Geistige in der Kunst* [The spiritual element in
art]; evidently Benjamin was attracted particularly to the mystical
elements of the theory contained therein. But he had little use for
catchwords in general and was less attached to schools than to
specific phenomena. The name of Kasimir Edschmid, at that time
universally regarded as one of the giants of Expressionist prose,
was for Benjamin a symbol of pretentious triviality; he would refer
to Edschmid in much the same tone of derision as he used for the
author Frida Schanz, whom he liked to refer to. To be sure, he
regarded Georg Heym as a great poet and recited for me verses

from his collection *Der ewige Tag* [The eternal day] from memory
—a very unusual practice for him. Thus there remains as an unsolved problem the poetry of Fritz Heinle, which for Benjamin
must have contained elements of greatness that set the poet apart
from the rest of the Expressionists.

This period also marked the beginnings of Benjamin's collection of old and rare children's books, which he described in a letter
to Ernst Schoen dated July 1918 (since published). The collection
was really launched by Dora's enthusiasm for the genre. Dora also
loved legends and fairy tales. She and Benjamin made each other
birthday presents of illustrated children's books until at least 1923,
the period of my close association with them, and they particularly
hunted for editions in which the illustrations were hand-tinted.
Benjamin showed me Johann Peter Lyser's things with a delight in
which the joy of discovery and pleasure at the artistic result were
commingled closely. He loved to give little lectures on such books
to Dora and me and to emphasize particularly the unexpected
associations that these talks brought out in the texts. In June of
1918 we found in a secondhand bookshop in Bern the first volume
of the *Bilderbuch für Kinder* [Picture book for children] by Friedrich Bertuch of the Weimar circle; subsequently Benjamin acquired
several additional volumes of this work. It constituted a particular
focus of his devoted absorption. His commentary on individual
pages already had begun to spark his pronounced sense of the
emblematical, although we were not aware of it at the time. The
illustrations in such books, which evoked so many associations,
already held the same fascination for him as Dürer's *Melencolia I*
and the emblem books of the sixteenth and seventeenth centuries
did later.

Benjamin's predilection for the imaginative world of associations, which was connected also with his profound interest and
absorption in the world of the child—an interest that dated from
the early years of his son Stefan—was also evident in his marked
interest in the writings of insane persons. In Bern he already owned
several works of this type. What primarily fascinated him about
them was the architectonic (today one would call it the structural)
element of their world systems and the fantastic tables often associated therewith, tables of coordinates that are no longer vari-

able, as they are with children, but are marked by the onset of a grim rigidity. His interest was not pathologic-psychological but metaphysical in nature. I heard him discuss this on a number of occasions, although never in connection with the technique of psychoanalysis, with which he was at least acquainted through his study of the works of Freud and some of the latter's earliest pupils. His relationship to painting, which I have mentioned already—it extended to include James Ensor long before his discovery by the Surrealists—probably belongs in this context also. He liked to visit exhibitions; this enhanced his great appreciation of art more than reproductions did. In Paris he led me, offering highly appreciative remarks along the way, to such places as the Cabinet des Illusions and also to Madame Tussaud's waxworks, whose unexpected juxtapositions of figures equally evoked his aesthetic-associative delight.

We hardly ever discussed aesthetic theory, which I had no interest in. I recall only two exceptions: his lifelong conviction of the importance of Alois Riegl's work *Spätromantische Kunstindustrie* [Late Romantic art industry] and his predilection for Jean Paul's *Vorschule der Ästhetik* [Primer of aesthetics], a work he read in connection with his study of Romanticism. I particularly remember a sentence from the latter work that Benjamin was fond of quoting as the epitome of witty profundity. Jean Paul referred there to the early Romantics as "a school now already half-decayed, whose most important programmatic writings, particularly Schlegel's, have, however, outlived their brief immortality."

Not infrequently we spent our time together taking walks through old Bern, but more often stayed in his large study, where he had gradually assembled much of his library. But sometimes we also took longer trips, for instance a nocturnal hike from Thun to Interlaken in late May 1918. We walked in silence, and when we began to talk, Benjamin soon stopped, since he greatly favored such a change of pace during a conversation. Then we would go on walking as we discussed more or less unimportant things, whereupon we would fall silent and then turn to "essential things" again. This is when I first noticed Benjamin's basic melancholy, the incipient depressive traits that later became more pronounced. (I never noticed anything manic about him.) At the same time I began to grow aware of the hysterical elements in Dora's behavior, which were sometimes suddenly triggered by the most insignificant events. Often enough these tension-laden scenes left me overwhelmed and perplexed, like a man who has seen more than he cares to see.

Beneath the previously mentioned disappointments on both sides and the disputes I have mentioned there lurked a deep-seated bitterness and disillusionment over the images of one another that we had fashioned for ourselves. Occasionally such feelings were expressed under the veil of an exchange of letters that the infant Stefan and I would leave out for each other. Stefan's letters were in Dora's handwriting, but they were written with Walter's knowledge and possibly even with his participation. On June 20—six weeks after my arrival!—Stefan wrote me with reference to a letter of mine that, as far as I recall, never existed:

Dear Uncle Gerhardt [sic]*:*

Herewith I am sending you a better photo of me which has arrived in the meantime. Thank you very much for your letter; various things may be said about it, and that is why I am writing you, for if I visit you, you will again tell me so many things that I won't be able to get a word in edgeways. Well then, first I must tell you that you ought to know I no longer remember. For if I could remember, I certainly would not be here, where it is so unpleasant and you are creating such a bad atmosphere; no, I long since would have returned where I came from. That's why I can't read the end of your letter. My mother read the rest to me. Incidentally, I have very strange parents; but more about that later.

When I was in town yesterday, something occurred to me: When I grow up, I'm going to be your pupil. Better start thinking now. Best of all, start keeping a little book in which you note everything down.

Now I will tell you something about my parents. I won't say anything about my mother, because she is, after all, my mother. But I have all sorts of things to tell you about my father. You are wrong in what you write, dear Uncle Gerhardt. I believe you really know very little about my Papa. There are very few people who know anything about him. Once, when I was still in heaven, you wrote him a letter that made all of us think that you did know him. But perhaps you

*don't after all. I think a man like that is born only once in a great
while, and then you just have to be kind to him and he will do
everything else by himself. You, dear Uncle Gerhardt, still think that
one has to do a great deal. Perhaps I shall also think that way when
I am a grown man, but now I think more like my Mama, that is, not
at all or very little; and so all this to-do and the great excitement over
everything seems much less important to me than which way the wind
is blowing.*

*But I don't want to be smart-alecky, for you know everything much
better. That's the whole trouble.*

*Many regards from
Stefan*

I started a reply:

Dear Stefan:
*Thank you for your photo. Why didn't you bring it along the last
time you came to my place, when I told you the story about the cat
and the three-quarter Jews? You see, your father is a strange man.
Learn about him critically, Stefan! He says making photos is an
immoral act—that is, he claims (I don't know whether you've learned
about this already) that it isn't proper for a respectable person, but I
suppose you've given him a good piece of your mind about that,
haven't you? One can tell from the picture that you don't want any
part of him. But let's be kind; he doesn't mean any harm, and he will
defend himself—clever as he is—by saying that you are only a child.
But that isn't true. Weren't you in heaven twenty-five years longer than
he was? Didn't you study the Torah there twenty-five years longer than
he did? (Actually, Stefan, I don't mind telling you that he already
has forgotten everything again.) But what are you going to do? Even
in heaven the Torah complained that he loved your mother Dora more
than he loved it. But with any luck we'll be able to bring him around,
won't we?*
*Dear Stefan, don't you go thinking that because I have your photo
you don't have to visit me anymore. That's not how it works with
photos. A picture is a dark mirror; we learned that in Talmud study
(you know, just when your father and your mother had quarreled in
heaven and he didn't want to study Torah anymore and was sitting*

in a corner with Michael, saying he was going to the Christian heaven, he was good and fed up with it, and Christian love was more enduring than Dora's—of course, he denied this later!). Anyway, if I tell stories to the mirror, it won't do you any good.

Dear Stefan, the two of us know what's what. Let's continue to pretend that we still don't understand anything. After all, we are the youngest in the family and have to stand together against the older ones, who only want to suppress us. They're squeezing us dry, Stefan! But we won't stand for that. Do you still remember Nekenyw [Wyneken] of the Teutons, who for the rest of his life read everything backward and therefore produced such junk? Remember how he screamed at your parents in heaven and even made such an impression in the Christian heaven that the Christ child wouldn't hear of your father anymore? That was some scene. . . . [At this point I broke off the drafted letter and instead wrote a sonnet, "To Stefan," which I have not preserved.]

In those days I wrote quite a few such poems, including one for Benjamin's birthday, which I left out for him along with the two books I gave him. I had told him a great deal about S. Y. Agnon, whom I had met in Berlin a few months before the Benjamins' wedding. As nothing of Agnon had been translated into German, however, it was hard to convey an idea of this extraordinary human being and his writings to someone who did not know Hebrew. In the spring of 1918, Max Strauss's wonderful translation of "Aggadat hasofer" [The legend of the scribe: "Die Erzählung vom Toraschreiber"] appeared in *Der Jude;* I had heard Agnon read it from the Hebrew manuscript in Berlin—an unforgettable experience. I still regard those pages as a high point in Hebrew literature. On a Friday evening in June, I read the translation to Walter and Dora. Benjamin was impressed profoundly, and in a long conversation he rated the first three-fourths of the work among the greatest things he had ever heard, although he raised vehement objections to the visionary ending. He said Agnon had no right to present a vision as the crowning point, since it could not surpass the reality of the preceding portions. "If the story *with* this ending is perfect, then I don't understand why there is a Bible. In that case we don't need the Bible." I made him a present of Agnon's story, which I had had bound especially for this occasion. I originally planned to give him *95 Thesen über Judentum und Zionismus* [Ninety-five theses on Judaism and Zionism], which I had actually written down over the preceding weeks, but in the end I was dissatisfied and did not present them to him. Instead I brought him the first draft of the *Philosophisches Alphabet* for the students of the University of Muri, whose "Second Edition, Revised in Accordance with the Latest Findings of Philosophy" I dedicated to him in a private printing in 1927. Benjamin was not only a great metaphysician but also a great bibliophile. The enthusiasm with which he was capable of discussing bindings, paper, and typefaces in those years frequently got on my nerves—at such birthday celebrations, for instance. Today it is hard for me to reconstruct the impression I received then, but I saw an element of decadence in it. I made this note about it: "Great though [Benjamin's] life may be in every sense—the only case near to me of a life being led metaphysically—it nevertheless harbors elements of decadence to a fearful extent. The way one leads one's life has certain hard-to-define boundaries, which decadence exceeds, and unfortunately this is definitely true in Walter's case. I deny that metaphysically legitimate insights can arise from this way of evaluating books on the basis of their bindings and paper. Walter has a lot of illegitimate insights as well. There's no way to change him. On the contrary; the only thing I have to guard against is the incursion of this sphere into my own through personal contact." Shortly before that I had made this note: "Of late I have been getting along with Walter very well again—probably because I now have found the locus from which I can tacitly resist him in my inner affairs. This way everything is all right; those scenes were, in the final analysis, nothing but moments at which he glimpsed a sphere of my condition that was not destined for him. After all, he did not reveal such things to me either, and our community consists precisely in each of us understanding the other man's reticence *without words* and respecting it."

Shortly after Benjamin's birthday I received the German translation of Agnon's first book, *Und das Krumme wird gerade* [And the crooked is made straight]. I lent it to Benjamin for his vacation in Bönigen near Interlaken. He wrote me about it: "I have finished the Agnon and can only express my complete liking for this book.

I have nothing to criticize about it and think it is very beautiful. The positive moments for me to say something about it would have to be furnished by you or perhaps by a second reading." From that time on his interest in Agnon never ceased, and the short tales I later translated, some of them from Agnon's manuscript, and published in *Der Jude* elicited his particular delight. Everything concerning Agnon's life and my relationship with him was assured of his interest as well. Benjamin knew next to nothing about Jewish affairs, let alone Eastern Jewish reality and literature. Thus he once sent me a postcard, on the occasion of my reading Theodor Lessing's *Philosophie der Tat* [Philosophy of action], inquiring how it was possible that a Jew was named Lessing. About details of Jewish history he was totally uninformed. In Muri our conversations often were on Jewish theology and the basic concepts of Jewish ethics but hardly on concrete matters and situations. Arguments about revelation and redemption, justice, law, the fear of God, and reconciliation frequently enough played a central role in those conversations, and these conversations are reflected, though in altered form, in many of his notes and publications.

Once the three of us had a long conversation about the Ten Commandments—Dora had asked whether one might transgress them—and the significance of the precepts of the Torah. I read them notes on the concept of justice as "action in deferment"; these evoked a strong reaction from Benjamin. They wanted to know why, despite my religious attitude, I did not adopt an Orthodox way of life—a step I have repeatedly considered and have always rejected with mounting determination. At that time I formulated my explanation something like this: for me that manner of life was connected with the concretization of the Torah in a false, premature sphere—as evidenced by the paradoxes of the tricks that become manifest in the process and that are necessarily inherent in such a false relationship. Something is wrong with the application; the orders clash. I said I had to maintain the anarchic suspension. Only later did my historical perspective change—in a direction that disposed of the problem, for my understanding of the sense in which one may speak of revelation had changed. At that time kabbalistic considerations hardly were involved, although I had begun to reflect on them from time to time.

On an earlier occasion, in June, we had had violent arguments about the "Open Letter" [printed in *On Jews and Judaism in Crisis,* pp. 54–60] I had written as a response to Siegfried Bernfeld's invitation, which had been extended to Benjamin as well, to contribute to *Jerubbaal,* a Zionist monthly he was editing in Vienna. At the same time my letter was a farewell to the Jewish Youth Movement, whose lack of radicalism made me hit the roof. Bernfeld was an old acquaintance of Benjamin's from the time of *Der Anfang* and the radical school reform but since had joined the Zionist fold. At first Benjamin and I considered signing such a letter jointly, but Benjamin withdrew from the idea. We had long discussions about the text, which I then wrote and published by myself. Benjamin said, "In such things it is a matter of having the metaphysical laughs on one's side." That, however, my letter would not accomplish, for in it I was loudly demanding silence. "In the *methodos* of silence, silence itself must not occur. One writes this sort of thing to free oneself, but one does not print it." He said he agreed with the intent of what I had said but that it had to be protected from profanation.

On July 22 there had been another scene with Dora. In a long conversation afterward we "traced the matter to its roots." Shortly thereafter I received another letter from Stefan:

Dear Uncle Gerhard:

You will not expect any letter from me after such a long time, and that's why I am writing you. You see, I am doing very well now, and Mama has a bit more time, too. There actually is no point in thanking your for your magnificent poem, for it's too beautiful for that. But when I'm bigger I'll probably write one to thank you.

Some very exciting things are happening. Mama and I celebrated Papa's birthday. I hear you turned up with terrific presents, too. Of course, I didn't see anything, for they never let me get close when there is some fun, so I can't tell you much about it.

One evening, when I was long asleep, there was a terrible row. First I thought it was another thunderstorm, but no, somebody was bawling and screaming so much that the walls shook. Do you have any idea what that was? I don't dare ask Mama, because she has been sad ever since. When I talk about you she usually gets snappish.

Also, a book I prize very highly is missing from my library. I can't imagine who might have taken it. Now take care of yourself. I'm already quite anxious to go to the mountains. When, oh when will I finally get there?

Come and pick me up for a lesson soon.

Kindest regards
Stefan

I think the book mentioned here was William Beckford's *Vathek*, which an enormously wealthy twenty-two-year-old Englishman is said to have written in French in the space of two or three days in 1782, only to fall silent for decades. Benjamin thought highly of this book, which he owned in German translation.

While Walter and Dora were in Bönigen, I went to Adelboden. There I had a difficult time with Erich Brauer, who was deformed and extremely sensitive. I wrote about this and my problems to Walter and Dora. In response I received a letter, which a few days later Benjamin described as "sensible and perceptive far beyond Stefan's years." It was, of course, in Dora's handwriting and read in part as follows:

Bönigen, Sept. 8, 1918

Dear Uncle Gerhard:

Thank you very much for your affectionate and beautiful letter, which gladdened my heart despite the many sad things you told me. Dear Uncle Gerhard, we are all a bit deformed, to say nothing of our deficient stature. So don't worry about your friend. But what you write about his inability to understand you is worse. This is all the more sad because I did notice how glad you were at the time to escape my father's tutelage. I've figured it out already: one can't scream and drink at the same time.

I'm fine. I'll be five months old in a few days, and then I'll finally have to get on the bottle. I'm very sorry for my mother, for she is taking it very hard. As if this meant that I stopped being her son! But it's just that I'm hungry.

You write that she never has time for you. I gave that a lot of thought once, and I believe I even wrote you about it. I believe she would have time if things were different; not having time is only a pretense, I think. I don't think it's like my mother not to have time because of external matters. After all, she always has time for Papa and me, and earlier, when she still wasn't feeling particularly well, people of your age, though not of your importance, would come and sit with her for as long as the Good Lord made the light shine, often even into the night. For all these she had time. But when I asked her in your name and we talked about it, suddenly many things became clear to us. It's hard for me to tell you, for I wouldn't want you to believe that your relationship with my Mama isn't all it should be. It is quite all right, but only on its own terms, as it were, for you would like it always to be something else. What you want from my mother she cannot give you, because you don't love her; she has known too many people who did to be mistaken about this. You could, however, get a great deal from her, but you don't realize this, because you want other, inadequate things. That's why she has no time for you, for now this would be lost time. There would be quarrels too often, for the aforementioned reasons.

This has been awfully hard for me, almost too hard for my little brain. Fortunately I slept the whole time. My very best to you, dearest Uncle Gerhard. We all wish you a happy Roschhaschanah [*New Year*], *even if we are still too dumb to spell it correctly.*

Yours,
Stefan

When I wrote Benjamin in response to this letter that it had depressed me greatly and worsened my already bad mood, he suggested that we take a long hike together if I felt strong enough. "It was and still is my intention perhaps to climb the Faulhorn on September 28, to descend to Meiringen from there, and then take a hike through the Rhone Valley. . . . I have spent the last few days getting in shape for a fine hike, and I have rested and recuperated in every sense of the word. I did not work much and thus did not tackle the Ethics, but I did occupy myself with Goethe a great deal, reading, among other things, his Metamorphosis of Plants. . . . I continue to hope that we shall climb the Faulhorn together and thus offer its demon the sacrifice that will induce him to spare us all winter."

This big trip did not materialize, and we climbed the Schynige Plateau instead.

When we returned from our vacation we no longer lived next door to each other. The Benjamins moved into a four-room apartment in the Marzili district, down by the Aare River; I changed my room a number of times. They did visit me occasionally, but our get-togethers became less frequent. For one thing, Dora and Walter successively succumbed to the widespread Spanish flu; for another, Benjamin was working very intensively on his dissertation and rather overexerted himself; then too, there was renewed tension, particularly with Dora, and this created difficulties. There were scenes in which all of us participated in turn. Sometimes Walter and Dora clashed for mysterious reasons while I visited them, and I silently withdrew. Then again there were great heart-to-heart talks and reconciliations.

My diary entry of November 5, 1918, describes one of these scenes from my perspective: "At about 5:00 P.M. I went to Walter's place to play chess with him. Dora was continuing on the mend [after her flu] and we conversed through the open door. Walter was very nice; after his deserved defeat he read us some really beautiful sonnets [on Heinle's death], and everything was fine. I was supposed to have supper with them. At eight o'clock he went into Dora's room, and after a short time a terrible row started—I have no idea what it was all about, as is unfortunately often the case. But today it was especially bad and excruciating. At first I stayed in my seat in the next room; then I was ashamed to be witnessing this and went downstairs, for usually things blow over quickly and Walter joins me. Today nothing of the sort happened. For three-quarters of an hour I sat in the dining room; of course I didn't want to eat alone while they were quarreling upstairs. When Walter didn't respond to the maid's repeated knocking, I left without any supper. I am very sad that there are such frequent scenes in a marriage like this one. I am the only witness to these things, and that is precisely why it is agonizing in the extreme. What is going on between them? Why this frantic running around and screaming? There is a terrible atmosphere in a house where there is quarreling. The maid doesn't dare leave the kitchen, the soup gets cold, one can hear only Walter's excited footsteps upstairs, and finally one is overcome by shame. In all this they have absolutely no consideration for me; I am not asking for any and shall never say a word, but it bothers me that it doesn't occur to them to think of me. After all, I'm not a eunuch to whom people expose themselves as they wouldn't to anyone else. Thus I sat there quite pointlessly for two hours, for I really wanted to leave after the chess game. Without the moving sonnets that echoed within me through it all I would have despaired completely of such togetherness." In contrast to this I quote my entry of November 9: "Yesterday and the day before I was at Walter and Dora's, and it was very nice. After a half-year of being together our relationship—the most decisive one of my life (with a man, at any rate)—appears in a clearer light to me. I am sure I have written a lot of nonsense about it in these pages, and in essence that is all wrong—simply because one only can keep silent about it. My sonnet for Benjamin's birthday was my only foray into language. I am beginning to grow inexpressibly fond of Dora again."

In November, at my initiative, they invited Erich Brauer along with me, and the evening turned into a terrible fiasco. Something in the atmosphere troubled Brauer; he sat there in a daze and hardly spoke a word. The mood was very oppressive. Walter and Dora attempted to get him to unwind, but it was no use. Later they were justifiably annoyed because I could not bring myself to discuss that dreary evening with Brauer. But there were very happy evenings as well. Dora had a piano in the new apartment, and on festive occasions she would sing settings of Eichendorff's poems, being very fond of such lieder as "O Täler weit, o Höhen" [O valleys wide, O heights] or "Durch Feld und Buchenhallen" [Through fields and halls of beeches]. When she was in high spirits she also sang songs that did not suit her at all, such as "Ich gehe meinen Schlendrian bis an mein kühles Grab" [I shall drift along to my cold grave]. As far as I can remember, Walter never sang. In general we got together only on weekends during the winter of 1918–19. In February and March, Dora took a position in an office as an English translator in order to earn some money, and consequently even Walter saw her only in the evening. In those days they had a live-in maid, who also took care of Stefan. They led a very secluded life; there was virtually no social activity in their home.

Until March 1919 I met only two guests there: a musician named Heymann, who sometimes played music with Dora, and (in March 1919) Wolf Heinle, the younger brother of Walter's late friend. Heinle came to visit from Germany and stayed with them for a month. He wrote very enigmatic Expressionistic-esoteric works, which I did not understand.

The Bolshevik Revolution and the collapse of Germany and Austria, as well as the ensuing pseudorevolution, brought current political events into our conversation again for the first time since we had agreed on our attitude toward the war. Between November 9 and 11 we witnessed the general strike, which the Swiss government put down by force of arms, but it hardly engaged our attention, although we did concern ourselves more with the events in Russia and Germany. I was not deeply involved, however. In December I wrote to Werner Kraft: "Palestine certainly excites and interests me more than the German revolution." In any case, we had discussions about dictatorship; I represented the more radical point of view and defended the idea of a dictatorship—which Benjamin then still completely rejected—provided that it was a "dictatorship of poverty," which to me was not identical with a "dictatorship of the proletariat." I would say that our sympathies were to a great extent with the Social Revolutionary Party in Russia, which later was liquidated so bloodily by the Bolsheviks. We also discussed the question of republic and monarchy, and to my surprise Benjamin opposed my decision in principle in favor of the republic. According to him, such a decision could be made only in relative terms after weighing the prevailing circumstances, and even under present conditions a monarchy might be a legitimate and acceptable form of government.

After the revolution, Werner Kraft, in whose fortunes we took a lively interest, wanted to make an attempt to join us in Switzerland. There were deliberations with Walter and Dora on how that might be effected. The project finally came to naught, because it was so hard to gain entry into Switzerland. Early in 1919, Benjamin made the acquaintance of Hugo Ball and Emmy Hennings, who lived in a neighboring building. Ball, one of the first pillars of the Dadaistic Cabaret Voltaire, was also one of the main contributors to the *Freie Zeitung*, a journal published by German pacifists. Ball was an extreme republican but not a Socialist or a Communist. He was a fanatical hater of everything Prussian. Toward the end of the winter Benjamin gave me a thick, passionate pamphlet entitled *Zur Kritik der deutschen Intelligenz* [A critique of the German intelligentsia]. It impressed both of us with the acuity of its hatred, but other parts of it, such as the immoderate attacks on Kant, only made us shake our heads. Ball's wife, Emmy Hennings, was one of the fieriest women poets of the heyday of Expressionism. From another liaison she had a daughter who was about twelve years old at the time; the girl painted religious portraits, which Benjamin judged to be of astonishingly high artistic quality. Both mother and daughter were extremely pious Catholics. Benjamin frequently told me about his visits to their home.

In March or April 1919, Ball introduced Benjamin to Ernst Bloch, who was then living at Interlaken and had also contributed to the *Freie Zeitung* during the war. I still own a pamphlet by him that appeared at that time. I was not present at these encounters, but Benjamin evidently was greatly impressed by Bloch's personality, although as yet he was unacquainted with his philosophical writings. He did not read the first edition of *Der Geist der Utopie* [The spirit of Utopia], which had appeared in 1918 and which Bloch undoubtedly told him about, until the fall of 1919. The title of this book aroused my attention, and Benjamin told me that it really was not Bloch's; the author had originally wanted to call his work *Musik und Apokalypse,* but Ludwig Feuchtwanger, the editor of the Duncker and Humblot publishing house, had rejected it because it might scare readers away. Benjamin described to me Bloch's impressive appearance and told me that Bloch was now working on his magnum opus, *System des theoretischen Messianismus* [System of theoretical messianism]; he grew wide-eyed when he mentioned this. He said that Bloch was also very receptive to questions of Judaism, although he did not say what his orientation was. At any rate, the relationship between the two men developed so rapidly in the spring of 1919 that Benjamin told Bloch about me and arranged that I visit Interlaken. Benjamin also told me that Bloch had him in mind as the specialist on the "theory of categories" for a projected general survey of philosophy. I made an appointment with Bloch and visited him on May 18, when we were together from 6:00 P.M. to 3:30 A.M. Most of the time (and often tempestuously) we discussed Judaism, past and present, and I read to him Agnon's "Legend of the Scribe." When I entered his study, I saw on a shelf on his desk Johann Andreas Eisenmenger's two-thousand-page *Entdecktes Judentum* [Judaism unmasked], the most scholarly anti-Semitic work in the German language, published in two fat volumes in 1701. In response to my surprised look, Bloch said that certain large portions of it were the finest writings about Judaism he knew; the author, however, had been a nincompoop who had quoted and translated the most wonderful, most profound things in order to ridicule them or decry them as blasphemies. He said one only had to read those things from the opposite point of view to have an eminently worthwhile experience. I liked this assessment very much, and when I acquired my own copy of the work two years later, I found it confirmed.

In general, however, this long visit was evidently not very successful, though Bloch was very cordial and said at parting that he hoped to see me again soon. Later Benjamin told me he had vigorously complained about me and called me an ass. I myself had noted: "Relatively speaking, it was good to talk with him, but in the final analysis I have little in common with such views. At times I saw a real iron wall. He explained Benjamin as an analyst of form. Whether I shall see him again is not clear to me; in any case, though our conversation was quite serious and profound, it is a temporary rather than a permanent relationship."

In his conversation with Bloch and Ball, Benjamin was confronted with the question of political activity, and he declined to engage in such activity the way they urged him to. The Munich soviet republic of April 1919 came into his purview only because Felix Noeggerath, whom he highly esteemed as a philosopher, was arrested for participating in it—something that greatly excited Benjamin. He regarded the Hungarian soviet republic as a childish aberration, and the only thing about it that touched him was the fate of Georg Lukács, Bloch's closest friend; at that time people (mistakenly) feared that he had been arrested and might be shot. In those days Benjamin, who had read only Lukács's pre-Marxist writings, such as *Die Metaphysik der Tragödie* [The metaphysics of tragedy] and *Theorie des Romans* [Theory of the novel], and thought very highly of them, still regarded the volume of Dostoevski's political writings which he owned in the Piper edition as the most important modern political work that he knew. In the months preceding his doctoral examination he used to study together with Hans Heyse, a fellow student of ours in Herbertz's seminar. Later Heyse became one of the most notorious Nazi philosophers and from 1935 on brought the journal *Kant-Studien* into line as an instrument of "philosophical training for the German people." The three of us got together on a number of occasions; at that time Heyse was a very pleasant and polite man who had come to Switzerland as a seriously disabled person on an exchange basis. He told me that few people had impressed him as profoundly as Benjamin.

At the beginning of February, Elsa Burchardt, who would later become my first wife, arrived for a visit and I introduced her to Walter and Dora, who soon became friends with her. She was an uncommonly quiet person but had firm convictions; it was precisely this combination that Walter and Dora liked very much. These two months laid the foundation for the subsequent very amicable relationship between her and them. After her departure in early April I went to Locarno for ten days. Following my return I spent the Passover holidays in Zurich where Benjamin, in the indirect way so characteristic of him, induced me to meet a young man of twenty from the circle to which he had formerly been close. "When you get to Zurich, you might call up Hyne Caro and give him my regards." I replied: "So you assume it would be worthwhile meeting him." "I could imagine it." Caro was generally called Hyne [*Hüne*, giant] because he was uncommonly small. This was the beginning of a strange acquaintanceship. Soon after my return to Bern there was a terrible incident with Wolf Heinle at the Benjamins' home which led to Heinle's sudden departure for Germany within two days. Dora told me they were in terrible straits and she would perhaps be able to tell me later what had so disturbed her. She did look disturbed. No one adverted to this matter again, however, and Heinle's relationship with Benjamin, who urged everyone he knew to aid him when a grave illness had rendered him indigent, continued until Heinle's untimely death in 1922. Compared to Heinle's profound melancholy which I witnessed during our encounters, Benjamin was almost a sanguine person. Such promises of later revelations were also made by Walter on a number of occasions. Thus he told me on one occasion when the conversation turned to Simon Guttmann and his destructive influence on him and Dora in the days of the Youth Movement: "Some day, when you and I are old people, I shall tell you about Simon Guttmann." But this never happened.

In our Swiss period we read Karl Kraus's periodical *Die Fackel* [The torch] almost regularly. I no longer recall when Benjamin started concerning himself with Kraus; I believe it was around 1916 under the influence of Werner Kraft's boundless enthusiasm. Particularly in 1919 we had many conversations about Kraus, his prose, and his *Worte in Versen* [Words in verse], the first volumes of which were then appearing. Later still we were enchanted by Kraus's play *Literatur oder Man wird doch da sehn* [Literature, or we'll see about that] with its parody of Werfel and its mockery of an Expressionism that went haywire in the revolutionary period. The matchless dialogues in this play could cause us to choke with laughter. When we were discussing the Munich soviet republic and I told Benjamin about efforts to reform the press with reference to Karl Kraus, he said: "Kraus was to be preferred, for he had only one position: 'Écrasez l'infâme.' "

Early in 1919 I had translated from Hebrew, at Buber's invitation, Hayyim Nahman Bialik's great essay on Halakhah and Aggadah, the two categories that shaped talmudic writing. When this essay appeared in *Der Jude* in April 1919, it made a lasting impression on Benjamin as well, and its influence may be discerned in a number of his writings. He regarded it as "quite extraordinary," and it really was. I also read him my (unpublished) translation of the polemic against this article which the important Hebrew writer Y. H. Brenner had published. Benjamin, however, was gripped much more by Bialik's magnificent intent. In those days I also translated quite a bit of medieval religious poetry; I read these translations to him and he encouraged me to publish some of them. In connection with our numerous conversations about laments and lamentations he was particularly taken with my translation of a famous medieval lamentation about the burning of the Talmud at Paris in 1240, a rendition which I had made under the influence of Hölderlin's translations.

Around the middle of May I informed Benjamin of my decision to make a radical change in my academic goal and to regard Jewish studies rather than mathematics as the focus of my future efforts. According to notes I made at the time, I had realized that "my true goal is not mathematics but to become a Jewish scholar, to be able to occupy myself truly and completely with Judaism; this would yield a great deal worth the effort. My passion simply lies with philosophy and Judaism, and for this I have a great need for philology." I told Benjamin that I would seek to complete my mathematical studies, which I did (so that I might earn my bread as a teacher of mathematics in a school in Eretz Yisrael), but that I wanted to take my doctorate in Judaic studies. In those months I decided to tackle the study of kabbalistic literature and write a dissertation on the linguistic theory of the Kabbalah. For some time I had had some daring ideas on this subject, and I wanted to confirm or refute them in my dissertation. The combination of philosophy, mysticism, and philology in a Judaic theme stimulated all my aspirations. Benjamin reacted very enthusiastically to this decision. Considering the decline of the German currency which was then already beginning, the two of us could not count on being able to remain in Switzerland much longer. Hence I considered going in the fall either to Göttingen to complete my mathematical studies or to Munich to start my new studies. Munich had the largest collection of kabbalistic manuscripts in Germany. While still in Switzerland I decided in favor of Munich, where Elsa Burchardt was already studying.

In May 1919 I attended a philosophical lecture by the international chess champion Emanuel Lasker and then complained to Benjamin about the utter emptiness of that talk. Benjamin looked at me wide-eyed and said: "What do you expect of him? If he had said anything, he would no longer be the world chess champion."

On June 20 he sent me to Heyse's oral doctoral examination, and it was a real farce. Thus I was able to reassure Benjamin who, as I noted, lived in "downright indecent fear" of this examination. In those months the tensions that had marked our relationship gradually and finally abated. On June 27, Benjamin passed his own examination *summa cum laude,* and that evening we celebrated. Benjamin had not, however, permitted me to attend his exam. He said that Herbertz, Häberlein, and Maync had been extremely humane and even enthusiastic. Dora was high-spirited and happy as a child, and we told one another nothing but meaningless-meaningful stories about Pappelsprapp, as Dora's fantasy place was called. While Benjamin was preparing for his examination, on May 31 and June 1 he and I had hiked from Biel to Neuchâtel amid many conversations. We had a long discussion on whether his manner of living and mine were the same; he was convinced that they were and I denied it. We also talked a lot about politics and socialism, and expressed great reservations about socialism and the position of the individual if it was ever put into practice. To our way of thinking, theocratic anarchism was still the most sensible answer to politics. At that time I had written a long critique of *Hapoel hatzair* [The young worker], the Hebrew periodical of the Palestinian People's Socialists, and I had a gloomy presentiment concerning the fate of intellectuals under socialism. "In such an order the intellectual could be conceived of only as a madman"— this sentence I reread with profound horror fifty-five years later in my diary entry of June 29, 1919.

In the hotel at Biel where we spent the night we had a conversation about *Anschauung* [intuition]. I noted down Benjamin's definition which he presented for discussion: "The object of *Anschauung* is the need of a content announcing itself in the senses as pure to become perceptible. The perception of this need is called *Anschauung.*" My protest against this theological transfer of *Anschauung* to the acoustic sphere was rejected. He said this was just the point: the spheres could be separated and there was no pure *Anschauung* that was not a perception—though not a perception of a voice but of a need.

It was part of Benjamin's mystery-mongering, which was incomprehensible to me, that for six weeks he absolutely insisted on keeping the completion of his doctorate secret from everyone. It probably had something to do with financial considerations vis-à-vis his parents. His attitude at that time was a very ambiguous one —between having to earn a living at any cost and a *Privatdozentur* [unsalaried adjunct lectureship]. On July 1, Walter and Dora went to Iseltwald on Lake Brienz for their vacation and stayed there until the end of August. I visited them there on July 22, when we belatedly celebrated his birthday and admired Dora's presents. On that day I had written as follows in a reflection about myself with obvious reference to Benjamin: "My talent lies in the interpretation of those who can be interpreted." As a gift I had sent him the new edition of Avé-Lallemant's *Das deutsche Gaunertum* [Criminals of Germany], a book which contained an extensive discussion of the Jewish underworld in its relationship to the German one—a subject considered taboo by Jewish historiography but one that began to attract me greatly as complementary to the Jewish "upperworld" of mysticism. "The crooks as God's people—that would be a movement"—so I wrote at the time.

Benjamin's parents unexpectedly came to Iseltwald for about three weeks in August, and my projected second visit was canceled. That was the beginning of the unceasing, difficult, and sometimes bitter arguments about financial problems and Benjamin's future which pervaded his life during the coming years and made his relationship with his parents very delicate, if not to say largely ruined it. However, prior to my departure from Switzerland Benjamin came to Lungern on the Brünig Pass for a two days' visit at the end of August, and he brought along a note of his piece "Analogie und Verwandtschaft" [Analogy and relationship]. Once more we had long conversations about our mutual plans. After receiving his doctorate he had visited Herbertz in Thun and raised the question of a possible *Habilitation* at the University of Bern; Herbertz had expressed interest but was going to think the matter over.

I recall two things from my last visits in Bern. Benjamin had begun to read, probably as a follow-up to his conversations with Ball and Bloch, Georges Sorel's *Réflexions sur la violence*, a book that he commended to me also. Coming to grips with Sorel occupied him for a long time to come. On his desk there was also Mallarmé's *Un coup de dés* [A throw of the dice] in a special quarto edition whose graphic form was clearly in keeping with the title. The words in various type sizes rolled back and forth over the lines like dice, alternating between black and white (and, I believe, red as well). The whole thing was a most astonishing sight, and Benjamin told me that he did not understand the text either. In my uncomprehending soul there remained engraved only the visual image of a pre-Dadaistic product.

The First Postwar Years
(1920–1923)

After my return to Germany three months passed before I heard from Benjamin again. I had meanwhile resumed my studies in Munich and delved into the kabbalistic works and manuscripts in the state library. Agnon, too, spent that winter in Munich, and we often got together. On September 15, Benjamin wrote me to Berlin from Klosters:

Because of a certain feeling of unease, which may be attributed to persistent misfortune and highly uncertain prospects for the future, I am not in a position properly to inaugurate our correspondence herewith; rather, this letter is intended to propose that you do. . . . Tomorrow we leave here to spend a few weeks in Lugano before departing from Switzerland. I hope that Dora will finally find pleasure and new strength there. No one must know about this. I am telling it to you only because it would be even harder for me to write you and keep our whereabouts a secret than it is to address to you once again the request for complete secrecy which my present circumstances impose upon me. Let this suffice. We are greatly looking forward to this trip: from Thusis via the St. Bernhard's Pass to Mesocco by mail coach and from there to Lugano by train. Yesterday and the day before we had

*snow here and it was only a few degrees above freezing. Today a
wonderful sun is shining again and all the mountaintops are covered
with snow. Dora has made a good start on her detective novel. For the
past week I have been reading intensively Bloch's* Geist der Utopie,
*and I may emphasize its praiseworthy features in public—for the
author's, not the book's, sake. Unfortunately I cannot by any means
approve of everything in it. In fact, it sometimes makes me impatient.
Bloch himself, I am sure, is already beyond this book.* [Briefe *1, 217.
The middle portion of this letter is published here for the first time.*]

They departed at the beginning of November. Before that
Benjamin visited Herbertz once again, and the latter opened up to
him sure prospects of a *Habilitation,* possibly even an adjunct
lectureship in philosophy. "My parents are very pleased and have
no objections to my obtaining my *Habilitation* there"—so he wrote
me on November 16—"but they cannot as yet make a financial
commitment. The next project that I have in mind is a *Habilitation*
thesis, probably on a specialized epistemological subject. I plan to
do preliminary work on this project here." In the meantime he had
gone to Vienna for a short visit with his in-laws, and he spent the
period from around November 9, 1919 to the middle of February
1920 with Dora on the Semmering in a sanatorium owned by
Dora's aunt (though there were some stays in Vienna in between).
In early March they left Vienna and returned to Berlin, whereupon
a rather lively correspondence again developed between us.

After our return to Germany our relationship became very
harmonious, and the tensions of the Swiss period never recurred.
Was it the physical distance that guarded the rising curve of our
friendship against disturbances and made the much more infrequent days we spent together so positive? Was it (as it sometimes
seems to me in retrospect) that three young passionate, gifted
people who were almost completely dependent on one another and
were seeking the road to maturity had to use one another as release
mechanisms in the private sphere? Were there in this "triangle,"
of which we were unaware, unconscious emotional inclinations and
defenses that had to be discharged but which we were not able to
recognize in our "naiveté," that is, owing to our lack of psychological experience? I could not answer these questions even today.

In January 1920, Benjamin wrote me that he was working on a detailed review of Bloch's book. I still have my reply (dated February 5):

In recent days I have read major portions of Bloch's Geist der Utopie. *I have great expectations for your review and hope that it will demonstrate to me quite clearly what is good about the book. I have no doubt that good features do exist, but I must confess that I seem to have perceived some highly questionable things. Since you are planning to deal with the book's faults only esoterically, perhaps I may voice my criticisms openly so we can clearly establish whether we are of the same opinion. The following remarks are based mainly on the sections entitled "Über die Juden" and "Über die Gestalt der unkonstruierbaren Frage" [The form of the unconstruable question]; to the extent that I have understood these correctly, I most violently reject them. I have the impression that here Bloch encroaches, in the worst fashion and with inappropriate means, upon an area whose boundaries the book might at most define. With the gesture of a magus (and, woe, I* know *the sources of this magic!) he makes statements about the stories of the Jews, history, and Judaism, which clearly bear the terrible stigma of Prague [in my linguistic usage, that meant Buber]; it's no use, even the terminology is from Prague. The Jewish generation that Bloch has invented does not exist; it exists only in the intellectual realm of Prague. It is absolutely impermissible to use a philosophy-of-history method in which witnesses and testimonies are invoked (and here the author himself is nothing more than a witness who expresses things more emphatically)—not for [Jewish] demonism and demonology, but for the living light and dark heart of things— witnesses and testimonies that derive from the German-Jewish or Jewish-German sphere and thus prove nothing but this original sphere. Once again the only thing successfully done here is the ontological demonstration of the existence of the Devil. It is evident that Bloch disdains philology, but the fact that he does so without at least meeting its requirements as a matter of course in reflections on the philosophy of history (separation of sources!!!) is highly dubious. And it is even more dubious if he thinks that he can dispense with philology for his purposes and that it is all right for him to intermingle testimonies indiscriminately. In an almost sublime disconnectedness, Jewish cate-*

gories become part of a discussion that is totally inappropriate for them, and so, of course, they cause as many misunderstandings as gave rise to them: kiddush hashem *[sanctification of God's name] (in its most pitiful misinterpretation, deriving from* Das Buch vom Judentum *[The book of Judaism]); the name or names of God—not to mention numerous other things. But all these are only emanations of the central Christology that is foisted upon us here. To conceive of* corpus Christi *in any sense as the substance of our history is not possible for me, and I look in vain for credible evidence bespeaking a decline of the "traditional awe" before the founder of Christianity among the Jews—if I (presumably with justification) disregard evidence from the hybrid spheres. Whatever else Bloch's remarks may possess, in these portions they lack the most significant thing: justice. Everything has been virtually displaced, and in point of fact, it is an old axiom that these virtual displacements in the heart of Jewish history always yield things Christian as their labile indifferent state. There is a terrible mechanical law in all philosophical-historical perversions, and I wish my apprehension that this law is at work also in this book, notwithstanding its depth, could be allayed and refuted. Perhaps everything I am writing here will be self-evident to you, or it may be too peripheral for you; if so, then all the better. But I cannot rejoice at any intention to treat a great subject which is then realized in such a dubious intuition. Bloch's world certainly is not upside down, but there is evidence to indicate that it is only semblance, of that semblance which is only a differential away from reality (and here this semblance does not seem to have originated in language). This impalpability of the distance is, if I may say so, my moral objection to what I have read of the book.*

Benjamin's response, in which he expressed his full agreement with my critique, has appeared in print (*Briefe* 1, pp. 234–37).

After a "complete break" with his parents, Benjamin and Dora, who had in early April already toyed with the idea of a move to the Munich area, moved under difficult conditions to Grünau-Falkenberg near Berlin, where they lived in Erich Gutkind's home, a colorful little house built by Bruno Taut. In those days Benjamin made his first attempt to learn Hebrew from Gutkind, my former pupil; Dora wanted to join them but was not able to, having obtained a position as an English translator in a telegraph office. She asked me for a Hebrew primer of the kind that Walter had received from Gutkind, in order to study Hebrew secretly and surprise Walter on his birthday. She claimed that Walter was already making Hebrew jokes and had characterized the most influential man of the Falkenberg colony, its founder Adolph Otto, as *melekh hagoyim* [king of the non-Jews]. They remained there for at least three months, during which time Dora's parents came to Berlin in order to act as conciliators. At that time Benjamin made the personal acquaintance of Agnon. For Walter's birthday Dora had in the spring acquired Paul Klee's picture *Vorführung des Wunders* [Presentation of the miracle]; it subsequently hung in his room, but I have no recollection of it. To earn money Benjamin had resorted to graphology, a field in which he had considerable ability. In Bern I had once shown him a letter from my closest friend in the Zionist Youth Movement, whose character I thought I knew intimately. Benjamin looked at the letter briefly but closely, rather excitedly said, "Idiotic probity," and refused to make any further remark, as though he found that type especially infuriating. As a matter of fact, probity was precisely what that person radiated.

That year Walter and Dora resumed their close contact with Ernst Schoen, a schoolmate of Benjamin's who had become a pupil of Debussy. When I came to Berlin in the late summer, they introduced me to Schoen. A natural gentility that was inherent in his reserved manner greatly impressed me from the start, and this was strengthened by his halting speech. He was the only one from the group of Benjamin's schoolmates who remained tied to him in friendship, and he sometimes told me about their shared experiences between 1910 and 1915.

After the debacle with Erich Brauer, Gustav Steinschneider was the only other friend of mine whom I brought together with Benjamin. He had been in the same company with me during my military period at Allenstein, and I cared a great deal about his fortunes. Benjamin was taken with this very strange person. The situation he came from was very similar to mine with respect to my brothers. Steinschneider's older brother was a Communist, his second brother a staunch Zionist and one of the first pioneers from Germany who went to Eretz Yisrael. Steinschneider himself vacillated between these camps, and in a very calm and thoughtful manner. Benjamin and he had an excellent rapport. Dora especially liked Gustav, and they frequently invited him over. He had something of the natural nobility and musicality of Benjamin's friend Ernst Schoen, but he was utterly unworldly and incapable of doing anything "practical." His speech was a very slow, melodious drawl; he inclined toward hypochondria, and his narrow, somewhat weary face betrayed the potential philosopher. I was fascinated by the contrast to his grandfather, Moritz Steinschneider, one of the most important Judaists of the nineteenth century, whom I admired greatly in many respects. When I came in contact with his writings, I often spoke of him to Benjamin as one of the major figures in the group of erudite liquidators of Judaism. In those days I reflected a great deal about the suicide of Judaism through the so-called *Wissenschaft des Judentums* [Science of Judaism], and in 1921 I planned to write an essay about it for Benjamin's periodical *Angelus Novus*.

During that year I thought that Benjamin's turn to an intensive occupation with Judaism was close at hand. However, I was also aware of the impediments that stood in the way, and in my letters I implored him not to miss the propitious and proper moment. His letter on this subject has appeared in print (*Briefe* 1, pp. 248–51). Meanwhile Walter and Dora had moved into his parents' house in the Grunewald section of Berlin again, though I no longer know under what circumstances. Dora played Mozart, Schubert, and Beethoven for him on the piano. In a very cordial letter dated February 1921 she wrote me: "Do not turn away from us. I hope with all my heart that we shall meet on the common ground of things Jewish, and sooner than we all think. Everything I do is only a fight for the means." But at all times his other projects prevented him from entering the world of Judaism, even during the period when we drew especially close to each other. Characteristic of that period is the short prose piece which Adorno published as "Theologisch-politisches Fragment" (not Benjamin's title) and erroneously assigned to the year 1938. Everything about this two-page essay is exactly in keeping with his thinking and his specific terminology around 1920–21.

On November 4, 1920, Benjamin wrote me about his efforts

to obtain for me works of Scheerbart that I still lacked and told me that he had been taking a Hebrew course at the university. "Instruction is based on Strack's grammar. The teacher is probably less than mediocre in every respect—except, maybe, the pedagogical one. There are only about fifteen students. Tomorrow I shall apply for admission to Troeltsch's seminar on Simmel's philosophy of history in order to be able to use the seminar library. I prefer this to Erdmann's seminar on the psychology of thinking and Riehl's on Plato—for several reasons, among which Herr Troeltsch himself ranks last."

That year we met in October and again during the Christmas vacation, when I was in Berlin. At these reunions he received me with the greatest warmth and an open heart. He suffered under the fact that he had not carried out his promises and his own plans to learn Hebrew at this first attempt. Yet his reaction to this was not increased irritability but, rather, greater openness. During that year he had acquired a number of Judaic titles from the Jewish secondhand book dealers in Berlin, with a view to his projected studies. I told him that I had changed my dissertation subject on the Kabbalah and that my reading of kabbalistic works on linguistic mysticism, particularly the writings of Abraham Abulafia, had induced me to choose what seemed to me a less pretentious subject than the linguistic theory of the Kabbalah. How wrong I was is evidenced by the fact that I was not able to present until forty years later my projected introduction to the old text which I had translated into German from the manuscripts and provided with a commentary. Since Benjamin was intensively pursuing his interest in the philosophy of language in connection with his projected *Habilitation* thesis on epistemology, and since these interests had also played a role in the resumption of his personal relations with the philologist Ernst Lewy, whom he continued to esteem, the information I gave him about this area was extremely valuable to him.

After his return to Germany he continued to lead a very secluded life, though he began to appear again in the circle of older and new acquaintances. He had not published a line in years, and it was not until 1920–21 that he took some first steps to emerge from this literary obscurity.

The year 1921 was a turning point in his life. His published letters indicate this only imperfectly, though otherwise they are very revealing about his intellectual life during that period. Through his friend Jula Cohn he had met the poet Ernst Blass, editor of the periodical *Die Argonauten,* and this meeting had also brought him in contact with its publisher Richard Weissbach, who was interested in issuing Benjamin's Baudelaire translation. The two men started a lively correspondence about this enterprise, and Benjamin's letters came to light only after the publication of the *Briefe.* At that time he wrote his essay "Critique of Violence," which inaugurated the series of his "political" writings and which in its discussion of Georges Sorel strikes all the themes that had agitated him in his Swiss period—his thoughts on myth, religion, law, and politics. But the *Weisse Blätter,* for which the essay had been written, turned it down, and so it appeared in 1921 in a sociological journal among whose articles Benjamin's essay seemed quite out of place. He also tried hard to place his review of Bloch's book, of which he sent me a copy. That he ultimately did not succeed was probably due to the fact that this rather long essay was couched in such esoteric terms that the critic's own views—which were, after all, what mattered to the editors—remained virtually concealed.

After my return to Munich I attended a lecture by Rudolf Kassner. It was entitled "Betrachtungen zur Physiognomik" [Reflections on physiognomy], and I was very eager to hear it. In a letter to Benjamin I vehemently complained about what I termed Kassner's "uncontrollable profundity," and in his reply Benjamin even topped this by speaking of the "immoderate mendacity" of Kassner's writings. Around that time I began to reflect on the philological aspect of a study of mystical ideas and texts, both its positive and problematical features, and I wrote Benjamin a long letter about this. To my surprise I learned from his response that although he certainly was no philologist, he had long reflected on these things.

In April 1921 the disintegration of Walter's and Dora's marriage became evident, and I was confronted with it during my visit. Between July 1919 and April 1921 I had known nothing about its status and had no idea of the extent of the deterioration of their relationship. Only when the explosion was already at hand (and afterward) did I learn about it in conversations with Dora. When Ernst Schoen renewed his amicable relationship with Walter and Dora in the winter months of 1921, Dora fell madly in love with him and for a few months was in an altogether euphoric mood. She discussed this quite openly with Walter. In April, the sister of his school friend Alfred Cohn, Jula Cohn, with whom Walter and Dora were already friends in the Youth Movement and before their departure for Switzerland (though I am not sure how close the friendship was), came to Berlin, and Benjamin saw her again for the first time in five years. He developed a passionate attachment to her and probably plunged her into confusion for some time before she realized that she could not commit herself to him. There developed a situation which, to the extent that I was able to understand it, corresponded to the one in Goethe's novel *Elective Affinities*. When I came to Berlin, Walter and Dora let me in on this state of affairs and asked me to counsel and assist them as a friend in a situation in which both were considering marriage to someone else. Neither marriage materialized, but with this crisis the dissolution of Benjamin's marriage had entered an acute stage. That summer was a period of great tension and expectations. Both of them were convinced they had now experienced the love of their lives. The process that began at this time lasted for two years, and during that period Walter and Dora resumed their marital relationship from time to time, until from 1923 on they lived together only as friends—primarily for the sake of Stefan, whose development Walter followed with great interest, but presumably out of financial considerations as well. In the following years, until their divorce, this situation remained unchanged and was interrupted only by Walter's long trips and by periods in which he took a separate room for himself. From then on they went their separate ways, but they discussed with each other everything that affected them.

In the critical months when their marriage was beginning to break up they both, as far as I was able to witness, acted with a touching and loving friendliness toward each other. I never saw either treat the other person with such infinite considerateness and profound understanding as in those April days and the following year. It was as though each was afraid of hurting the other person, as though the demon that occasionally possessed Walter and mani-

fested itself in despotic behavior and claims had completely left
him under these somewhat fantastic conditions. My encounters in
those days with them and Ernst Schoen—Dora came to Munich
with him for a few days on her way to Breitenstein on the Semmering—are among the most beautiful that I remember. During my
remaining period in Germany, Dora was still greatly attached to
Walter, and yet she started speaking about him in a new tone. Not
that she doubted his gifts and his genius that meant so much to her,
but she began to speak about features that had never before been
voiced between us, including her experiences in the marriage. She
labeled Walter a person suffering from an obsessive-compulsive
neurosis, and this came as a surprise to me, for both of them had
great reservations about psychiatric terminology. Later I heard this
term from her on a number of other occasions, though I could not
really corroborate this diagnosis on the basis of my own experience.
Dora, a very sensuous woman, said that Walter's intellectuality
impeded his libido. Breaking away from his intellectual sphere, to
which she was to remain attached for a long time to come, proved
very difficult for her and brought about a radical change in her life.

Later I spoke with several other women who personally knew
Walter Benjamin very well, including one to whom he proposed
marriage in 1932. They all emphasized that Benjamin was not
attractive to them as a man, no matter how impressed or even
enchanted they were with his intellect and his conversation. One
of his close acquaintances told me that for her and her female
friends he had not even existed as a man, that it had never even
occurred to them that he had that dimension as well. "Walter was,
so to speak, incorporeal." Was the reason for this some lack of
vitality, as it seemed to many, or was it a convolution of his vitality
(which often enough burst forth in those years) with his altogether
metaphysical orientation that gained him the reputation of being
a withdrawn person?

In that year a circle which was forming around the strange
figure of Oskar Goldberg began to play a role in our letters and
conversations—a circle that was bound to interest us from altogether different angles. While quite a bit has been written on the
beginnings of Expressionism and the Neopathetisches Kabarett,
the obscurity surrounding this circle, which later (from 1925 on)

appeared in public as the Philosophische Gruppe, a forum for the discussion of vital problems of philosophy, is still as great as it was in the twenties and particularly during the period preceding my departure for Eretz Yisrael. Among the Neopathetics were Oskar Goldberg (1887–1951) and Erich Unger (1887–1952), later the circle's outstanding personalities. Goldberg had been a medical student, but as far as I was able to determine, he never practiced medicine. He was a small, fat man who looked like a stuffed dummy, and he exerted an uncanny magnetic power over the group of Jewish intellectuals who gathered around him. There were also two or three non-Jews as marginal members; one of them, Peter Huchel, told me: "I was Goldberg's *shabbes goy* [non-Jew who performs chores in an Orthodox Jewish household on the Sabbath]." Goldberg, who came from a very pious family and had an excellent knowledge of the Hebrew Bible, had as a young man already delved into numerological speculations about the construction of the Torah from God's name. Above all, however, it was the visions which he had over a long period of time in schizoid twilight states before awakening and the revelations about the Torah to which he laid claim that had made him an absolute authority for the initiates of this circle. The only thing he had published at that time was a thin booklet entitled *Die fünf Bücher Mosis, ein Zahlengebäude* [The Pentateuch, an edifice of numbers, 1908]. Goldberg disseminated his teachings in private courses, and if one of his adherents was asked about his observance or nonobservance of some aspects of the Jewish ritual, the answer was: "That is what Oskar told us to do." No questions could be directed to Oskar, for he was in the enlightened possession of revelation. He did not lack philosophical training and interests, and from biological and ethnological categories then current in the world of scholarship he had fashioned for himself a sort of biological Kabbalah which was intended to demonstrate the ritual of the Torah—the *Wirklichkeit der Hebräer* [The reality of the Hebrews], the title of his major work, published in 1925—as a continuum of perfect magic. These ideas did not lack a demonic dimension, nor should one underestimate the fascination exerted by a commentary which explained Judaism as a sort of theological state of decline of the ancient magical Hebraism and in so doing shrank from no conclusion and no absurdity. What Goldberg aimed at was the restoration of the magic bond between God and His people (of which he viewed himself as the biological center), and things that he did not deem capable of realization in our time were shunted aside unconsidered. Goldberg's formulations were uncommonly incisive and presumptuous, and they had a certain Luciferian luster. Goldberg had first devoted himself to theosophy, but he soon struck out on his own, availing himself of the considerable philosophical gifts of Erich Unger, who became his chief spokesman and interpreter. Unger and Simon Guttmann, who has already been mentioned in several contexts, were his closest confidants. At the same time that Benjamin resumed his association with these people, whom he had known in his youth, I made the acquaintance of some of Goldberg's adherents, and they sought to induce me to join this circle. Goldberg spoke little, and as the head of the sect he was, as it were, untouchable. Benjamin felt such a strong antipathy toward him that on one occasion he was physically incapable of grasping the hand Goldberg had extended in greeting; he told me that Goldberg had been surrounded by such an impure aura that he had simply been unable to manage it. Unger, on the other hand, was humanly agreeable and philosophically quite interesting to him. Benjamin first drew my attention to the earliest publications of the Goldberg circle and particularly those of Unger which were appearing at the time. These demanded, among other things, "the stateless founding of a Jewish people" [*die staatslose Gründung eines jüdischen Volkes*] by metaphysical means in contrast to empirical Zionism, which Goldberg's circle opposed. At the Lichterfelde home of Elisabeth Richter-Gabo, a close friend of Dora's and a patron of the Goldberg group, Walter and Dora sometimes got together with Unger, Goldberg, and others.

These people found me interesting not only because I had access to the Hebrew sources, but primarily because an old friend of mine had told them that I was studying the Kabbalah. The Kabbalah was highly regarded among them—not so much because of the religious and philosophical aspects that attracted me to its study, but because of its magical implications, about which Goldberg had the most extravagant notions. My wholly negative attitude toward the attempts to draw me into this circle, and toward the pseudo-Kabbalah that was presented to me in Goldberg's name, caused Benjamin considerable embarrassment on several occasions, for while he was not interested in Goldberg, he did care about maintaining his connection with Unger. During the next years we had much occasion to talk or correspond about the publication and other activities of the Goldberg circle which, among other things, campaigned for a mass emigration from Europe to "primitive" peoples—that is, those who were, according to Goldberg, capable of magic. Their negation of the bourgeois world brought them close to social-revolutionary movements, particularly in their printed announcements, whereas they were actually concerned with the realization of a new worldwide theocracy, and Goldberg believed he was pulling the strings.

When I arrived in Jerusalem, I became friends with Ernst David, who had financed the publication of Goldberg's magnum opus. He was a man of noble character whom Goldberg's spell had caused to remain in the circle for years, and who had broken loose from it with great difficulty, infringing Goldberg's taboo on emigration to Eretz Yisrael and participation in Zionist reconstruction. From David and his wife I learned a great deal about the exoteric and esoteric aspects of this group. After *Die Wirklichkeit der Hebräer* had appeared, I wrote a long, critical letter about the book; Benjamin and Leo Strauss disseminated copies of it in Berlin, and it won me no friends among Goldberg's adherents. That others were impressed, indeed entranced, by the imaginative verve of Goldberg's interpretations of Torah and sometimes even by their rather sinister aspects is evidenced not only by the writings of the paleontologist Edgar Dacqué but above all by Thomas Mann; the first novel of the latter's Joseph tetralogy, *The Tales of Jacob,* is in its metaphysical sections based entirely on Goldberg's book. This, to be sure, did not keep Mann from making Goldberg the target of his irony a few years later in a special chapter of his novel *Doctor Faustus.* There Goldberg appears as the scholar Dr. Chaim Breisacher, a kind of metaphysical super-Nazi who presents his magical racial theory largely in Goldberg's own words. Benjamin's interest in this Jewish sect, if I may so describe it, accompanied him right into the Hitler period.

After the abovementioned incidents between Walter and Dora,

which also marked the beginning of the familiar form of address among the three of us (the *du* used by friends), I went back to Munich. I had tried to encourage them to clarify, as far as possible, not only their feelings but also the direction in which they wanted to go, and, above all, to gain a clear understanding of whether the fulfillment of their lives really lay in new marital commitments. I regarded such new commitments as entirely possible but not very probable. I knew Ernst Schoen personally, but all I knew of Jula Cohn at that time was what Benjamin had told me about the magic she radiated. The following letter from Benjamin, dated May 26, 1921, refers to these events and some others, including a renewed encounter between Ernst Bloch and myself in Munich (the last until 1968):

Dear Gerhard,

I sincerely and most cordially hope that your inability to work and your depression have by now abated and are not dependent on a clarification of the occurrences among us. For nothing has been decided here, and it is not even certain when a decision will be made. Of course it is possible, as you write, that some day inner clarity will come, and more quickly than we realize, but there certainly is no guarantee that any kind of solution will promptly manifest itself definitively, i.e., among other things, in the reestablishment of a stable way of living. Naturally, the two of us will in no way let ourselves be tied to an unending chain of upheavals, doubts, and torment; instead, we shall try to keep on enhancing the composure which we have maintained up to now. The bad thing about all this is that I fear an unfavorable effect on Dora's health if she does not get some peace. The doctor made a definite diagnosis of pleurisy, which is not in itself serious, but does mean that she needs rest. In recent days the outward symptoms have greatly abated, and Dora hardly coughs anymore, though that does not mean too much. She will see the doctor again before her trip. Whether or not you will see her in a few days is apparently not quite certain yet (or perhaps again), for as long as Dora has not made definitive arrangements, she is not sure whether she will visit you on the way to her destination or on the way back. It also depends on E.S., but I believe you will perhaps see her now after all. In any case, I would like her to take a four-week rest cure in Breiten-

stein regardless of her other trips. You will in any event see me this summer as well, though it is not yet certain where and when. . . . I don't understand your reference to my essay on violence. I did give you a copy—and Bloch was already acquainted with it. Did he borrow it from you again? When is he going to Vienna? I would like to see him this summer also. There is a possibility that I shall go to Austria, though not until later. I believe I shall go to Heidelberg [where Jula Cohn lived] only temporarily; in any case, I shall meet J.C. in some other place first, probably toward the end of June, and in the meantime I shall stay here with the Gutkinds. I may also take a trip to visit [Ferdinand] Cohrs [a friend from the Freie Studentenschaft period] and the Rangs.

The project with S. Fischer, a very shrewd and timorous gentleman, is pending and hinges on the support given by my sponsor [Moritz Heimann or Rudolf Kayser?]. And you know by what complex fraudulence this is in turn determined. Thank God, the pace has slowed down considerably. When I visited Fischer I did not make a bad impression; fortune favored me.

To my great joy and relief I was recently able to write the preface to the Baudelaire translation "Die Aufgabe des Übersetzers" ["The Task of the Translator," in Illuminations, *pp. 69–82]. It is completely finished, but I don't know yet how I shall have copies made.*

Shortly thereafter Benjamin came to Munich on his way to visit Dora on the Semmering. On that occasion he bought Klee's watercolor *Angelus Novus* for 1,000 marks (14 dollars!). In my essay "Walter Benjamin und sein Engel" ["Walter Benjamin and His Angel," in *Jews and Judaism in Crisis,* pp. 198–236] I have given a detailed account of this acquisition and Benjamin's close relationship to the picture. At the end of June he returned to Munich and stayed with us in the apartment which I shared with my wife-to-be, Elsa Burchardt (called Escha by her friends), and where the Klee picture hung for the time being. I was then working on a detailed discussion of the mystic poetry of the Jews. This was the subject of *Die Lyrik der Kabbalah* [The poetry of the Kabbalah], a book that had been written by an excellent Hebraist, Meir Wiener, but that had been corrupted by Expressionism and now called forth all my polemical spirit. I told Benjamin what the Talmud and the

mystics of that period had to say about the hymns of angels, and
my words fell on very fruitful soil. In those days he was in excellent
spirits, and Escha and he outdid each other in humorous-ironic
dialogues. He told us about his encounters with Salomo Friedländer who, like him, viewed the activities of the Goldberg group
as an outsider with a considerable amount of philosophical cynicism (later he was a very strict Kantian in ethics). Benjamin
brought me as a present Friedländer's major philosophical work,
Schöpferische Indifferenz [Creative indifference], which he esteemed
highly. That was when I first told Benjamin about *Der Stern der
Erlösung* [The star of redemption], Franz Rosenzweig's important
religiophilosophical work which had appeared in late 1920 and
which had begun to occupy me. With reference to my publications
in *Der Jude* I told him he would have no other choice but to
subscribe to the periodical, and we sent in his subscription.

After about a week he went to Heidelberg to see Jula Cohn, and
on July 9 he sent us a humorous certificate recommending Elsa
Burchardt's inn, especially for the Sabbath. "The proprietress has
substantial facilities, an academically trained porter, and inexpensive beds. A garage for angels is available upon request. . . . An
address book (angelology) and political promotional literature *(La
révolte des anges)* are at the disposal of our honored angel guests
at all times." The nouns in the certificate were presented in rebus
form, and some were translated into embryonic Hebrew. Benjamin
signed "For the Committee" as Dr. Nebbich, the self-pitying or
ironic name he liked to apply to himself for playful purposes. When
he was in a good mood, this tendency toward playfulness often
manifested itself. The following letter was enclosed with the certificate:

Dear Gerhardt [sic]
    *In my official capacity it is my duty to send you the enclosed
euphonious certificate. My personal antipathy to Fräulein Burchardt
remains unaffected by it. Yours, Dr. Nebbich.*
*P.S. The trip was very pleasant on the whole, though this time too I
had to listen to conversations that made my head swim. Immediately
after my arrival I went to the Hotel Tannhäuser, where I was given
a room. By evening that hotel was fully booked.*

The weather here is heavenly and the city much more beautiful than I remembered it. Last night we had supper at the Wolfsbrunnen Inn; and I am planning to take long walks to the valley or the mountains every day until I feel inwardly well again. Here I am occupying the two rooms of Herr Leo Blumenthal [read Löwenthal] who is out of town for a few months. I feel very comfortable in them. They are on the ground floor on a quiet street (the Schlossberg), and with a very pleasant desk virtually entice one to work. Any day, therefore, I may ask you to send me Der Stern der Erlösung, but I shall wait to keep you from doing so unnecessarily.

At Fräulein Cohn's I found Agnon's new novel complete in individual issues of Der Jude. Unfortunately I must report that my forced subscription to the journal gave her great pleasure.

Herr Blumenthal [Löwenthal] was considerate enough to leave his small, choice, and well-kept library out here for my use. So you see that I have gone from one pleasant stay to another, and things go well for me. I shall be very well. With cordial regards to you both,
                                                        Walter

(Leo Löwenthal, who is mentioned in this letter, was an ardent Zionist in his student days; later, after his emigration, he worked with Benjamin as one of the chief associates of the Institute for Social Research.)

Benjamin stayed in Heidelberg until the middle of August and while there started preliminary work on his great essay on Goethe's novel *Elective Affinities.* During this period of heightened spirits and renewed productivity he celebrated his birthday with Jula Cohn, and as a present I sent him my poem "Gruss vom Angelus" [Greetings from the angel] about the Klee picture which I had had a chance to view for so long. On August 4 he gave me an important bit of news: the publisher Weissbach had offered to bring out a periodical entirely reflecting Benjamin's spirit beginning January 1, 1922, and it was to bear the title of Paul Klee's picture. He regarded my collaboration as essential to this journal's success, and he wanted to visit me in Munich at once to discuss the new situation. The high expectations which Benjamin had for my collaboration were rather embarrassing to me. After all, I could not conceal from him the fact that I did not feel impelled to collaborate on a

German periodical in what seemed to me like an especially visible manner while my mind was on quite different things and goals— something that Benjamin certainly must have been aware of. Thus there were difficulties and disappointments, which are reflected in letters from that period, including a few satirical letters from Dora to me. In response to Benjamin's urgent request I had expressed my readiness to help but also my misgivings. His reply of August 8, written after Elsa Burchardt had stopped in Munich for two days to visit him, sheds some light on the situation:

Dear Gerhard,

    Your letter came on Sunday morning after Fräulein Burchardt had left and half an hour before I went to see Weissbach to sign the contract. Your letter is hesitant, but my confidence in you must remain all the more unhesitant, because I could hardly have undertaken the project without it. You will now speak with Fräulein Burchardt sooner than with me and will receive the first information from her. To give you an idea of the more precise details that I had hoped to tell you about in person, I am enclosing my draft of a contract which coincides in all points with the one I am signing. According to the plan, which is entirely of my devising, a periodical is to be founded which will not concern itself in the least with a commercial readership and will thus be able to serve an intellectual one all the more unequivocally. It is for this reason that the number of subscribers which the budget could count on had to be pegged as low as possible, for any attempts to base a periodical such as I have in mind on a substantial number (1,000 at the very least) of subscribers paying a modest subscription fee (about 50 marks a year) would be doomed to failure. The people who can "take" periodicals won't even take such a publication for free, and many—perhaps most—of those for whom it is intended could not afford it even if it cost only 30 marks. Thus there is only one possibility: to regard the "subscription" as a nonprofit institution—so the journal won't have to dance to the public's tune. If those hundred copies do not suffice for the real, nonpaying readership, then the free copies can be increased. This cannot cause any problems, because the free copies will be stamped "complimentary copy." For the time being the periodical will print nothing about the title's reference to the Klee picture.

I hope this has dispelled a substantial part of your misgivings. Now to mine. True, I am limited to 480 pages a year only as a maximum and can stay below that, but I don't have a lot of really important prose in prospect. Fräulein Burchardt told me in response to my question that Agnon probably would like to see his German translations appear in Angelus—*for one thing because they will be available for free there, and for another because he might even like the idea of having them in a periodical that is not specifically Jewish. If that is true, I would like to print "Die neue Synagoge" [The new synagogue; a slip for "Die alte Synagoge" (The old synagogue)] in the first issue. And I beg of you to do your best to bring this about. Then, too, it would be important for me to get a chance to see your letter to the editors of* Vom Judentum *[On Judaism]. Couldn't you send it to me? Also, the letter which you wrote to Siegfried Lehmann several years ago should be published, if memory serves.*

Today I wrote to Lewy, duly called his attention to your plans to visit him, and told him that I would like to be present. I also told him about Angelus *and bespoke his goodwill in every way. If you answer me promptly, your letter will probably still reach me here. Your proposals for September are all right with me. With cordial regards,*

Yours,
Walter

We have bought for you here: Deutsch-Hebräisches Wörterbuch. . . . zum Gebrauch des hebräischen Handelsstandes ausgearbeitet von C. G. Ewert Pfarrer *[German-Hebrew dictionary . . . compiled for the Hebrew trading class by Pastor C. G. Ewert]*, Reutlingen 1822. *For six marks. The preface reads as if it were by Dukes.*

In 1920 I had translated into German several short stories by Agnon which seemed absolutely perfect to me and read them to Benjamin, who was delighted with them. Agnon was a great master of very short narratives, and in this he was in many respects closely akin to Benjamin. In 1920 the editors of *Vom Judentum*, a volume published in Prague in 1913, had decided in view of changed conditions to issue another volume with the same title, and they invited me to contribute to it. I responded with a vehement invective against the pseudoreligious and pseudorevolutionary element

of Prague Zionism, and I read this polemic to Benjamin. The letters
to Siegfried Lehmann, which I had written in the fall of 1916 after
a stormy debate in the Jüdisches Volksheim [Jewish community
center] that Lehmann directed, were already in the same vein,
culminating in a comparison between Buber and Ahad Ha'am, to
the latter's favor. When I read these letters to Buber in early 1917,
they met with his strong approval. Incidentally, Kafka was informed of this debate with Lehmann in a letter from his fiancée,
and as I found out to my great surprise more than fifty years later,
he reacted by expressing his agreement with the demands and
proposals of "Herr Scholem." As for Leopold Dukes, he was a
nineteenth-century Jewish scholar who combined the strangest eru-
dition in matters regarding old and rare books with an embittered
style that was lapidary, bordering on the pathological. I had come
across his writings, and on Benjamin's visit in Munich I had read
him a long preface to one of these, which sounded like a voice from
another planet.

Our visit to Ernst Lewy came about owing to the coincidence
of two different circumstances. One was Benjamin's desire to interest Lewy in contributing to the projected periodical, and the other
was my intention to visit Leni Czapski-Holzman, a young painter
with whom I had been friends since my Jena days. She was married, lived with Ernst Lewy's family in a remote little village—
Wechterswinkel in the Rhön mountains—and had invited me to
visit her husband and herself. We were there from September 8 to
10, 1921, spending two memorable days in a fine old house with
a large fairy-tale garden and a pond with water lilies. The whole
property had once belonged to the bishop of Bamberg. Lewy, who
was still *Privatdozent* in Berlin, spent only his vacations there.
There was something uncanny about his wife, who spoke slowly
and little: she had the attracting power of a swamp, the magic of
an orchid, and the sucking and frightening quality of a clinging
vine. They told me about their daughter, a girl of about twelve who
was a sleepwalker. Mrs. Lewy dominated her husband in a
strangely quiet way. The atmosphere was an enchanting one and
affected all of us. We soon learned that the Holzmans had been
bothered by it for a long time and wished to leave. Michael Holzman was a cousin of Oskar Goldberg, and in his youth, long before

the First World War, he had shared a room with him for a time, experiencing at first hand Goldberg's schizophrenic character and his claim to power over others which manifested itself even then. Holzman gave us a long account of this on our first evening, and to us, who had just had so many discussions about Goldberg, it was as surprising as it was enlightening.

We were housed in a large room with a huge double bed. When we awoke in the morning, Walter said to me: "When I opened my eyes just now, if you had been a girl lying there, I would have thought I was the bishop of Bamberg." The next day he presented his ideas on the nature of *Angelus*—as they have been preserved in the "Ankündigung" [announcement] of the periodical. In the literary sphere it was clear that he wished to center it on the production of Fritz Heinle and his brother Wolf. As for prose, he was interested in presenting authors who had no literary exposure or were only marginal figures and whose orientation toward language was akin to the one that dominated Benjamin. It was this orientation that brought together in Benjamin's spirit people like Agnon, Florens Christian Rang, Ernest Lewy, and myself—quite apart from what the subject of a contribution might be. Although Benjamin's ideas about language went far beyond his own, Lewy was greatly taken with them and suggested as his own contribution to the periodical a linguistic critique and analysis of the speeches of Wilhelm II. He owned the five Reclam volumes of these speeches which unmistakably betrayed the authorship and personal style of the Kaiser, and he gave a wonderful reading of a few of them, accompanied by his commentary. In his analysis of the metaphors and the syntax he expressed the whole "Wilhelminian" disorder. We were all enthusiastic about the idea of such an essay, which he was modestly going to call "Bemerkungen zu Reden Wilhelms II" [Notes on speeches of Wilhelm II]. From this outline there developed a long conversation about the Jews' relationship to language. There were lively discussions about Heinrich Heine, Karl Kraus, and Walter Calé (who after his early suicide was touted as a great genius, though there was not much to him), as well as philosophers of language like Lazarus Geiger, Haim Steinthal, and Fritz Mauthner. From very different points of view we discussed the thesis whether the Jews' special attachment to the world of language might be traced to their thousands of years of occupation with sacred texts, with revelation as the linguistic basic fact and its reflection in all spheres of language. Karl Kraus, with whose attitude toward, and indeed addiction to, language Benjamin was already beginning to concern himself, was the subject of a heated debate. I had for a long time reflected on the derivation of Kraus's style from the Hebrew prose and poetry of medieval Jewry—the language of the great halakhists and of the "mosaic style," the poetic prose in which linguistic scraps of sacred texts are whirled around kaleidoscopelike and are journalistically, polemically, descriptively, and even erotically profaned. Benjamin often requested that I elaborate on these reflections in writing, but neither my study of this subject nor Lewy's analysis of the speeches of Wilhelm II ever assumed definitive written form.

Holzman was himself a painter, inclining toward the Expressionistic orientation which was then prevalent. Benjamin and he had long conversations about painting. However, the uncanny atmosphere that surrounded the Lewy family really got on Benjamin's nerves, and especially on the last evening he became jumpy and irritable. In such things he was very sensitive. In Lewy's wife he sensed a reserve and half-concealed antipathy which produced irritated conversations between him and Lewy and spoiled much of what the day had brought. He felt that a rejection was impending. Meanwhile Holzman and Lewy recommended some of their friends and acquaintances as potential contributors to *Angelus.*

In point of fact, Benjamin, who spent most of September and October in Berlin, soon received a rather aggressive rebuff from Ernst Lewy, and this led to an alienation between the two men and what was for a considerable period only a formal relationship between them. As he often did under such conditions, Benjamin wrote diplomatic letters to Lewy under Dora's inspiration and guidance. I, too, was in Berlin in September, and under the influence of Holzman's detailed reports about Goldberg there was a row between me and this circle when Goldberg's fiancée (and later wife), Dora Hiller, visited me in an effort to convert me—the last such attempt made from that quarter. The lady paid me great compliments, but when I gave her my opinion of Goldberg in very harsh terms, she took back everything she had said and swept out of the room. I gave Benjamin a detailed account of the scene, and I also discussed Goldberg with Hyne Caro, who was on the fringe of that circle. Upon my return to Munich I received from Benjamin a letter as a [Jewish] New Year's greeting in the name of the Angel, in which he described in a manner very characteristic of him his behavior during the crisis that I had precipitated (printed in greatly abridged form in *Briefe* 1, pp. 273–75).

. . . Your conversation with Dora Hiller, you see, has borne rich fruit the thickness of hailstones, and it has all fallen on my head. I am not sure why she came to see you, but I suppose she conducted a little espionage interview with you under some pretext and at her own risk, and thus without a real assignment from the "opposing party"; perhaps you were under no illusions about that. I don't know what threads run from this visit to what follows, and it really doesn't matter; you will probably have a clear view of the situation. On Tuesday, the day of your departure, Mr. Unger took Hyne Caro aside at the home of Dr. Zacharias (Unger's brother-in-law) and asked him when he had seen you last and whether you had said anything against the "circle" (that is, Goldberg). Little Caro thought he remembered—whether correctly or incorrectly—that your anti-Goldberg remarks were made with reference to me, and he was quite right to regard this reference as confidential. He therefore said that he knew from nothing—to which Unger replied only, "Strange." On the same evening the devil got into me and I cut Goldberg in rather ostentatious fashion. At my next meeting with Unger, when we were going to talk about Angelus, *he prefaced our discussion by asking what my attitude toward Goldberg was and said that his own relationship with him was an extremely close one. He hinted broadly that he actually knew the truth and expected from me only a purely formal declaration that I was "indifferent" toward Goldberg. As for me, however, since my experiences at Wechterswinkel and my unhappy experiences with Bloch (which I shall tell you about later), I haven't been able to see such an abyss without jumping into it out of fear, and so I ruined everything—to my horror as well as his. In short, it was a complete break. Dora, who—unlike me—immediately recognized that the whole thing was a matter of prestige, then involved Unger in a diabolically clever conversation and explained my antipathy as a personal idiosyncrasy, thus saving the day. After these*

conversations, of course, Unger is better informed about my true atti-
tude than before, but he now has the desired salving of his conscience.
This long account is by way of motivating my request that you do not
tell the "circle" anything about my position or about your conversa-
tion with Caro. There will be time enough for that if some day
Goldberg's follies come out in the open somewhere.

At that time Benjamin's relationship with Ernst Bloch began
to grow strained. His oral reports and later his letters reflected a
constant fluctuation between personal attraction and revulsion, between admiration for the energy that was at work in Bloch and his
great intellectual potential on the one hand and an often profound
disappointment at his literary production on the other. Among
these disappointments was *Thomas Münzer,* a work that had recently appeared. Some of Bloch's essays, such as his review of
Georg Lukács's *Geschichte und Klassenbewusstsein* [History and
class consciousness], he praised very highly, while many of Bloch's
contributions in *Die Weltbühne* [The world stage] made him fly into
a rage.

The coming months were filled with Benjamin's efforts to obtain studies adequate to the spirit of *Angelus.* It was at that time
that I first presented to him my critical reflections on the *Wissen-*
schaft des Judentums and its function in Jewish history, which were
aimed at clarifying the problematical character of these bourgeois
efforts for so unbourgeois a phenomenon as Judaism. Benjamin
tried to induce me to present these reflections in an essay for the
periodical. I wrote that essay more than twenty-two years later in
Hebrew, and it belongs to those of my writings that have had an
enduring effect. Its formulations were so tempestuous that I could
never bring myself to present the original version to readers not
familiar with Jewish affairs, and so I published only a greatly
watered-down, overly compromising German speech on the subject
—something that is still a source of irritation to me.

At Benjamin's urgent request I had also to give an expert
opinion on Rang's great essay interpreting Goethe's poem "Selige
Sehnsucht" [Blessed longing], a profound and significant study
which was, however, so preoccupied with gnostic elements that I
had to counsel Benjamin against printing it in *Angelus.* Numerous

remarks in Benjamin's letters give evidence of the continuing activities of the "University of Muri." In November 1921 I received the following "notification":

The Rector's Chambers
Muri

Dear Colleague:

Regarding your several urgent reminders to remit to you the honoraria due you from last semester, I herewith notify you for the third time that your lecture course on THE INVENTION OF THE FRETSAW as well as your seminar PRACTICAL TRAINING IN FRETSAW WORK did not attract any students. However, we shall continue to recommend your courses to all students.

Further, I am pleased to be able to tell you that at the last examinations Herr stud. bub. Martin passed and was awarded the degree of Buber. His application for the venia lebendi *[permission to live—a pun on* venia legendi, *permission to teach] was approved. Within a year's time he intends to offer the following course: Weekdays, 7–8 A.M. Martin Buber: "Rabindranath Tagore" (with guided tours).*

*Also, the entire faculty voted in unanimosity [*eingrimmig*] to permit Prof. Scheler to lecture as a visiting professor. He is announcing the following courses: "Life and Works of St. Johann Maria Farina" (publ.) [the inventor of eau de cologne]; "Seminar on the Conclave" (for the advanced).*

The following new work was acquired for the library: Arthur Kutscher, Herrschaft und Dienst *[Authority and service]. The photograph of Fräulein Burchardt which you kindly sent us for our art collection is returned to you with many thanks, since the collection is being extensively renovated.*

Salve!
The Rector Magnificus

I. Kaut
Warder

Benjamin was fond of telling a joke that circulated about Hermann Cohen, the head of the Marburg neo-Kantian School. In

Marburg even pharmacists who wished to obtain a diploma had to take an examination in philosophy, cursory though it might be. One day such an examinee was sent to Cohen, and he asked him with his characteristic intensity, "What do you know about Plato?" The candidate had never heard the name. "Can you tell me something about the main doctrines of Spinoza?" Silence. Cohen, by now in despair: "Can you tell me who the most important philosopher of the eighteenth century was?" The pharmacist's face brightened and he started hemming and hawing. Cohen vigorously encouraged him. Finally the candidate said, "Kaut, Mr. Privy Councillor." Cohen is said to have burst into tears.

Over the Christmas vacation of 1921 Benjamin and I were both in Berlin. I had little time to speak with Walter and Dora, however, since family matters detained me—there was a political trial involving my brother Werner—and I was dictating my dissertation to a typist. Benjamin sent me an allusive invitation to stay with them; it was in the form of an "Aramaic fragment" from the "Cimelia of the Bibl. Berol." [Treasures of the Berlin Library] entitled "Of the Man Gershom Who Lived among the Daughters of Balaam by the Banks of the Buber." On the reverse Dora had written: "*Komm komm komm / Platz ist und Willkomm / kannst auch bei Ernst bleiben / Wenn dich von hier tut der Angelus vertreiben*" [Come, come, come / There's room and welcome / With Ernst you could stay / Should Angelus drive you away].

In the succeeding months, between November 21 and February 1922, Benjamin wrote in Heidelberg his study of Goethe's *Elective Affinities,* which he dedicated to Jula Cohn. In addition, he tried to establish contact with university circles to explore the possibility of a *Habilitation,* of which he saw some prospect, and he participated in the philosophical-sociological evenings that took place in Marianne Weber's house. There he read a paper on poetry which presumably was taken from the introduction to his projected edition of Fritz Heinle's poems. This presentation was an utter failure, meeting with total and embarrassed imcomprehension. Nevertheless, he was able to establish a fairly friendly relationship with Karl Mannheim, one of Max Weber's gifted pupils. In Heidelberg, Benjamin once saw Stefan George taking a walk on the Schlossberg, and George's appearance made a great impression on him. Jula Cohn's attachment to George's circle, to which she had been introduced by Robert Böhringer in 1916, for a long time kept alive in him a certain interest in the figure of George.

The completion of my dissertation and the preparations for my examination kept me busy. At the end of January 1922, Benjamin wrote me from Berlin: "I believe that our mutual prolonged silence has kept us informed abut each other pretty well, meaning that we both have our hands full." And about himself he wrote:

I have done a lot of work, but in the process I once again picked up my noise psychosis, be it from actual noise or the excessive strain of concentration. As a result I am completely run down, every voice, especially the "western ones" [?], infuriates me, and I have to consider working only at night, which would mean a great deal of inconvenience. Do other people manage to have peace and quiet or don't they?
. . . In the meantime the "Announcement" of Angelus *has been completed, and you will receive it as soon as a typewritten copy is available. Now I am working on completing the critique of* Elective Affinities *in the near future. This is a study of which I speak with respect. It is claiming all my time and energy. If you are not acquainted with the novel, I would have to ask you to read it before reading my study. —The other day Herbertz wrote me such a touching letter (about divorces, financial matters, and the essay on violence) that I have nominated him as a* corresponding *member of Muri Academy. On the other hand, the efforts of certain gentlemen to appoint Deputy Scholem [my brother] Chairman of the Bacteriology Department after his release from jail are encountering serious opposition. —Starting tomorrow I am to give a* Backfisch *[teenager] who lives next door in the Grunewald district graphology lessons at 30 marks a throw. At the KDW [Kaufhaus des Westens, West End Department Store] I bought myself a magic wand, with the aid of which I hope to make this a very long-drawn-out affair. . . .*

> *Be thanked and warmly blessed*
> *By Walter, who's depressed.*
> *—Goethe*

He and Dora complained that I had not yet sent in my contribution to the first issue of the periodical, though it was supposed to be printed in the spring, a plan that never materialized, however, due to the runaway inflation. Walter wrote me that the first number would contain thirty blank pages with this heading: "Gerhard Scholem: The Empty Promises."

Benjamin's work on *Elective Affinities* marked a new turn in his intellectual life, from systematically oriented thinking to commenting. He must have had a deep-seated predisposition toward this, and I am far from believing that our conversations of those years —particularly in Switzerland and subsequently—about the central significance of commentary in Jewish literature had more than an indirect influence on this reorientation. In those years I still studied a portion of the Talmud almost daily, especially in Munich with the rabbi of the small Orthodox synagogue, Dr. Ehrentreu, who was an absolutely first-rate Talmudist and nothing short of an ancient Jewish sage. I used to commend to Benjamin the virtues of the commentators, particularly those of Rashi, whose work represents in the Jewish tradition the greatest achievement in commentary, and I would often tell him in jest: Actually, you ought to become the new Rashi. His productivity increasingly shifted in this direction, and he became the commentator of important texts around which his thinking was able to crystallize. His speculative talent was aimed no longer at devising something new, but at penetrating something existent, interpreting and transforming it. This surely was not a deliberate shift in emphasis, at least not in the beginning, and he continued to engage in reflections that were more aimed at a system. Only gradually did he become clearly aware of this tendency, and in 1927 I found it fully developed in him.

In early March I passed my doctoral examination, and my two major professors, the Semiticist Hommel and the philosopher Bäumker, immediately suggested that if I presented an appropriate dissertation I could qualify for an appointment in Judaic studies at the University of Munich (which would have been a first at a German university at that time). Although I did not seriously consider it, I was able to employ this prospect to complete my studies (with the *Staatsexamen* in mathematics) and prepare my emigration to Eretz Yisrael, and in this regard I was more successful in dealing with my parents than Benjamin was with his. Thus we were able to compare our prospects of *Habilitation* in the spring of 1922 and conclude that our situations were quite different. Both of us stood at a crossroads. Benjamin was still pursuing his aim of achieving an academic career via a *Privatdozentur;* this was his clear-cut ambition, and because he sought to obtain the resources for it from his parents, his relations with them were in constant turmoil. To me, however, the renunciation of ambition was a primary factor in my decision to go to Palestine, a plan that now approached the stage of realization. Anyone who went over there in those days could not think of a career, and that I would have one later could not be foreseen. The Hebrew University in Jerusalem was not yet in existence, and no one believed that it would become a reality in the foreseeable future. To be sure, I had published a few German essays that had made some impression, as well as a book that no one was going to read. But I had to expect that in Judaic studies there would be far more thoroughly trained experts than I, one of the first in my generation who had taken up such studies quite independently and without any intention of becoming a rabbi. I believe it was the moral element in this decision that contributed to Benjamin's great trust in me, a trust that he continued to entertain for a long time to come.

In April 1922, I returned to Berlin for a year, and we spent the next three months together. Walter and Dora, who lived together very peacefully in those days, asked me to enable them to participate in a seder (the home celebration on the eve of Passover) according to the strictly Orthodox ritual. Thus I induced my friend Moses Marx, the brother of Agnon's wife, to invite the Benjamins, along with my brother Werner, who was at that time the youngest member of the German Reichstag and had gone over to the Communists with the larger part of the Independent Social Democrats. This company represented many contrasts, but held together by the ancient ritual, it made for a very pleasant evening. Walter and Dora felt very comfortable in the huge library and were greatly attracted to Moses Marx, who embodied a mixture of Jewish spirit and Prussian bearing, something that was not all that rare in those days. Marx shared with Benjamin the passion of book collecting. The fact —as I had told Benjamin in advance—that this businessman and collector could not really read or understand the Hebrew works which he tended so zealously and had so beautifully bound by

Berlin's best bookbinder made that scene seem straight out of Scheerbart. From then on Benjamin and Dora visited the Marxes on a number of occasions. In the summer of 1922 at the Benjamins' home I met Lotte Wolff, a young medical student who had befriended them; Dora called her an especially close friend of hers. She was a rather unattractive, downright mannish, very slender, quick-witted, and lively person who evidently found Benjamin very impressive. At that time Lotte Wolff had a lively sense of her Jewishness and had probably heard about my Jewish studies from Benjamin. We had several conversations on the subject. This was the period when Benjamin emphasized publicly as well his particularly strong affinity for things Jewish. When he met Franz Hessel, the editor-in-chief of the Rowohlt publishing house, Benjamin and Lotte Wolff published Baudelaire translations in Hessel's short-lived periodical *Vers und Prosa*. The picture of Benjamin that Lotte Wolff later drew in a few pages of her memoirs *Innenwelt und Aussenwelt* [Inner world and outer world, 1971] bespeaks her clear vision and her understanding, even though some things are out of focus and distorted in her recollection. This presentation is the only account of Benjamin from the years before 1924 that has been available up to now.

Benjamin's relations with Ernst Schoen, whom I frequently met at their home, and with Jula Cohn, whom Walter had courted in vain the preceding year, had either faded or receded into obscurity. It was evident to me that Walter's attachment to Jula Cohn was unchanged. I had met her only once on Walter's initiative, in Berlin in the late summer of 1921. Dora sometimes mentioned this attachment to me. Benjamin's farewell letter of 1932 and his prose sketch "Agesilaus Santander," which I published in "Walter Benjamin and His Angel," are a confession of this love after ten years. He himself almost never adverted to her in conversation.

In the fall of 1922 both the projected periodical (which the publisher Weissbach dropped in October) and Benjamin's dim prospects of *Habilitation* in Heidelberg (to the extent that these had existed at all) finally came to naught. On the other hand, Benjamin's friendly relations with Florens Christian Rang were intensified from 1921 on. Wolf Heinle's death in early 1923 and Rang's at the end of 1924 were heavy blows to Benjamin. In Rang, Benjamin saw a personification of the true German spirit; he represented in an outstanding and noble way those qualities which were antithetical to Benjamin's. This polarity was probably the basis of the mutual attraction between the two men. Rang was an irrepressible, tempestuous, and eruptive person. Impatient and given to making extreme demands in his personal life as well, he was, in the final analysis, a gnostic Christian. He regarded Buber and Benjamin, to whom he felt equally close, as incarnations of authentic Jewishness and found it hard to comprehend the unusually great reserve which kept these two apart. As the harshness of Benjamin's judgments on Buber mounted, so did his admiration for Rang's character, which remained unshakable through all upheavals. Benjamin respected the literary lava left by these upheavals and eruptions, and, surprisingly for him, he found himself in profound agreement with Rang on the highest political plane, beyond the differences in their religious and metaphysical outlook. The approval which he so touchingly bestowed on Rang's political work *Deutsche Bauhütte: Ein Wort an uns Deutsche über mögliche Gerechtigkeit gegen Belgien und Frankreich und zur Philosophie der Politik* [German stonemasons' guild: a word to us Germans concerning possible justice for Belgium and France and on the philosophy of politics] permits one to gauge the full magnitude of the altogether contrary decision in favor of, or at least possible prospect of, radical Bolshevist politics which Benjamin made a year later.

At the beginning of 1923, Benjamin started making efforts for *Habilitation* in Frankfurt, this time in the field of modern German literature. Gottfried Salomon, associate professor of sociology there, interceded very vigorously with a number of influential senior professors. I was able to observe these early efforts at close range, since I spent the spring and summer months largely with Benjamin in Frankfurt. He knew that I was determined to emigrate from Germany in the fall and that my life would take a new direction or, more accurately, that the direction it had been taking for years would only now fully come into its own. Benjamin himself displayed an attitude of reserve toward Palestine precisely in the year in which the catastrophic development of inflation and the general breakdown of interpersonal relationships rendered the prospect of emigration acute for him. "As regards Palestine, at this time there is neither a practical possibility nor a theoretical necessity for me to go there," he wrote to Rang in November when I was already there (*Briefe* 1, p. 311). In 1922 and 1923 his material existence was made possible largely by the fact that Dora found positions as a journalist and translator from and into English. Anyone who was paid in foreign currency in those days, as Dora was, could keep afloat despite the precipitous decline of the mark.

As the last thing before my emigration I wanted to study the kabbalistic manuscripts in the great collection of the Frankfurt municipal library, and so I went there for four months. Every day I "learned" Talmud for an hour, and for pleasure I read texts from the Zohar, the Book of Daniel, and stories by Agnon within the framework of Rosenzweig's Freies Jüdisches Lehrhaus [Free Jewish academy] with a few young people like Ernst Simon, Nahum Glatzer, and Erich Fromm. At that time Ernst Simon quoted to me the verse about his friend Fromm—then still a strict adherent of the Orthodox tradition of his father—which was circulating as "Gebet der kleinen K.J.Ver" [Prayer of the Zionist student organization]:

> *Mach mich wie den Erich Fromm,*
> *Dass ich in den Himmel komm.* *
>
> [Make me just like Erich Fromm
> That into heaven I may come]

Fromm and Benjamin later became colleagues at the Institut für Sozialforschung [Institute of Social Research], when Fromm was one of the most influential advocates of a synthesis of psychoanalysis and Marxism. In those days Agnon had taken up residence in Bad Homburg together with a number of important Hebrew writers like Ahad Ha'am and Bialik. I often went out there, and once or twice I took Benjamin along. Shortly before my emigration I frequently met at Agnon's home Fritz Sternberg, who later established a relationship with Benjamin in the circle around Brecht to which Sternberg preached Marxism from 1925 on. He lived in Homburg and was already working on his first major work, *Der Imperialismus*

---

*A punning reference to a child's prayer. *Fromm* is the German word for "pious." —TRANS.

(1926). A short time earlier he had broken away from Buber and the Zionist "Volkssozialisten" [People's Socialists] among whom he had been a leader between 1918 and 1922, and during the next three or four years he sought a Marxist road within Zionism among the Poalei Zion [Labor Zionists]. He was still considered one of the ablest minds of the younger generation of Zionists. Like me he was a great admirer of Agnon, and he took a lively interest in my future projects in Palestine, a country whose socialist reconstruction he had written so much about. Sometimes I would go directly from a visit with Benjamin to Agnon's home, where Sternberg would be sitting with his wife, Genia. I could have no idea, of course, that Benjamin, who would not have been interested in Sternberg's works at that time, would a few years later meet Sternberg under entirely different circumstances and that Sternberg would be one of his Marxist mentors. I never saw Sternberg again, heard nothing about him, and was very surprised in 1938 when in response to a question I posed about the attitude of the Brecht circle and the Institut für Sozialforschung toward the Communist Party, Benjamin casually mentioned Sternberg (who would not have anything to do with the KPD). I said in astonishment: "Do you mean the Fritz Sternberg of *Der Imperialismus?*" "Of course," Benjamin replied. "Do you know him?" "Of course," he said, "through Brecht." "You could have had that acquaintance a few years earlier, at the home of another great writer."

Once Benjamin also took me along on a visit to Siegfried Kracauer of the *Frankfurter Zeitung* who was in the hospital with a minor malady, and there was a disputatious conversation in which Kracauer, despite all his respect for Benjamin, expressed distinct reservations about his "ontology." All of us had fairly sharp intellects. Much later Adorno told me that he had been present at the hospital visit as a young student, and had met me for the first time on that occasion.

The abyss which Germany faced in 1923 and the measure of desperation that filled Benjamin when he contemplated German conditions found its full expression in the farewell present that he handed me in Berlin shortly before my departure. It was a closely written scroll which bore no title but which he termed "A Descriptive Analysis of the German Decline." With minor revisions this text was included as "Reise durch die deutsche Inflation" ["A Tour of German Inflation," in *Reflections*, pp. 70–76] in his book *Einbahnstrasse* ["One-Way Street"; selection under this title in *Reflections*, pp. 61–96], which he wrote four years later. The scroll still reflected the immediate horror of the experienced present. It was Benjamin's first writing on the situation of the moment—addressed to an emigrant, "zur glücklichen Ausreise" [to a happy emigration], as the dedication to me read. It was hard for me to understand what could keep a man who had written this in Germany. As evidenced by his Frankfurt enterprise, however, he wanted to pursue to the end the possibility of an academic career which might have been able to provide his intellect with material backing. When we took leave of each other, he happened to be rather optimistic in that regard. He did not know as yet that "intellect cannot be habilitated"—to quote Erich Rothacker's wickedly insolent statement about him.

Trust from a Distance
(1924–1926)

The essence of our relationship in the years from our separation to Benjamin's death is expressed in the detailed letters concerning Benjamin's work and many aspects of his life, and the most important of which are collected in *Briefe*. With few exceptions they are distinguished by complete frankness, a frankness based on trust. I had settled down in Jerusalem, married, and found work at the Jewish National Library. Thus I was far removed from the sphere in which Benjamin's life evolved in the coming years and not involved in its ups and downs; it was due at least partly to this fact that Benjamin opened his heart to me as he did to hardly anyone else. Only his relations with women were virtually omitted from his communications, though I was able to make sense of many a dry elliptical statement and later received some information from a few of his lady friends. At times of great emotional stress or when working very hard he sometimes did not write for months; at other times his letters would come thick and fast, as for instance during the half-year he spent in Italy in 1924 following the rehabilitation of the German currency. He had dreamed about such a trip—which was to bring him relief from the increasingly unbearable burden of conditions in Germany—the entire preceding fall and winter, and his letters to Rang are full of references to this. In the fall

Benjamin's father became gravely ill and had to have his right leg amputated. The relationship with Dora also became difficult, and Benjamin moved into a rented room for a prolonged period.

Benjamin's chances for *Habilitation* in Frankfurt seemed surprisingly favorable. The authorities there awaited his submission of the study of German tragic drama *(Trauerspiel)* of the baroque age, which he had proposed.* His letters reflect the transformation that this project underwent in his mind. The two years he devoted to its composition were among the most turbulent of his life. Soon after my emigration, the volume of his Baudelaire translations appeared; its foreword, "Die Aufgabe des Übersetzers" ["The Task of the Translator," in *Illuminations,* pp. 69–82], represents a high point in this period, during which his approach to the philosophy of language was openly theological in orientation. He attached particular importance to these pages, viewing them as something like his credo; to be sure, the study contained all the ingredients that gained for his writings the reputation of incomprehensibility. The utter silence with which this essay was received constituted his first great disappointment on the literary plane. The sole exception was a ludicrously vacuous statement by Stefan Zweig, which Benjamin complained about in a letter to me on June 13, 1924:

. . . Something terribly annoying has recently happened to me. Herr [Siegfried] Kracauer of the Frankfurter Zeitung—*you probably know him—months ago had promised through a friend a favorable review of the Baudelaire, and I finally had prevailed upon Weissbach to send out a review copy. Thereupon the book was, through some editorial maneuver, pilfered from behind S.K.'s back, as it were (his mouth opens to promises more than his columns fulfill those promises), and it was sent to Stefan Zweig. That author's Baudelaire translations have been housed in the poison cabinet of my library for years. I could see it all coming, but my protests to the* Frankfurter Zeitung *were fruitless, and nothing could be done. When I was beginning to hope that the whole matter would be dropped, the review appeared (it had to be on a Sunday morning, of course, when all of Frankfurt could*

---

*This study ultimately was published under the title *Ursprung des Deutschen Trauerspiels* (Berlin: E. Rowohlt, 1928); reissued in 1962 (Frankfurt/M.: Suhrkamp Verlag). An English edition appeared under the title *Origin of German Tragic Drama*, translated by John Osborne (London: New Left Books, 1977).—Trans.

enjoy it at great menucha *[leisure]), and it really was a beaut. It had a well-tailored objectivity that precludes any understanding of the context on the part of any uninformed person. The review might have been a bit worse, but it could not possibly have been any more harmful. Being too superficial and too short, it may not make a great impression on people who know the book. The preface is not ignored; it is, rather, mentioned in a snide remark: ". . . the difficulties of which he was aware, as is evidenced by the foreword" (that's typical of the style!). I was so distressed that I misplaced the paper immediately after reading it and now cannot find it.*

When Benjamin wrote these lines he had been on Capri for two months with Ernst Bloch, Erich and Lucie Gutkind, and others who, like him, not only sought relief in the atmosphere of Italian life and the Italian countryside but also wished to enjoy the benefits of the unusually inexpensive life on Capri.

Was it an accident or something more that produced in Benjamin a change in the first year after our separation and provided the first impetus for his "insight into the relevance of a radical communism" as a highly legitimate possibility of political life? His letters from Capri were full of cryptic allusions to Asja Lacis, whom he never mentioned by name but presented to me as "a Russian revolutionary from Riga, one of the most outstanding women I have ever met" or as "an outstanding Communist who has been working in the Party since the Duma revolution." In his letters he did not say that he had fallen in love with her, but I was able to put two and two together. These initial statements about the "political practice of communism," which he now saw for the first time "in another light as a binding commitment," certainly gave me pause. There was no need for me to discuss the theoretical problem of communism with him at that time, because then and for some time to come he still dissociated himself from Marxist theory and declared that the aims of communism were pointless. But I knew more than he did about the practices of the Communists—not only through my brother, with whom I had had long and rather heated discussions about them before my emigration, but also on the basis of my own experience in Palestine. I did not conceal my misgivings and apprehensions from Benjamin. When he sang the praises of

Lukács's major work *Geschichte und Klassenbewusstsein* [History and class consciousness], a book Bloch had drawn his attention to, I wrote that precisely this work had come under vehement attack from the theoreticians of Russian communism and had been branded a relapse into bourgeois idealism. On Capri he had not read Lukács's book as yet, but he wrote that he would study it as soon as he had a chance, "and I would be surprised if the foundations of my nihilism did not manifest themselves in the discussion from a point of view opposite to the Hegelian concepts and the anticommunist statements of dialectics" (*Briefe* 1, p. 355). To me, communism in its Marxist form constituted the diametrically opposite position to the anarchistic convictions that Benjamin and I hitherto had shared politically.

This was the beginning of a split in Benjamin. At first it remained virtually invisible, manifesting itself only marginally in his writings during the next five or six years. Then, however, as he picked up theoretical ideas from the Marxist heritage, this split gave his writings that gleam of ambiguity that years later I attacked in principle in a letter. The struggle between his metaphysical mode of thinking and the Marxist mode into which he sought to transform that thinking shaped his intellectual life only after 1929, molding it in an absolutely unmistakable manner—but more about this later. His book on tragic drama, during the incubation period of which his new Communist perspective worked only as an inhibiting factor, contains no references or allusions to that perspective. The philosophical background he gave to this book and the theses he developed there on the dialectics of the phenomenon of *Trauerspiel*, remain rooted in the metaphysical realm from which they derive in their execution as well. Marxist categories do not figure in this work. Still, it was completed during a period when Benjamin seriously questioned whether he should join the German Communist party—a question he did not finally answer in the negative until shortly before he left Moscow early in 1927, after weighing all the pros and cons. But the duality of his thought was already manifest during this period of his encounter with Communist ideas, and that duality would pervade his writings more and more pronouncedly to the end. From his return to Berlin to his last period, references to the experimental, heuristic nature of his association with the thought world (or, as it seemed to him, the practice) of communism recurred in his letters to me and in the remaining conversations that I had with him. This was by no means a tactic he used to defend himself against fundamental objections; rather, as evidenced by his entire literary production up to the end, it was exactly in keeping with his true convictions, which at no time permitted him to write finis to an old way of thinking and to start a new one from a freshly gained Archimedean point. Instead, there now appeared an often puzzling juxtaposition of the two modes of thought, the metaphysical-theological and the materialistic, so that the two became intertwined. This interlocking of two elements that by nature are incapable of balance lends precisely to those of Benjamin's works that derive from this attitude their significant effect and that profound brilliance that distinguishes them so impressively from most products of materialistic thought and literary criticism, noted for their uncommon dullness. His new outlook produced a ferment in his ideas for which he did not find adequate expression for a long time, causing him to postpone more precise written discussions until a later date. These began with the (published) letter of December 22, 1924, written after I had asked him to specify the factors that had brought about his shift on Capri. In that letter (published in *Briefe* 1, pp. 365–69) he first spoke of "Communist signals" that, as he put it with a graceful tortuousness, were "signs of a shift that has aroused in me the desire no longer to present the topical and political elements in my ideas in an outmoded disguise but to develop them, by way of experiment, in extreme form." How much emphasis he placed on the phrase "by way of an experiment" is evidenced by the next passage, in which he reduces the continuation of his exegetic writings to the defense of "the genuine against expressionistic misrepresentations," thus ascribing to this work a preserving, conservative character even in its already emerging metaphysical dialectics—because for the time being it was not given to him, "in the position of commentator, which is appropriate to me, to get at texts of entirely different meaning and totality." In the context of the conversations and discussions we had had over the preceding six years, this remark clearly referred to Hebrew texts of the Jewish literary tradition whose commentary represented a sort of utopian vanishing point to him. In the meantime, so he wrote, his reflections on the political plane (which he clearly viewed here in contradistinction to the theological sphere) had, to the surprise of his characteristic non-materialistic way of thinking, "renewed contact in various places with an extreme Bolshevist theory" (*Briefe* 1, p. 368).

I continue to find it very strange that around 1930 Benjamin told at least two men (Max Rychner and Theodor Adorno) that only someone familiar with the Kabbalah could understand the introduction to his book on tragic drama—which for all practical purposes left me as the only reader who was close at hand. Each of the two men independently had heard him make this remark and asked me twenty years later whether this was correct and, if so, to what extent. But to me, who would have been, so to speak, the most likely recipient of such a message, he never directly expressed himself in this vein either in writing or in person, unless he did so implicitly in my dedication copy of his book: "To Gerhard Scholem, donated to the *ultima Thule* of his kabbalistic library"— as though that work somehow belonged in a kabbalistic library. Did he perhaps believe that this contiguity with ideas of the kabbalistic theory of language, even though greatly modified, should be obvious to me and required no explanation—which is true to a certain extent—or was he indulging in a game of hide-and-seek with me? Did he succumb to the temptation to indulge in some showing off, or did he wish to shroud the reproach of incomprehensibility that this introduction must have suggested to him, like few other pages in his writings, by referring to something even more incomprehensible (which is how the Kabbalah must have seemed to these men)? I do not know. I am reminded of one of my own statements, also from the thirties, that students of mine used to quote. Apparently I told them that in order to understand the Kabbalah, nowadays one had to read Franz Kafka's writings first, particularly *The Trial.*

At any rate, Benjamin's letters of the ensuing years, and not only those addressed to me, hewed totally to his earlier line. The "shift" that had occurred in him presented itself at first as a virtual displacement, but hardly in the form of completed thought processes.

I do not know whether Asja Lacis accompanied him to Germany in the fall of 1924, but in any case he visited her in Riga for a time in late fall of 1925. That year brought important events in his life: the completion of his *Habilitation* thesis and the definitive collapse of his academic plans, a collapse that corresponded to the deep inner resistance to such a career, which I had diagnosed in an earlier letter to him; then there was the resumption of his journalistic activity, first in the *Frankfurter Zeitung* and in *Der Querschnitt* [The cross section], but particularly in the newly founded journal *Die literarische Welt,* where Willy Haas, despite all interference, afforded him a rather wide latitude. Benjamin quite regularly sent me long and short essays and reviews, so I was able to start an almost complete archive of his publications. Hand in hand with this went his rather close relationship with Ernst Rowohlt, who, to be sure, kept only in part the far-reaching promises and assurances he gave Benjamin, though he did recognize his extraordinary talent and the new note in criticism that Benjamin represented.

Beyond this, two personal relationships grew closer in that year: the correspondence with Hugo von Hofmannsthal, which Benjamin carried on with considerable diplomatic care and with equally great respect for the man; and the correspondence with Franz Hessel, with whom Benjamin undertook the grand project of an adequate German translation of Proust's great novel. Hofmannsthal, who thought very highly of Benjamin, as his letters attest, and who was the only writer of great stature and reputation to support him vigorously, sent Benjamin his problem child, the first version of his play *Der Turm* [The tower], about which Benjamin wrote a lengthy review. What he wrote me illuminated the diplomatic element in this relationship: "I have not read the thing yet. My private judgment is already set, and so is my journalistic judgment, which is the opposite." Benjamin thought very highly of Franz Hessel, the man even more than the writer, whose *Spazieren in Berlin* [Strolling in Berlin] stimulated him in a similar way. In his youth Hessel had been close to the circle around George, Klages, and Schuler, and he was one of the authors of the *Schwabinger Beobachter* [Schwabing observer] in which the "giants" of this circle were lampooned. He gave Benjamin much inside information about that period in Munich (1903–4), which he could not have received from anyone else. Benjamin later shared some of it with me in Paris.

In 1925, Jula Cohn married the chemist Fritz Radt, a brother of Benjamin's first fiancée, Grete Radt. The two then lived in Berlin, and Benjamin stayed in touch with them for a long time. Once or twice he traveled with Fritz Radt to Zoppot and in the local casino indulged a passion for gambling that sometimes came over him. On one of those trips he lost all his cash, down to the last pfennig, and had to borrow money for the return trip to Berlin.

An innate wanderlust, inner unrest, and dissatisfaction with the conditions of his life as *homme de lettres* combined to explain the many changing addresses and places of residence from which I received letters and postcards during the coming years. Whenever possible, Benjamin went traveling. The growing alienation between him and Dora probably was a contributing factor, as was perhaps the death of his father in July 1926. From that year on, however, Paris captured a firm place in his heart; he spent the major part of 1926 there, working on his Proust translation. He felt a lively attraction to that city and returned to it whenever possible. His professional obligations, however, repeatedly required prolonged sojourns in Berlin, and his letters from there bear the mark of unrest, while those from Paris are much more relaxed and even cheerful. In the meantime he had read Lukács's *Geschichte und Klassenbewusstsein* and, under the enduring influence of this book, the chapter about the fetish character of merchandise from the first volume of *Das Kapital* (a chapter obligatory for all intellectuals of Marxist hue) as well as a few Communist analyses of current politics, such as Trotsky's *Wohin treibt England?* [Whither is England drifting?]. He sought ways to get to Russia, and in this he was motivated equally by his objective interest in what was going on there and his personal decision to establish closer ties with Asja Lacis. He was able to carry out this intention after overcoming considerable bureaucratic difficulties, which almost caused him to abandon his travel plans. He was in Moscow from December 6, 1926, to February 1, 1927, financed by various advances for pieces he had promised to write, among them a long essay about his trip that had been commissioned by Buber for *Die Kreatur*. His extensive diary—a strange mixture of his personal relations with Asja Lacis (which by no means developed according to his wishes), his encounters with her acquaintances and various cultural officials, as well as detailed descriptions of the city's physiognomy and Soviet life for the projected essay—has been preserved; it reflects faithfully the mood that underlay his subsequent decision not to join the Communist party. Understandably enough, his letters from Moscow were as sparse as they were reserved; some were written on miserable paper, whatever was available in Moscow, and, in contrast to his usual practice, in pencil.

When I read the letters he wrote in the three years between his trip to Capri and our reunion in Paris in August 1927, I am dismayed to note to what slight extent the new shift discussed earlier was manifested on this level of personal and confidential communication. We were in the habit of recommending to each other books and essays that either of us felt were important or at least noteworthy for the world of the other. But his letters are as meager in pertinent recommendations as the list of the books he actually finished reading—a list he kept with astonishing care—is in relevant titles. If on his trip to Moscow he had desired to establish literary connections with Russia, he managed to do so to only a very limited degree; the disappointments he brought home in this regard did not encourage him to abandon his metaphysical orientation. The inspiration he had derived from Asja Lacis had not yet come to fruition.

In the meantime my situation in Jerusalem had undergone a surprising change. The generosity of some wealthy patrons of the idea of a Hebrew University in Jerusalem a scant year after my arrival had provided a fund that made possible the founding of an Institute for Judaic Studies as the nucleus of a School of Humanities. This was an important step toward the establishment of a center that would be free from any fixed theological orientation but devoted to a living, historical-critical investigation of Judaism. Such a center could give rise to great expectations for a regeneration of the *Wissenschaft des Judentums* (about whose state I had considerable misgivings, as I have mentioned already). At first, the committee in charge had in mind merely a research institute, which only gradually was to develop into a teaching institution that also would give formal examinations and—*horribile dictu*—diplomas. It is well to remember that in the twenties, when vocational retraining was of primary importance to the Zionist cause (there being a large "academic proletariat" among the Jews), titles and diplomas held a slightly contemptible connotation. I need not speak here of the rather dramatic efforts to establish such a Judaic institute. In any case, a few months after the festive opening of the university (in early April of 1925) I was appointed lecturer in Jewish mysticism, a field in which virtually no scholarly work had been done up to that time, and from age twenty-seven on I was able to devote all my energies to a field of research that my recently deceased father had deplored as "unprofitable pursuits."

Thus the beginning of my university career, which opened up so unexpectedly, coincided with the miscarriage of the career that Benjamin had pursued now for six years. I simply had better luck, for it is hardly an exaggeration to say that the committee that appointed me knew no more about my work than the one that turned down Benjamin's thesis. Gottfried Salomon, who had championed Benjamin so vigorously, later informed me that Hans Cornelius and Franz Schultz, who had the final say on Benjamin's application for *Habilitation,* had told him that they did not understand a word of his book. And yet no one could have accused them of ill will in their attitude toward Benjamin.

Paris (1927)

When Benjamin and I met again in Paris in 1927, our reunion took place under circumstances that had outwardly changed our lives in opposite directions. I had been granted a semester's leave for the study of kabbalistic manuscripts in England and France, and I looked forward to the projected reunion with Benjamin with great expectations. After all, four years was a long time in the lives of young men. We met together in the final days of April, while I was en route to London, and exchanged our experiences of those years. Benjamin said that he would like best to settle permanently in Paris because he found that city's atmosphere so much to his liking but that this was next to impossible for someone in his circumstances. There was no periodical or publisher that would appoint him "literary correspondent" for French affairs. Besides, he said, it was extremely difficult for a foreigner to establish really close contact with Frenchmen. To be sure, writers were ready to give interviews for *Die literarische Welt* or other journals or to carry on a pleasant discussion with a foreign critic about literary matters and perhaps even his plans and desires, but one soon realized that nothing would come of that. I do not know whether Benjamin's judgment in this case was true generally or only reflected more specific personal experiences; at any rate, he kept returning to it. As the only exception he named Marcel Brion, the editor of the *Cahiers du Sud,* whom he esteemed very highly. Benjamin invited Brion one evening together with me, and he was evidently fascinated by Benjamin's personality. On another evening we went to a Chinese restaurant that he frequented and praised highly.

I took Benjamin to see Robert Eisler, an astonishing figure in the world of scholarship. I had already introduced them in Munich, where I saw Eisler on a number of occasions. Eisler was one of the most imaginative and—if one looked at the inconceivably erudite store of quotations in his books without checking them—one of the most learned historians of religion. For all unsolved problems he had in readiness brilliantly false solutions of the most surprising kind. He was a man of unbridled ambition, ceaseless diligence, but rather unstable character. Benjamin was interested in him for a long time, and I often reported to him on Eisler's quotation-laden leaps into scholarly adventurism, with enterprises that at various times were as sensational as they were unsuccessful. Around 1925, through the good offices of the great English philologist Gilbert Murray, Eisler was named head of the League of Nations' Section de Coopération Intellectuelle, headquartered in Paris; he had accepted that appointment without first consulting with the government of Austria (whose citizen he was). When I arrived in Paris, Benjamin told me about the scandal this appointment had caused. The Austrian government had lodged an official protest, while Eisler, confident of future official duties, had taken an enormous apartment on the rue de Lille. The visit we paid Eisler in the deserted rooms of his luxury apartment—the "official people" already had dissociated themselves from him—was a depressing experience for us. Eisler, however, cheerfully discussed his great discoveries about the person and role of Jesus as the leader of a political revolt, the subject of the *cours libre* he was then giving at the Sorbonne. At that time he was developing the ideas he later wrote down in his voluminous work *Jesus Basileus ou Basileusas.* It was an eerie scene. Benjamin, who had a special feeling for situations of that kind, was spellbound. We also attended a session of Eisler's course, which was taken by Salomon Reinach's pupils and friends. The highly un-Christian hypothesis with which Eisler took up Kautsky's theories on the origin of Christianity (in an uncommonly ingenious, self-assured manner), supporting them with unexpected interpretations of equally unexpected sources, was received with considerable acclaim by the freethinkers of the Cercle Ernest Renan. But we realized that we were witnessing a sad turning point in the life of an unusual human being.

Soon after my departure Dora visited Walter in mid-May. He showed her around the city for a few days. Dora wrote me about it on a postcard, attempting to imitate Walter's minuscule handwriting, glossed by him as "a significant bit of modern Kabbalah." He thereupon went to the Riviera with her and spent a few days in Monte Carlo, where he won so much money that he could afford a week's trip to Corsica. After his return he wrote me in July:

*You will have gathered from a little postcard that I was on Corsica. The trip was wonderful and did me a lot of good. On the debit side of the ledger, however, is the fact that on this trip I lost a bundle of irreplaceable manuscripts—*en l'espèce *preliminary sketches, made over a period of years, for the "Politics," the original manuscript of "One-Way Street" (which, to be sure, contains only very little beyond what is available in copies), and diverse tomfoolery. As I probably wrote you, I took a plane from Corsica back to Antibes, and this brought me up to date on the latest human means of transportation. I am pleased that your leave in England was so productive, but less pleased about your delayed arrival here. At present I am virtually alone and in two weeks' time I shall be absolutely so. For the time being I am applying my invigorated energies to an essay on Gottfried Keller's works that has been due for a year, and I flatter myself to have included in it some things that have been knocking about the alleyways of my brain for a long time.* Die literarische Welt *will probably find it too long—at least I am reckoning with that possibility—and then the journalistic* misère *will start up again.*

At the middle of August I went to Paris again, and we spent several weeks together—up to the middle or end of September. Before my arrival, from August 12 to 16, Benjamin had taken a short trip through the Loire castles at Orléans, Blois, and Tours. He arranged to take this trip with a Parisian woman he had met

about four weeks earlier and with whom he had fallen in love—
something he did rather easily and frequently in those years. She
stood him up, however, and he went by himself, though he was
depressed by the "torment of loneliness that especially besets me
on trips." He was undecided whether he should go at all, but as
he wrote: "If Scholem were not arriving today, I probably would
not have gone. But I fled. Right now I could not bear his sometimes
rather ostentatious self-assurance." He had not seen me in four
years, and could not have known that after my experiences in Eretz
Yisrael, which were very much on my mind, my "self-assurance"
was no longer so great. When we met on August 17, however, he
was perfectly charming to both of us. For in the meantime my wife
had come to Paris for a week on her return trip from Hamburg, and
the three of us got together on several occasions. Once we also
visited him in the shabby Hôtel du Midi on 4, avenue du parc
Montsouris, where he inhabited an equally shabby, tiny, ill-kept
room that contained hardly more than an iron bedstead and a few
other furnishings. We mostly met in the cafés around boulevard
Montparnasse, especially in Dôme and La Coupole. From morning
to late afternoon I pored over the manuscripts in the Bibliothèque
Nationale, but we spent many evenings and weekends together.
Several times we went to the movies, because Benjamin especially
admired the actor Adolphe Menjou and automatically went to every
film he appeared in. Twice he dragged me to the Grand Guignol,
a kind of horror show, which supplemented his predilection for
mystery novels.

This period fell under an unexpectedly lucky star, at least as
far as I was concerned. In those years certainly something had
changed in our relationship to the world. When I left Benjamin in
1923, I took with me the image of a man driven by a beeline
impulse to fashion an intellectual world of his own, a man who
unswervingly followed his genius and who knew where he was
headed, no matter what the exterior entanglements of his life might
be. I was heading for a world in which everything still seemed
disorganized and confused, in which amid severe internal struggles
I was seeking a stable position where my efforts to understand
Judaism would more clearly fit together into an integral whole.
When we saw each other again, I met a person caught up in an

intensive process of ferment, whose harmonious view of the world was shattered and in disrepair and who was in transit—to new shores he was as yet unable to determine. That original impetus toward a metaphysical weltanschauung was still alive in him but had fallen in a state of dialectic disintegration. The revolution that had appeared on his horizon had not yet managed to mold this dialectic into specific forms. The Marxist terminology in some of the notes for "One-Way Street" that he read to me struck me as merely a kind of distant thunder.

Benjamin was uncommonly relaxed and had an open mind to suggestions. By comparison, I was bound to appear as the more secure person, a man who had been guided by a more accurately functioning compass in his absorption in Jewish studies. At the same time he was greatly taken with what I had to tell him about my studies and some of my experiences in the new country. Thus those days in Paris were a period of great receptivity and fruitful tension between us.

As a welcoming present he handed me, an old admirer and zealous reader of Anatole France, the inaugural address of Paul Valéry, who had taken the deceased writer's seat in the Académie Française. Benjamin explained to me that a newly elected "immortal" was required to include in his address a eulogy of his predecessor, but that Valéry, who despised Anatole France, had managed the sensational feat of not mentioning the name of France even once in his entire speech. Since he thought very highly of Valéry as a thinker, poet, and prose writer, he also gave me a work he especially admired, *La Soirée avec Monsieur Teste*, in order to acquaint me with this phenomenon. The other side of the coin of his admiration for Valéry was his burning interest in the Surrealists, who embodied much of what had erupted in him during the years just past. What he sought to penetrate and master in intellectual discipline he found noteworthy precisely in the antithetical forms of an untrammeled surrender to the explosions of the unconscious, and it stimulated his own imagination. The immoderation of the Surrealists attracted him more profoundly than the studied pretentiousness of literary Expressionism, in which he discerned elements of insincerity and bluff. To him Surrealism was something like the first bridge to a more positive assessment of psychoanalysis, but he was under no illusions about the weaknesses in the procedures of both schools. Benjamin read those periodicals in which Aragon and Breton proclaimed things that coincided somewhere with his own deepest experiences. What happened here was similar to his encounter with what he called "extreme communism." Benjamin was not an ecstatic, but the ecstasies of revolutionary utopias and the surrealistic immersion in the unconscious were to him, so to speak, keys for the opening of his own world, for which he was seeking altogether different, strict, and disciplined forms of expression. Louis Aragon's *Le Paysan de Paris* [The peasant of Paris, 1926] gave him the decisive impetus for his projected study of the Paris Arcades from whose first drafts he read to me in those weeks. He had in mind an essay of about fifty printed pages, in which he wanted to project, still altogether beyond dialectic materialism, his historical-philosophical physiognomy onto a plane that would reflect as well his metaphysical experiences (or whatever part of them was in flux in the above-mentioned process of dissolution). At that time he spoke of completing this work in the next few months. We had no idea that this project would be in severe and finally irreconcilable competition with another project that emerged in our conversations: the resumption of Benjamin's Hebrew studies, which, as he thought, would give legitimate expression to his metaphysical intentions from an entirely different vantage point. He said that as soon as this project was completed, there no longer would be any reason for him to put Hebrew on the shelf.

I brought up communism and Benjamin's grappling with Marxist ideas and methods, a question that had arisen in our correspondence, and was quite surprised that he evaded a deeper discussion of this matter, saying that he was still not ready to talk about these things. He added that he could not imagine any conflict between the form in which the radical-revolutionary perspectives could become fruitful for his work and the approach he had been taking, albeit in dialectical transformation. He said he needed texts of canonical importance in order to develop his philosophical ideas adequately to comment on them: everything else could serve only as a preliminary stage for him. I told Benjamin about the progress of my research on the development of Jewish mysticism, a pursuit that engaged all my energies and—though this still was largely unexpressed in my philological writings—all my ideas as well. We spoke about the angelology and demonology of the kabbalists, which I had begun to study in handwritten texts. Benjamin was the first person I told about a very surprising discovery I had made: Sabbatian theology—that is, a messianic antinomianism that had developed within Judaism in strictly Jewish concepts. This discovery, which I made in the manuscripts of the British Museum and the Bodleian Library at Oxford, later led to very extensive research on my part.

I never shall forget the evening after Escha's departure, which I spent at the Café Dôme with Benjamin and Franz Hessel, who evidently had a very amicable relationship. Hessel had the nonchalance of a man of the world. There was a marked contrast between the two men's physiognomies, heightened by Benjamin's thick hair and Hessel's completely bald pate. Only when both of them showed passionate interest in my discussion of Cardozo and Berdyczewski did it dawn on me that Hessel was also a Jew, something I had not at all taken into account. In Abraham Miguel Cardozo's writings in defense of the Sabbatian heresy, which I talked about on the basis of my Oxford studies, smoldered a flame that leaped from me to my first audience. The perennial question as to what Judaism was all about—a question that had been given an entirely new turn in my studies, at least for me—combined in that conversation with a long account of Micha Josef Berdyczewski (1865–1921), the strangest figure of Jewish "modernism," an influential Hebrew and Yiddish writer who, however, published his scholarly works (above all *Die Sagen der Juden* [The legends of the Jews] and *Der Born Judas* [The fountain of Juda]) in German translation, a man who, though deeply rooted in the Jewish tradition, regarded Judaism basically as designed to be known. Was Judaism still alive as a heritage or an experience, even as something constantly evolving, or did it exist only as an object of cognition? This was the question that thrust itself upon me at that time in the confrontation of those two figures, for which I expected a solution only from my new life in Eretz Yisrael; it was the question I grappled with, under varying emphases, for years. It was a memorable evening, and Benjamin later adverted to it on a number of occasions as a high point of our encounter.

Another high point of a very different kind was the encounter, somewhat later, with Judah Leon Magnes, chancellor of the Hebrew University in Jerusalem, on which occasion Benjamin held the floor. When Benjamin told me about his readiness to study Hebrew, I told him about the still rudimentary plans for the establishment of a School of Humanities in Jerusalem, where he might find the sphere of activity that was denied him in Europe. Benjamin was greatly taken with this possibility, and I suggested that I arrange a meeting between Magnes and us, who happened to be in Paris. I went to see Magnes and told him what I thought of Benjamin's genius and how Jerusalem might offer a fruitful solution to the intellectual dilemma he had to surmount. Magnes was a man wide open to all living aspects of Judaism. A rabbi and public figure, he had behind him a many-faceted career as one of the characteristic leaders of American Jewry before coming to Jerusalem in 1922 and devoting himself body and soul to the cause of the Hebrew University. He was exactly the right man to take a warm interest in a man like Benjamin. Thus the three of us had a two-hour conversation, during which Benjamin, who was evidently well prepared for this encounter, presented his intellectual situation in magnificent formulations, specifying his wish to approach the great texts of Jewish literature through the medium of the Hebrew language not as a philologist but as a metaphysician and declaring his readiness to come to Jerusalem, whether on a temporary or a permanent basis. Magnes, who had taken his doctorate twenty-five years earlier at Heidelberg, spoke German fairly fluently, so there were no difficulties in communication. I remember the tenor of Benjamin's presentation very well. He said that in his thinking about philosophical and literary matters, which had occupied him for fifteen years, he had encountered the problem of where and on what subjects he could develop most legitimately the ideas that had formed in him. He had realized that his ideas on the philosophy of language could not find their focus in the German and French literature accessible to him. He said that his friendship with me had contributed to the increasing realization that his focal point would lie for him in an occupation with the Hebrew language and literature. Benjamin explained to Magnes his studies of the Romanticists, of Hölderlin and Goethe (he said that he had studied the latter only partially but very intensely), as well as his fascination with Baudelaire and

Proust and the translations he had devoted to them. It was particularly his work as a translator, he said, that had prompted philosophical and theological reflections whose resolution he expected from his immersion in Hebrew. He said that it was precisely these things that had made him ever more clearly conscious of his Jewish identity. He had already done what he could as a critic of significant texts; here he also mentioned his book on German tragic drama. But he thought that he would be able to reach an entirely new level only as a critic of Hebrew texts. Benjamin said that his position had found virtually no response in Germany and that he wished to devote his productive work to things Jewish. True, he knew little about the Jewish intellectual world, but what he did know of it had appealed to him profoundly: the Bible, fragments of rabbinic literature that he had become familiar with, and thinkers like Moses Hess, Ahad Ha'am, Hermann Cohen, and Franz Rosenzweig. He, too, had in view the religious world of Judaism as a central subject of his own work. He said that he had a positive intellectual attitude toward the reconstruction work in Eretz Yisrael, though he had not concerned and identified himself particularly with the political aspects of Zionism.

I myself was surprised by the firm, positive way in which Benjamin presented these thoughts. Of course, they had been expressed in one form or another often enough on previous occasions, and I had a certain share in them. It was a vibrant avowal of the chances of rebirth for the Jewish people and Judaism (which I certainly would not have been able to differentiate at that time) that I, along with so many others, hoped for in Eretz Yisrael and only there. Never before had Benjamin placed himself so decisively in this context, nor did he do so on any subsequent occasion. He also talked of his trip to Russia and promised Magnes that he would send him his essay "Moskau" ["Moscow," in *Reflections,* pp. 97–130], which had just appeared in Buber and Victor Weizsäcker's *Die Kreatur.* Magnes, a profoundly religious person and politically far on the left, had undergone strong metamorphoses in both his Jewish and his general political positions. He was greatly moved by Benjamin's personality and his presentation, and he confirmed this to me when I saw him the next day. He asked Benjamin how he imagined his preparation for a possible activity of this sort.

Benjamin replied that if it were made financially possible for him, he would prefer to come to Jerusalem for one year. There he would devote himself exclusively to a study of the language and have a chance to find out whether he would be capable not only of delving into the sources but also of expressing himself adequately in Hebrew as a university teacher. Magnes promised to think the matter over and agreed with Benjamin that such a trial ought to precede a final decision. He asked whether there were scholarly and literary authorities of stature who would be prepared to give a written evaluation of Benjamin. It was agreed that the two men would be in touch with each other both directly and through me. Benjamin was impressed by Magnes and ecstatic about the prospect that this meeting had opened up. He outlined to me plans for the completion of his various literary obligations, including an anthology (which never materialized) of Humboldt's writings on the philosophy of language. He thought of coming to Jerusalem in the summer or fall of 1928; there my wife, who was an excellent teacher, would guide and support him in his studies. The conversation with Magnes undoubtedly constituted the high point of our Paris reunion.

This encounter is more fantastic in retrospect than it seemed at the time. What appeared natural and possible to both of us at the time—a decision on the part of Benjamin to pursue a career and future within the Jewish fold—must seem all but incredible to present-day readers of Benjamin's later writings. He was highly satisfied with his conversation with Magnes and regarded it as a possible turning point if it led to practical results. His Socialist activity was still embryonic and, as far as I am able to judge, remained so for years to come. In Paris I saw only one instance of this. On the evening of August 23, 1927, I accompanied him to the great demonstrations that were held for many hours on the northern and northeastern boulevards against the execution of Sacco and Vanzetti, which was taking place in Boston that night. Things were rather violent. For the first time in my experience Benjamin wore a red necktie and a somewhat shabby suit. He said it was unthinkable not to be present on that evening. To my questions about the justification for this demonstration—the innocence of the two men, that is—he replied that even if they had committed the murder it was intolerable to execute them for the deed seven years later. He said that a six years' wait for death ought to preclude the execution of a death sentence. On the justification of capital punishment in principle he had no firm views, saying that the decision depended entirely on the historical circumstances and not on philosophical principles. That evening was tempestuous. The police, most of them on horseback, proceeded to attack the demonstrators. We found ourselves in a big melee and barely managed to escape the truncheons of the *flics* by reaching a side street off the boulevard de Petersbourg. Benjamin was very excited. That was the only evening I can remember when, very much against my custom and in order to calm him down, I drank quite a lot of wine with him.

In those days Benjamin had two books on press, but they did not appear until the beginning of the following year: the book on German tragic drama and his aphoristic collection of notes, which after several title changes finally appeared as *Einbahnstrasse*. (Ernst Bloch not inaccurately described the collection as a "philosophy in the form of a revue.") He had not yet read the proofs, was rather angry at Rowohlt's delays, and read me a considerable number of excerpts from his handwritten notes. The wonderful prose piece about Karl Kraus, "Kriegerdenkmal" [War memorial], he read with an almost Georgian solemnity in an inimitably raised voice. It made a profound impression on me, and to this day I regard it as one of the most beautiful pages he wrote. In the Café des Deux Magots we spent a long evening discussing the meaning of symbols. We tried to refine our concepts experimentally, and though Benjamin's book on tragic drama was his point of departure, I remember that the conversation far transcended its formulations. The conversation constituted a continuation of his remarks to Magnes; since he had operated with the concept of symbols, I questioned him about the significance of that presentation. Benjamin was in especially good spirits. When we parted, he asked me to make some kind of record of our conversation; he said that we had touched on dimensions of the matter that far transcended the presentation in his book and he wanted to use them as the basis for further reflections. I did make such a record and sent my notes to him in Berlin in December 1927. Unfortunately I did not make a copy, and the notes were lost in 1933.

Another evening I spent with Benjamin, Helen Hessel (Franz

Hessel's wife), and a friend who wished to meet me, whom Benjamin had brought along after making sure it was all right with me. It was Hans Radt; I could surmise only that he was connected with Grete Radt, Benjamin's former fiancée. We sat in a restaurant for a long time and spoke about literature. The conversation turned to Joseph Roth, who was being discussed widely then, particularly in the circle of the *Frankfurter Zeitung*. Benjamin and Roth did not like each other, though Walter used to claim in relaxed moments that he had an a priori predilection for Galician Jews, of which species Roth seems to have been a truly convincing specimen, though in a very individual variant. As evidence for his liking, Benjamin cited the fact that he even forgave Galician Jews for baptism, which was repugnant to him. (This was correct. I remember his having shown me years earlier a postcard on which the writer Ignaz Ješover, an old acquaintance of his who had introduced him to Erich Gutkind and with whom he remained in touch until around 1930, informed him in solemn words that he and his wife had received "holy baptism" on the previous day. Benjamin's showing me this postcard was his entire commentary.) On our way home that evening Benjamin suddenly said, wide-eyed, "That [he meant Hans Radt] was the brother-in-law of Jula Cohn." After 1923 he had never mentioned Jula Cohn in his letters. I asked, "Are you still in contact with her?" He replied, "Yes, very much so," and while we were still walking he started to tell me about her, obviously still with great involvement. He spoke of her marriage and her career as a sculptor. This ran completely counter to his usual custom. Not that he spoke of his continuing attachment to her, but the special emphasis he gave his statements about her made it clear what was going on inside him. I avoided asking him questions, though his first statement had deliberately provoked my first question, making it evident that he wanted to speak about her.

On an entirely different plane was the conversation I had with him about sound analysis, a method originating with the Munich attorney Otmar Rutz and subsequently taken up by the then-famous Leipzig Germanist Eduard Sievers. This method is forgotten today, but over the preceding fifteen years it had played a considerable part in critical investigations of the homogeneity of literary works and had touched off great debates, not only regarding Sievers's examinations of Middle High German texts but also concerning his use of sound analysis to test the authenticity of the Pauline letters in the New Testament and the various "voices" that were supposed to become discernible on examination of several parts of the Hebrew Bible. The fundamental notion was that on the basis of written reproductions of speeches or literary documents, conclusions could be drawn about the full-dimensional voice embodied there. This notion was bound to appear basically plausible to Benjamin because of his own occupation with graphology and its theoretical premises, and the matter was of great interest to him. But he did not arrive at a judgment of his own, at least not then, and I never discussed it with him again.

GERSHOM SCHOLEM

With Escha, Jerusalem, March 1924

With Escha, Jerusalem, Sukkoth 1926

Paris, 1927

Berlin, September 1927

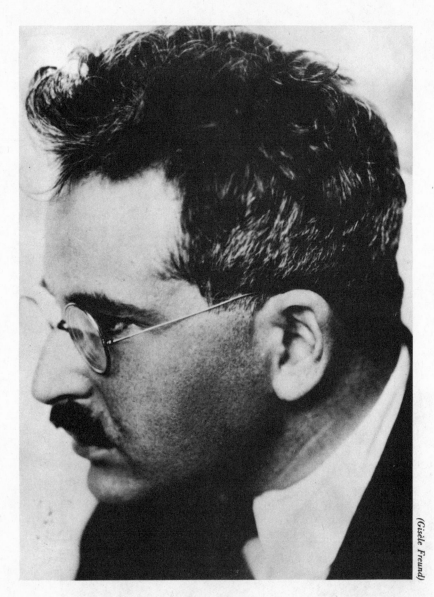

(Gisèle Freund)

Paris, 1937

Paris, 1939

Dora, with son Stefan, around 1925

Dora, around 1930

(from Asja Lacis:Revolutionär im Beruf, Rogner & Bernhard, Munich)

Asja Lacis

*Before Bertolt Brecht's house,
Svendborg, Summer 1938*

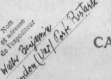

Jacket of
Einbahnstrasse

(Ernst Rowohlt Verlag: Sasha Stone)

*The cemetery
at Port Bou*

(Helga Niemeyer)

The Failed Project
(1928–1929)

The following two years were, as far as our relationship was concerned, largely dominated by a plan for Benjamin to study Hebrew with a view toward an eventual teaching appointment at the university in Jerusalem, though, as earlier, many other things were discussed in addition. After parting in Paris we never saw each other again, though I spent October in Berlin, where I was often with Dora. Benjamin did not return from Paris until November, by which time I long since had returned to Jerusalem. He kept postponing sending Magnes a packet of typewritten copies of his writings (as had been discussed in Paris), because he expected to send him in a few weeks his book on tragic drama as well as four of his best essays (these were, in his opinion, the ones on Keller, children's books, *Elective Affinities,* and the task of the translator). When he sent his book to Magnes at the end of January, he wrote in his covering letter that he hoped it would "come at a propitious moment . . . when its first pages will awaken for you the memory of our Paris conversation, which is uniquely present and alive in me."

At the end of November 1927 he wrote me that by way of celebrating the appearance of my Philosophical Alphabet from the

Archives of the University of Muri, which my brothers had printed for the "Berlin Bibliophiles' Evening," he wished to produce a few contributions of his own and had in mind a new version or type of literary wall calendar such as he had devised for *Die literarische Welt* the previous year. "For the rest, I haven't felt well for the past week, especially today, and am suffering from an indefinable flulike condition for which a great deal of unfinished paperwork constitutes the most dismal background imaginable. Yesterday there was a Parisian enclave in my new Berlin existence: a Romance writer was captured and interviewed. This hunting scene gradually loses its nobility; they come around in droves to bend the ears of the poor Germans. There was something beautiful I wish you could have seen: a play by Ford, a pre-Shakespearean dramatist, in an indescribably decent performance. One of the best dramas. Subject: love between siblings. Otherwise the usual sensational performances in the theater that put one to sleep." I had written him earlier that Dora had joined me for the premiere of one of the Nelson revues then fashionable in Berlin West, which I had found dismally boring. In his letter Benjamin also wrote me that in the same issue of *Neue Deutsche Beiträge* [New German contributions] that contained the first printing of the chapter on melancholy from his book on tragic drama I would "find an essay by Leopold Andrian entitled *Die metaphysische Ständeordnung des Alls* [The metaphysical corporative system of the universe] that made Hessel and me shake with laughter for hours." In a postscript to that letter he informed me that his flu had suddenly turned out to be a rather severe case of jaundice. "And this right now, when I ought to be showing my face around in honor of the pieces of mine that are appearing. It is, to be sure, more honorable when people call on one. This honor presumably will be done me by Wolfskehl one of these days." Enclosed with his letter was a small slip of paper with the following:

Idea for an Arcanum
    To present history as a trial in which man as an advocate for mute nature makes a complaint against the nonappearance of the promised Messiah. The court, however, decides to hear witnesses for the future. There appear the poet who senses it, the sculptor who sees it, the

musician who hears it, and the philosopher who knows it. Their testimony thus diverges, though all of them testify to his coming. The court does not dare admit its indecision. Hence there is no end of new complaints or new witnesses. There is torture and martyrdom. The jury benches are occupied by the living, who listen to the human prosecutor and the witnesses with equal mistrust. The jurors' seats are inherited by their sons. At length they grow afraid they may be driven from their benches. Finally all the jurors take flight, and only the prosecutor and the witnesses remain.

This brief note, whose contrast to the much later notes on the theory of history is as unmistakable as its messianic context, constitutes the first evidence of the influence on Benjamin of Kafka's novel *The Trial.* He had concluded the various postscripts to the above-mentioned letter with this lapidary sentence: "As an angel of illness I have Kafka at my bedside. I am reading *The Trial.*" The Arcanum, however, which takes up Kafka's *Trial* on another plane, was not written as part of the letter, where there would have been ample space for it, but enclosed on a separate slip. This was the beginning of his meditations on Kafka, which were intended as preliminary studies for an essay on *The Trial.* That this work was to be dedicated to me was not surprising, for at that time he was still expressly concerned with theological categories in which the "levels of meaning of theology" were to be differentiated from the "levels of experience of dreams." At that time Benjamin already was acquainted with a note of mine about the writings of Agnon, which had appeared in mid-1928 and mentioned that in Agnon a revision of *The Trial* was discussed. In his work Benjamin wanted to produce a comparison between Kafka and Agnon, developing in his own way the category of deferment, which in a manuscript written in 1919, *Über das Buch Jona und den Begriff der Gerechtigkeit* [The Book of Jonah and the concept of justice], I had described as constitutive for Judaism—an idea that made a great deal of sense to him. Thus from 1927 on our thoughts on at least one central subject approached a single point.

That year also marked the beginning of the great essays in literary criticism, starting with the essay on Keller, which appeared shortly before our Paris reunion. After the long hiatus following

the completion of his study of *Elective Affinities,* Benjamin's genius
clearly was revealed in these essays. In January 1928 he sent me
his book on German tragic drama, which had just appeared. By
1930 there appeared "Der Surrealismus," ["Surrealism," in *Reflections,* pp. 177–92], "Zum Bilde Prousts" ["The Image of
Proust," in *Illuminations,* pp. 203–17], "Pariser Tagebuch" [Paris
diary], and the three essays on Julien Green, which were still
largely dominated by an absolutely pre-Marxist line. Only several
book reviews (especially from 1929 on), the first Brecht commentaries, and the major essay on Karl Kraus (which he sent me in a
typewritten copy prior to publication and later in the original
manuscript) heralded a shift directly labeled as Marxist, though
reflections of an entirely different nature continued alongside this
shift. These writings occasioned my letter of March 30, 1931,
which by no means contained "cautious objections," as has been
asserted, but a sharp frontal attack on his new shift and position.
What was striking about these works was that, with the exception
of the paradoxical case of his Brecht commentaries, there were
absolutely no commentaries in Benjamin's precise sense of the
word. To me, who had listened to Benjamin's speech to Magnes
about his task as a commentator on Hebrew texts—thus a utopian
program!—this was less astonishing than it seems in retrospect
today, when the commenting nature of many of his later writings
is so much more apparent precisely on a level far removed from
the Jewish plane.

Benjamin was an outsider in a dual sense: in regard to scholarship (which in large measure he has remained to this day) and in
regard to the literary scene. Only a few of his fellow writers had
any use for him; to many he was insufferable. And the feeling was
mutual. He had a particularly low opinion of the literary lights then
in fashion—with the exception of Heinrich Mann and later, after
The Magic Mountain and the overcoming of considerable repug-
nance, of Thomas Mann as well. This almost led to a break with
Brecht, who hated Thomas Mann. Authors like Lion Feuchtwanger
or Emil Ludwig, who were very well known at that time, did not
exist for him, and to the best of his ability he tried to avoid any
contact with them. But as late as 1938 he greatly reproached

himself for having missed Kafka when the latter was in Berlin.

Therefore, when Magnes asked me for names of important authors and scholars from whom he could solicit evaluations of Benjamin's writings, supplying these was by no means a simple matter. I corresponded with Benjamin about this, and at first he proposed only four men: Hofmannsthal; the Viennese Germanist Walther Brecht; the Munich scholar Fritz Strich; and the Bern professor Samuel Singer, an old friend of Benjamin's father-in-law. As a matter of fact, all four sent in very positive reports, and Magnes was most pleased. Benjamin had especially high hopes for a review of his book in Rychner's *Neue Schweizer Rundschau* [New Swiss review], which Hans Heinz Schaeder, an Orientalist in Königsberg and later in Berlin, may have promised Hofmannsthal, with whom he was in close touch. Schaeder, a man with uncommonly varied talents and interests, had known about Benjamin for a long time and had a quality rare in scholars: a predilection for praising the work of others. Benjamin was going to suggest that after the appearance of this review Magnes write Schaeder a letter from Jerusalem. He was completely mistaken about Schaeder's judgment, however. It may be illuminating for an understanding of the milieu that an intellect like Benjamin had to function in to print in full those portions of Schaeder's letter to Hofmannsthal of April 21, 1928, that refer to Benjamin. It shows how difficult it was for a scholar who was then quite liberal and certainly not without discernment to come to terms with Benjamin's book; Schaeder never did turn in a review. (This letter was kindly supplied me by Dr. Rudolf Hirsch, who found the manuscript among Hofmannsthal's literary remains.)

My dear Herr von Hofmannsthal:

. . . *A similar conflict* was created for me by W. Benjamin's important book. I distinctly remember being gripped and absorbed by his essay on student life, which I read while on active duty about twelve years ago, and later by his essay on* Elective Affinities *in your*

---

*The reference is to Schaeder's preceding sentences about the literary historian Josef Nadler.

Beiträge. *I approached his book, which the publisher was kind enough
to send me, with the highest expectations and soon had to experience
the most painful disappointment. Please allow me once more to refer
to your work. It is your absolutely sure feeling for the essence of the
historical and the style appropriate to it that gives every reader of your
essays on intellectual history a sense of security and clarity from the
first words on. You allow things to present themselves in their natural
order and system. What Benjamin, by contrast, does in his new book
is, it seems to me, the most dangerous thing one can do in intellectual
history: he does not present his subject, does not even wish to do so,
but instead seeks to grasp the supposedly ideational content of his
subject, eliminating the historical* hic et nunc. *The result could not
possibly be different from what we have before us now. Since I thought
highly of the author from earlier occasions, I took the trouble of at
least making some sense of the first chapter by reading it three times
and philosophically interpreting the individual statements. But I am
well aware of the fact that probably only a very small number of
readers will have sufficient patience and time to assimilate this altogether personal scholasticism, obscure to the point of incomprehensibility. It is, so it seems to me, no accident that the author sedulously
polemicizes against one of our leading intellectual historians, Konrad
Burdach, and against Benedetto Croce, one of the very few living
philosophers, if not the only one, in whom one can discern a genuine
orientation toward history and the intellectual world in its historical
manifestation—and in both cases, Benjamin polemicizes against the
fundamental positions of these two men. Pseudoplatonism seems to be
the characteristic feature of Benjamin's book; this is the most dangerous malady that can befall anyone who deals with historical matters
either* ex professo *or out of his own inclination. I have no more ardent
desire than to see a man of such acuity and profundity of thought
return from these paths, which can lead only to intellectual solipsism.
I hope you will not be offended by this unreserved presentation of my
attitude toward the book. I see an absolute divergence of intellectual
posture between Benjamin's efforts and your work, or the work of a man
like C. J. Burckhardt, whom you also mention in your letter. Burckhardt's* Kleinasiatische Reise *[Travels through Asia Minor] displays
such a perfectly evenly developed acuity of vision for landscapes and
people in their historically based unambiguousness and at the same*

*time an equally developed descriptive and linguistic power that I must
deeply admire this work of his.*

Our discussions of the Jerusalem project continued in 1928
and 1929. In our correspondence Benjamin made definitive plans
to come to Jerusalem to devote himself there to the undisturbed
study of Hebrew. Upon closer reflection I realized that it would be
important for him to gain access to Hebrew and Hebrew texts and,
while teaching at the university, to produce creative work in his
new surroundings; such studies, however, even under optimal conditions, would never suffice to give him competence as a university
teacher of Jewish studies. I discussed this with my wife as well as
with Magnes, and wrote Benjamin in February 1928 that if his
studies were successful, teaching activities in the field of modern
German and French literature would be a reasonable prospect, so
that he would have access to the Jewish world without constraint
and outer obligations. His reply of March 11, in which he of
course reacted very positively to this, was very moving. At any
rate, my insight into his situation had progressed to that point
even when I was enthusiastic about the idea of bringing him to
Jerusalem.

After all these years I am by no means unaware of the fact that
in this project and in Benjamin's conduct more complex motives
were at work. There was a genuine, I would say a utopian, vision
through which he himself believed in these plans, because in those
years he still could meaningfully imagine the theological categories
of Judaism as the vanishing point of his thinking, just as in the
handwritten addenda to his book on tragic drama he saw his real
achievement in the transfer of Goethe's concept of *Urphänomen*
"from heathen nature contexts" to the Jewish category of historical
contexts in the concept of origin. There was, in addition, a possibility he probably considered quite weighty: that of meeting me on
a level at which the two of us could have a great deal to say to each
other and could influence each other. On the other hand, there was
much self-deception in his insistence that he had exhausted his
European possibilities; in the course of the next two years I realized
this more quickly than he, since he did his best to avoid facing his
state of affairs. But his own notes from these same years prove how

all this continued to occupy him—deeply, intensely, and altogether productively.

Added to this was a matter about which I could gain no truly authentic knowledge from a distance and which he himself tried to pass over in silence—namely, the entanglement of his personal affairs. That these would soon militate against the project did not become evident to me until the end of 1928, when Asja Lacis came to Berlin. In January of that year he still could write me, alluding to our Paris conversations: "This may be the last moment for me to turn to Hebrew and everything this means for us with some chance of success. But it is also a very propitious moment—in regard to my inner readiness, for one thing" (*Briefe* 1, p. 455). In March 1928 he wrote in the same vein to Hofmannsthal, to whom he had spoken during a personal encounter in Berlin about his "relationship to things Jewish and thus the question of Hebrew." That spring we agreed that he would come to Jerusalem in the fall, and my discussions with Magnes concerned the financial guarantee for such a sojourn. Shortly before June 18, Magnes saw Benjamin in Berlin and promised to make available funds for his study of Hebrew. As late as the first of August, his "trip to Palestine amid strict observance of the course of study determined by Your Hierosolymitan Excellence" was "a definite thing" (*Briefe* 1, p. 478). He announced that he was going to stay in Jerusalem for four or five months, and that he would know the date within a few weeks. I did not know, of course, that behind this statement there was his correspondence with Asja Lacis, whom he had invited around that time to join him in Berlin. On September 20 I received from Lugano the following letter, which is revealing for his situation and work at that time:

Dear Gerhard

The stamp on the envelope and the crumpled margin of the notepaper are evidence that I am traveling. It happened suddenly and is only a short trip. All summer long I stayed in my cubicle out of an aversion to traveling alone, something to which I am traumatically sensitive at present. The itinerary in which I became wrapped up was all the more eccentric, and some day I really want to follow it: Then I was unable to get away for a long time. And finally, when I learned that Fritz and Jula Radt were down here, inclination and situation coincided. It has been nine years since I was last here. The countryside has all its old power and took its time about manifesting it. In front and in back of the St. Gotthard, everything was overcast on the first day. Even on the second day, when we made an excursion to Lake Como, all the peaks were covered by clouds. Since yesterday it has been clear, and I have hiked along favorite paths.

I thank you both for the instructions in your last letter and shall follow them exactly. Learn to read now, then. My daring essay on Goethe will be finished in a few days. Knowing that it will be published shortly still does not make me see its final form any clearer. And it is not yet certain whether despite the boldness of its approach it will not turn out all the more philistine. Then I shall start with the reading. At the same time I am returning to the study on the Arcades. It would be marvelous if the shameful hackwork did not also insist on reaching a level high enough for me not to get disgusted with it. I cannot say that I lack the opportunity to have trash printed, but despite everything I still lack a certain courage to write such things. In regard to this field, I feel secure only with book reviews. Now I am trying to spread the word about a French book, a novel that particularly gripped me. It is by Julien Green, a young Anglo-Saxon who lives in Paris and writes in French. The novel is called Adrienne Mesurat, *and it has appeared in German as well. Get it quickly so I won't have to give it to you as a birthday present.*

Regarding the Palestinian payments, I accept your proposal not to approach Magnes until I have really started intensive studies. You are quite right about this. But I would not want to have these payments explicitly tied to the date of my appearance in Palestine. I shall surely come for four or five months. But precisely because my stay will be a long one, the date of my trip is not easy for me to determine even now; it may be in January rather than December. A stay with you will be highly beneficial at any *stage of my Hebrew studies. In accordance with our agreements—I mean their spirit and not merely their letter —Magnes will agree with me on one point: that I may expect support from the moment I start my real study and make it the focal point of my work.*

After my return to Berlin I would like to try [Leo] Baeck myself if things cannot be set in motion any other way. Please let me have your and Magnes's directives for that.

I shall not go to Paris, at least not for a prolonged stay. Write soon and accept my cordial regards to you and Escha.

Yours
Walter

P.S. I must not forget to tell you that your letter about [Oskar] Goldberg's book [Die Wirklichkeit der Hebräer] *is, in my estimation, among the most important and successful writings of yours that I know. With your permission I shall read it to Hessel, who is still wide-eyed about our conversation on Bin Gorion [Berdyczewski]. I hope I can expect* Die Entstehung der Kabbala *[The origin of the Kabbalah] soon.*

Many thanks for your instructions regarding a passport. I shall follow them closely when the time comes.

It is appropriate to say something about "Goethe," the above-mentioned article that Benjamin had written as his first "materialistic" work during the period in which the Hebrew project was discussed, in the six months before Asja Lacis's arrival. In the spring of 1928 the editors of the Great Soviet Encyclopedia had commissioned an article on Goethe from him; until October 1928 this project greatly occupied him with the "death-defying courage of someone who is made to feel the spurs of a deadline." In August he wrote me that the article "could be produced only with blissful impudence" (*Briefe* 1, p. 481). In point of fact, this essay was a tour de force that was the last word in self-denial. It was the only fruit of his efforts in Moscow, for his hopes of being able to contribute to Russian periodicals independently—rather than as an anthologist, that is—came to naught. This relatively long contribution, in which he employed a Marxist vocabulary, sought to present in rather crude disguises objective insights about Goethe and the meaning of his major works. Naturally, it was in no wise in line with the orientation desired in Moscow and was put on ice. It appeared in 1929 only in a greatly abridged and heavily edited, denatured version. Benjamin was aware of course of the weaknesses of such a reduction of the Goethe phenomenon, a reduction that had to put up with many absurdities, but he clearly enjoyed working on this essay. At any rate, he never completely abandoned its intent. After the essay had been rejected in Moscow, he made only halfhearted attempts to publish it in Germany, as he counted on the possibility of a later, less rough-and-ready edition. He sent me a copy of the article; it amounts to forty typewritten pages and is still in my possession. When, much later in Paris, I voiced my astonishment at the leaps he had indulged in for the sake of putting some very original ideas in his essay, he said, "Why should only idealists be permitted to walk a tightrope, while materialistic tightrope walking is prohibited?!"

My wife and I regarded with much skepticism the plan of sending the monthly stipends to Berlin, even under Benjamin's conditions of concentrating on Hebrew. We had calculated that a sum of 300 marks under the prevailing conditions would permit our friend to live in Jerusalem without additional earnings—all the more so because the expense of Hebrew instruction would be eliminated. Escha, who was an excellent teacher and on the best of terms with Benjamin, was willing to take him on. The situation in Berlin would be quite different; the agreed-upon sum hardly would be sufficient and would necessitate extra, distracting work.

Thus our shock was great when, on October 18, Benjamin quite unexpectedly acknowledged receipt of the entire amount from Magnes and asked me to convey his warm thanks to him. From that moment on our confidence that we would actually see Benjamin in Jerusalem waned, and we already had gloomy thoughts about the situation that would arise now in Berlin. Our suspicions were quickly confirmed by Benjamin's letter of October 30 (published in *Briefe* 1). Only after the arrival of his "Russian lady friend" (who then actually did come to Berlin in November 1928) would it be decided where he was going to spend the coming months. He wrote that although he was free to start his Hebrew lessons, there would be somewhat risky competition from the necessary expansion of his study on the Arcades. In any case, he was now postponing his trip until the spring of 1929. Magnes's well-meant but in fact hardly appropriate action was one of the factors in the impending developments in Benjamin's life that contributed to the failure of the entire project—to the extent that this project ever had any chance of materializing.

That he was still far from starting his studies was confirmed by the letter—laconic on this point—he wrote me on November 23 in reply to my remonstrances. In it he said only, "So you can count on my coming in March at the latest." About the reception of his books—*Einbahnstrasse* had appeared in the spring of 1928 as well —he wrote, "My little collection of now almost forty sections of an often curious character will be of interest to you, and I shall place it at your feet in Jerusalem. A special showpiece is a very snide review in the *Berliner Tageblatt,* by a trueborn Berliner in whom [Alfred] Kerr can take pleasure." I picked up a copy of the review (dated November 11) with which Werner Milch—a trueborn Breslauer, not a trueborn Berliner—won his polemical spurs against Benjamin. Milch, a young specialist in Baroque literature and a fellow Jew, took as a target both books by Benjamin, a "clever fragmentist" whose "many-sided talent proves his undoing." He characterized Benjamin as a descendant of romantic theories of science. "But that would hit upon only one aspect of the problematical phenomenon of Benjamin, the interpretation of whom would require a longer essay. With their mixture of academic dryness, journalistic verve, philosophical filigree, and romanticizing somersaults, the two books are recommended to all lovers of clever outsiderism." (Did Milch later regret his malicious attack? He did not include it in his collection of *Kleine Schriften,* compiled in 1949, shortly before his death.)

In February 1929, Benjamin wrote me a letter that confirmed the apprehensions I had expressed to him in writing. In it he said that he had to reckon with no longer being taken seriously by me, since he had to postpone his trip to Palestine until fall. This, to be sure, was somewhat in keeping with my expectations and my feelings that combined loyalty to him with mounting skepticism regarding the whole project. It also had been the reason for my rejecting an invitation from the *Jüdische Rundschau* [Jewish review], whose editor-in-chief, Robert Weltsch, I had spoken to in Berlin about my conversations with Benjamin. The journal had asked me to write an essay about Benjamin's books "in order to say something in this context about Benjamin as a Jewish thinker or the relationship of his thought to Judaism generally." I dropped a hint about this to Benjamin, and he wrote me, "Why do you evade such a task?— But I know the reason quite well, and may Heaven bless you for it." That letter contained many interesting things about my work

and his, but not a word about Asja Lacis, with whom he had lived
on Düsseldorfer Strasse for a time and who led an active campaign
against his Palestinian plans; a few months later I received only
indirect information about this in letters from Dora. In her memoirs
Asja Lacis boasts of her success in preventing Benjamin's visiting
me. In doing so, to be sure, she erroneously shifts the events of
1929 to the Capri period in 1924, when Benjamin had harbored
no plans of this sort. He asked me to recommend a teacher for his
Hebrew lessons in Berlin, and I referred him to Max Mayer, whom
I had known very well since 1916; he was one of the few Zionists
from assimilated families who had really learned Hebrew
thoroughly.

But these daily lessons did not begin until the end of May. They
lasted less than two months, at which time Mayer went on vacation
and Benjamin took a short trip to Italy with Wilhelm Speyer. After
their return the lessons were not resumed. As was confirmed to me
from several sides, Benjamin actually ran around with a Hebrew
grammar during those weeks of studying. What really happened,
however, remained concealed behind his letters of those months.
He passed over everything that he called "external circumstances"
—that is, what concerned him, Asja Lacis, and Dora in their crises
—and wrote only about difficulties that had arisen from other
quarters. On March 23 he wrote:

*Yesterday I had an hour's discussion with Dr. Mayer that was extraor-
dinarily encouraging. He has a quite astonishing eye for what has
happened and was able to work things out for me, although I concealed
none of the difficulties from him. As you know, the greatest difficulty
is, to my mind, that preliminary studies for—not yet, by any means,
work on—the "Paris Arcades" cannot be interrupted at this moment.
Rather, I want to advance the preliminary work to the point where I
shall be free in Palestine to occupy myself with the study, or to
interrupt it, without aids or risks. As a consequence of that conversation I have had to make what is at present a hard decision: to stay
in Berlin. If I can at all bring it about financially, I want to set out
for Palestine via France in summer or fall.*

Two months later he wrote: "Because of my silence I have to reckon
with all sorts of volatile thoughts on your part. There was nothing

I could do"—because Mayer had fallen ill. Benjamin added that daily instruction now would resume and that he was writing his first Hebrew cursive letters. On June 6 he wrote to Magnes, expressing his expectation "that my presence in Jerusalem will strengthen your conviction of the seriousness of our Paris talks, even though my silence may have shaken it for a while." To me he wrote on the same day: "Unfortunately I am not able to counter your reproaches with anything at all; they are absolutely justified, and in this matter I am encountering a pathological vacillation which, I am sorry to say, I have already noticed in myself from time to time." There followed an allusion, which I could not immediately understand at the time, to the inhibitions "whose form and dimensions you actually know only in part and which, to the extent that they are purely personal in nature, will have to await an oral report" (*Briefe* 2, p. 493). From an excursion to Bansin on the Baltic Sea he wrote that he was less satisfied with his progress than his teacher. "You see, it becomes clearer and clearer to me how very rapid my progress could be if I had nothing else on my mind from early till late; which is impossible. I do an enormous amount of work in order to stay on top in both spheres of my activity. In Palestine a greater exclusivity in Hebrew automatically will develop. I think I shall leave Marseilles in the course of September, provided that nothing unforeseen intervenes." This was a veiled warning, which recurred in an obscure reference (on July 27) to a lawsuit that was placing all his dispositions in doubt. The warning had its denouement only with his brief but revealing statement that he had definitively moved out of his apartment "in clouds of dust and under a mountain of boxes," a piece of news that he shared with me on August 4, 1929, when he moved in temporarily with Hessel.

Crises and Turning Points
(1930–1932)

A week before Benjamin wrote the above-mentioned letter, Dora had written me that Walter, who had lived with Asja Lacis at Düsseldorfer Strasse no. 42 from December 1928 to January 1929, was living with her again and that spring had asked her for a divorce so he could marry Asja. Dora claimed he was doing so only to obtain German citizenship for Asja, who was having difficulties getting an extension of her permit of residence in Germany. I had my doubts about that, but from a distance I was not able to determine to what extent this was true and what the situation really was. Between June 1929 and March 27, 1930, the date on which their marriage was dissolved, there was a lawsuit over the question of blame and the related financial disputes based on Benjamin's obligations according to the marriage contract of 1917, on which Dora's parents had insisted at the time. This lawsuit was carried on by both parties with the greatest vehemence. All I shall say about it is that Walter lost. For about two years, until June 1931, all contact between them ceased; it was resumed by both sides very haltingly. Very slowly there developed a modus vivendi and later a more friendly and more trusting relationship between them.

In June, Dora wrote that I could not count on Walter's ever

coming. "All his friends say that he will not go to Palestine"—by this she meant primarily Ernst Schoen, Franz Hessel, Gustav Glück, and Ernst Bloch. At that time these men still were visiting her, but after the divorce they withdrew—under pressure from Walter, Dora thought. It stood to reason that the obvious victim of these events would be his Hebrew study, and Benjamin's letters from this period reflect some painful embarrassment. Before 1930 he could not bring himself to mention his divorce *expressis verbis,* with the exception of one letter, dated November 1, 1929. In that letter he wrote me: "It could not be foreseen that my separation from Dora would assume the cruel forms that it did. I am embroiled in an incalculable divorce suit, and . . . you will not expect to hear more about it from me in writing than this little bit, the telling of which I postponed for as long as I could. That's the way it is: for the time being I shall have to make all dispositions in my life exclusively with a view toward the requirements of this situation." What that involved no longer could surprise me. Nor was I under any illusions about a telegram of September 17, in which he announced his arrival on November 4. On several occasions in September and October he was in Frankfurt, where Asja Lacis was being treated by the neurologist Kurt Goldstein. There Benjamin established close contact with Theodor Adorno and Max Horkheimer. This relationship reached its zenith at the time in long conversations about Marxism, at which Asja Lacis and Gretel Karplus, later Adorno's wife, were also present.

I myself never met Asja Lacis, since I was not in Germany at the time of her various visits there. Most of those mentioned in these pages, however, were generally in agreement regarding what they later told me about her, her personality, and her behavior toward Benjamin. Her own report is highly selective. When I came to Europe in 1932, she had long since returned to Russia. As far as I know, she never saw Benjamin after that, although she continued to correspond with him until her arrest under Stalin. As for him, after his letter of September 18, 1929 (published in *Briefe* 2), he never referred to her again in his communications to me. Thus this side of his life remained completely dark to me.

Something that remained astonishing in this year of the greatest excitements, upheavals, and disappointed expectations in his life was his capacity for concentration, his openness to intellectual matters, and the harmoniousness of style in his letters. There was in him a store of profound serenity—only poorly described by the word *stoicism*—that remained untouched by the awkward situations in which he found himself at that time and the upheavals designed to throw his existence off course. The year 1929 constituted a distinct turning point in his intellectual life as well as a high point of intensive literary and philosophical activity. It was a visible turning point, which nevertheless did not exclude the continuity of his thought and of the motives governing his thought in the realm of the invisible—something that is more clearly discernible now than it was then. In the ensuing years I was able to discern this conflict clearly, possibly all the more so because I did so from a distance. This dual recognition of change and continuity in him, something that I was probably the only one to recognize at the time, shaped our relationship in the years to come.

In May 1929, Benjamin made the acquaintance of Bertolt Brecht, with whom Asja Lacis had professional dealings. Although he hitherto had made his Berlin literary acquaintances primarily in the circle of Franz Hessel and Ernst Bloch—he had met Gretel Karplus and Otto Klemperer through Bloch—Brecht brought an entirely new element, an elemental force in the truest sense of the word, into his life. Around that time his hitherto quite loose relationship with Adorno assumed a firmer form. As early as June 6 he informed me of his rather close acquaintance with Brecht: "There is a lot to say about him and about it" (*Briefe* 2, p. 494). Three weeks later he wrote: "You will be interested to know that a very friendly relationship between Bert Brecht and me has recently developed, based less on what he has produced (I know only *The Threepenny Opera* and the ballads) than on the well-founded interest one must take in his present plans." Even before meeting Brecht personally, he had pitted Brecht's poems against Walter Mehring's chansons, which he sharply attacked. The emergence of heavier Marxist accents from 1928 on evidently is connected with the influence of Asja Lacis and Brecht; Adorno and Horkheimer later led him to a further breakthrough in this direction at Königstein. Benjamin's conversations with Brecht, to which soon were added talks with Brecht's Marxist mentors Fritz Sternberg and Karl

Korsch (a close friend of my brother Werner, who by then had been expelled from the Communist party but was still a member of the Reichstag), had more to do with the Bolshevist theory of politics and aesthetics than with Brecht's published writings. Of those Benjamin apparently read only *A Man's a Man* in June 1930, before he was fascinated by Brecht's *Versuche* [Attempts]. As late as September 1929 he wrote me: "Brecht's new play *[Happy End]* does not do him very much credit" (*Briefe* 2, p. 502). I did not realize the full importance of this relationship for him until 1930, after his Hebrew plans had been put *ad acta* for good.

During this period of upheaval, he did a great deal of work. In the above-mentioned letter of November 1, 1929, he wrote: "I have been commissioned by the encyclopedia [*Encyclopaedia Judaica*] edited by [Jacob] Klatzkin to write on the subject 'The German Jews in the Intellectual Life of the Nineteenth and Twentieth Centuries' as a subsection of the entry 'Germany.' The deadline is the end of November. Until then this project will claim all my time. It would be important if you could advise me on it." Precisely this essay, the first one in which he expressed himself in concentrated form on a Jewish subject, evidently was so far removed from the expectations then popular and so markedly bore the stamp of complete independence that it appeared only in a completely adulterated version, greatly "revised" by Nahum Goldmann and Rabbi Benno Jacob. This was bound to be especially infuriating to Benjamin, as in many instances there appeared under his name the opposite of what he had written. Unfortunately, the original text has not been preserved. In addition to this work he wanted to finish an essay on André Gide; another essay, on J. P. Hebel, he had presented as a lecture in Berlin in September or October. But the untoward circumstances took their toll. He wrote me that in October he had suffered a breakdown connected with agitation over the divorce suit and had been completely immobilized for ten days. "I was not able to make a phone call and talk to anyone, let alone do any writing. Even this letter I am mailing reluctantly; true, I have recovered, but the letter is so silent on everything that could be said now that I can sense your dissatisfaction (not to mention more important feelings) on receiving it." He concluded his letter with a veritable sigh: "At the moment I am greatly dependent on the discretion and forbearance of my friends."

After that he fell completely silent for almost three months, before sending me—evidently after Asja Lacis's return to Moscow —the letter (published in *Briefe* 2) of January 20, 1930 (written in French!), the purport of which shocked me. He said he could not contemplate a journey to Palestine until the divorce decree at the earliest, and this decree was not so imminent. He also wrote finis to any hopes of learning Hebrew while still in Germany. It was now his ambition, he said, to become the most important critic of German literature. With this he renounced the hopes of earlier years as well as his own remarks to Magnes. The letter crossed in the mail with one of mine, written a few days earlier, which, as he put it, "restored the use of my mother tongue to me" with its attitude of friendship and its sympathetic interest in his situation. My thoughts on the situation thus created are contained in my letter of February 20, 1930, which concluded these discussions (*Briefe* 2, pp. 510–12). In it I wrote about the situation that was bound to arise "if it turns out that in this life you can no longer reckon with, and do not reckon with, a real encounter with Judaism except in the medium of our friendship. . . . To me it is far more important to know where you really are than where you hope to go someday, for the way your life is constituted it is certain that you, more than anyone else, will always wind up some other place than where you wanted to get." I was very moved by his reply for which I had to wait more than two months—something that could not surprise me in view of the prevailing circumstances. In that letter he wrote: "Living Judaism I have certainly encountered in no other form than in you. The question as to my attitude toward Judaism is always the question as to my attitude toward—I will not say toward *you* (for my friendship is no longer subject to any decision) but toward the forces that you have aroused in me." The next sentence bears witness to the depth of his self-knowledge: "No matter what this decision may depend upon, no matter how it may be embodied on the one hand in circumstances seemingly quite alien to it and on the other in that extremely tense vacillation that is my nature in all the most important situations of my life, it will be made very soon" (*Briefe* 2, p. 513).

Even after the divorce had been granted, there were three more months of litigation between Walter and Dora regarding the financial settlement, which caused him considerable difficulties. I wrote him that my wife, Escha, was going to come to Europe that summer and planned to visit him. I had asked her to remind him of the ticklish situation into which I would be put by his use of the sum granted him for a specific purpose, particularly if—as was to be expected—he never came to Jerusalem. He answered me on June 14 from a new temporary apartment:

Dear Gerhard:

You know that illusions, especially about myself, are not my strong suit. In your letter, which was waiting for me last night, I found more truth than both of us can desire. Your reference to Green was food for thought, especially since I have realized for a long time that at least the constellations in the family from which I come display a striking similarity to those encountered in Green's novels. My sister is a match for the unloveliest female characters there. And what a struggle I have had to wage against these forces—not only where they face me in her, as they do now, but also in myself! That is precisely why I am writing you. Surely anyone who touches the most limited and most questionable elements in me as deeply as you have hardly can disregard entirely the fact that I have taken up battle against them, even though belatedly and under disastrous circumstances. I doubt whether even you have a fairer and more positive picture of my marriage than I retain to this day and thus presumably forever. Without encroaching on this picture too much, I shall tell you (though perhaps I hardly need do so) that in the end (and here I speak of years) my marriage completely had become the exponent of these forces. For a very, very long time I believed I would never have the strength to find my way out of my marriage; when this strength suddenly came to me in the midst of the deepest pain and profoundest loneliness, I of course clung to it. Just as the difficulties stemming from this step at present determine my outer existence—it is, after all, not easy to be without property and position, home and funds at the threshold of one's forties —this step itself is now the basis of my inner existence, a foundation that feels hard but has no room for demons. Even this foundation is not yet secure—that is, I still cannot be sure that by assigning in

writing my entire future estate I shall see my burdens reduced to
tolerable dimensions; the coming days will bring a decision on that.
Before this happens, in the breathtaking, constantly shifting constella-
tions in which I have been caught up for months, now that the actual
divorce suit has ended in my disfavor and I have accepted the verdict
in the first instance, nothing really can be done. This much in response
to your letter. I shall stay in Berlin at least till the middle of July
and thus hope to see Escha. . . . I am yearning greatly for some
relaxation, since I recently have been burdened by an excessive amount
of work in addition to everything else. Right now I am preparing a
radio talk based on two fairly lengthy, still unpublished critiques
of the collection Krieg und Krieger *[War and warriors], edited*
by [Ernst] Jünger, and Der Dichter als Führer in der deutschen
Klassik *[The poet as leader in German classicism] by Max Kommerell,*
a pupil of [Friedrich] Wolters. In the course of this I had to deal,
somewhat later than you, with Wolters's unspeakable tome [the book
about Stefan George and the Blätter für die Kunst*]. In it there is a*
contrast between pupil and master that does credit to the former. For
my volume of essays I still am preparing a study of Karl Kraus. I have
signed a contract with Kiepenheuer for a volume of selected novellas
by Marcel Jouhandeau.

This extremely personal letter and my wife's report about her two
visits with Dora and Walter gave me a picture of the serious crises
and changes in his life, in which everything was coming to a head
at once. "I suppose you have heard a great deal," Walter said to
Escha when he visited her for a long conversation in my family's
summer house near Berlin. He had reason to suppose that she
already had met with Dora. On the contrary, Escha had, if anything, reacted defensively to Dora's readiness to tell her details.
When Escha described to Benjamin the situation I was sure to find
myself in if he did not come or failed to return the sum that he long
since had spent, Walter avoided giving a clear answer, for he
disliked having unpleasant situations arise in conversations of a
personal nature. The conversation also turned to his now obvious
Marxist approach to literary and philosophical subjects and to his
Communist inclinations in politics. In this connection he said to
her, "The fact of the matter is that Gerhard and I have convinced

each other." This was a memorable statement, which in view of our conversations during the winter of 1918–19 on the Russian revolution and theocratic politics, was not completely in accord with the facts but was in keeping with the different forms that our shared radical stance had assumed. The American novelist Joseph Hergesheimer, who had met Benjamin in this period of upheavals, said at the time, as Dora wrote me, that Walter gave "the impression of a person who has just climbed down from one cross and is about to mount another."

Around that time there already were spirited discussions in Berlin between Benjamin, the writer Soma Morgenstern, whom he had known since 1927, and Brecht on the major subject of Trotsky and Stalin and on the question of Stalin's possible anti-Semitism, which had been raised by Morgenstern, a man of strong Jewish feelings. (Morgenstern told me about this in a long letter.) At that time Benjamin also wrote to Adorno about "great chunks of conversation in meetings with Brecht, whose crashing surf has not reached you yet." The letters Benjamin wrote me about the project of a periodical that he planned to edit with Brecht clearly indicate the depth and significance his relationship with Brecht had assumed by then. Around the same time, Siegfried Kracauer, who regarded Benjamin's Marxist views with much greater sympathy than I, wrote me that in Berlin he had had "a very heated argument with him about his slavish-masochistic attitude toward Brecht" and promised to tell me about it later, "preferably in person." This was not the only controversy of the kind in Benjamin's circle.

A strange juxtaposition in Benjamin's letter of November 3, 1930, is an enthusiastic statement about the "sobriety with which the kabbalistic sources that you mention integrate the mystical states of affairs or raise them for discussion" and an emphatic reference to Brecht's *Versuche,* which he then also sent to me. "I admit the time has come to inform you about these things, because they have in the meantime made some progress on the road to public revelation. With my next communication you will receive the program and the statutes of a new periodical titled *Krise und Kritik* [Crisis and criticism], which is to be published by Rowohlt under the editorship of [Herbert] Ihering, with the first issue dated January 15, 1931. On the masthead I shall appear as a coeditor along with Brecht and two or three others. It will be a source of equivocal satisfaction to you to see my name as that of the only Jew among nothing but goyim" (*Briefe* 2, p. 519; one passage of this letter is published here for the first time). As he had written me a month earlier, he was fully aware of the "inherent difficulty of any collaboration with Brecht," although he supposed that "if anyone is capable of coping with him, I am that person" (*Briefe* 2, p. 518). The fact that despite my above-mentioned letter from the beginning of the year he still harbored hopes of a "definitive decision regarding the Palestinian attempt" that would be made within a year was, in my estimation, more of a manifestation of his continuing discomfort at his conduct, a discomfort that found expression in other letters as well.

Again three months passed, during which time I wrote a gloomy letter about the situation in Eretz Yisrael and the Zionist movement following the Arab disturbances of August 1929. On February 5, 1931, he replied:

Dear Gerhard:

Your letter came yesterday and made me very contrite. I certainly disapprove of the hiatus in my communications as much as I do of the reasons that occasioned it. And now the profusion of opaque allusions in my last letters that stood like a mass of flowers at the edge of my abysmal silence. To build a bridge across this abyss of three months I don't even mind using the instrument—revolutionary in our correspondence, as far as I know—into which I am dictating this letter, for otherwise many days would be lost again.

To begin with lesser matters, you received Spuren *[Tracks, by Ernst Bloch] at my behest; you don't seem to realize this at all. Tomorrow I am having dinner with Rowohlt and shall get [Josef Kastein's]* Sabbatai Zevi *for you. At about the same time as this letter a good-sized package containing some homemade goods, so to speak —my own writings—will be mailed to you. Among them will be a prose piece, which brings me right away to one of the reasons for my long silence: it is a carbon copy of the essay on Karl Kraus, on which I worked for an extraordinarily long period, almost a year, and during the past month amid complete disregard for all personal and financial obligations. It will bring to life for you all sorts of key words from a*

*period that, God knows, may perhaps already be called our "youth."
You should take it in this spirit if I reserve the manuscript, which
constitutes the fourth version of the entire material, for your archives,
to be sent you upon your request.*

*The package will contain also a printed sheet from Brecht's lat-
est book, which I happen to have on hand; even though this certainly
will not give you an idea of the projected periodical, it will convey
to you some inkling of what interests me most about it. The nature
of my involvement with it recently has become open again. Whether
I shall appear as coeditor depends on what form the first issue takes.
For a long time everything, including the very appearance of the
periodical, was in doubt, but in recent days things have assumed
more concrete shape, and April is supposed to be the publication
date.*

*Since owing to technical circumstances I do not have as much time
for this dictation as I would like, I shall now give you a brief outline
of the situation as a forerunner of a more detailed handwritten report.*

*There no longer is any inner indecision for me. I cannot expect
much of the German situation. My interest in it does not go beyond
the fate of the small circle around Brecht. It is perhaps more this lack
of interest in external matters—coupled with a more intensive application to my work, partly its oldest themes—than what you hypothetically call the "harder substance of my character" that brings about
a certain unchangeability in my situation. Lamentably enough, it is
unchangeable in an external sense as well. If you knew the amount
of the debts I have had to pay in recent months,* you could not help
having considerable respect for the negative of my financial portrait.
The short and the long of it is only that I have no freedom of movement
and do not have the 3,000 marks that would, according to a calcula-
tion made with Escha, constitute the basis for any rearrangement of
my life. A change in Germany's economic situation would give me that
amount. But that would be a tall order.*

I shall react to your remarks about Spuren *when I meet my
obligation, which I find somewhat oppressive, to review the book in*
Die literarische Welt. *But I cannot close without asking you to
expand on your gloomy references to the conditions in Palestine—
"more the internal than the external ones." Write me as soon as you*

---

*It was a matter of 40,000 marks.

*can at the above address. During the next twelve days I shall be in
Frankfurt to take care of some piddling radio matters. But your answer
will find me back in Berlin.*

With cordial regards to you and Escha,

as ever yours

Walter

*P.S. [handwritten] I have just reread your long letter of November and
feel that the key to the downcast references in your last letter may be
your detailed presentation of the Zionist situation. But I shall be
grateful for any more detailed information. I commend myself to your
Department of Foreign Correspondence with an especially good conscience because, as promised and planned, today I induced Rowohlt
to send you a copy of* Sabbatai Zevi. *Of course the book will not arrive
until a few days after this letter. By the way, in the same conversation
I managed to postpone by six months the appearance of my collected
essays that were to be published in the spring; this will enable me to
put them in better shape. For one thing, I still have to write the preface,
"Die Aufgabe des Kritikers" [The task of the critic], but I hope above
all to produce this summer my major essay on* Jugendstil, *the intellectual content of which lies partly in the realm of my essay on the
Arcades. So as not to neglect Escha in this long letter, you may promise
her in my name my next article in* Uhu *[Owl]. To say what it is about
does not belong in a civilized letter. ***

I copied the beginning of my reply, dated February 19, on the back
of the typewritten letter:

Dear Walter:

*Unfortunately I lack the necessary background for a motto, which
I really ought to place above your letter, received yesterday, in order
to retain the appropriate style and unburden my somewhat heavy
heart. Which of Goethe's or Lichtenberg's writings could I draw it
from? For although it is certain that the technical production of your
letter adds, as you say, what is undoubtedly an extremely modern,
revolutionary touch and tenor to our correspondence, as someone rather*

---

*It was "Der enthüllte Osterhase" [The Easter bunny unmasked], which did
not appear in *Uhu* until April 1932.

competent in this area I may say with equal assurance that this indirect form of communication appears simply and bluntly as a redoubled taciturnity; even though I would not want to make presumptuous speeches, I will say that probably no letter crying for a fountain pen was ever less suited to being dictated to a stenotypist. But since, as amply evidenced by your specific remark, you are aware of all this far more clearly than I, there arises with all the more urgency the need to respect a silence or, rather, a falling silent (even a verbal one), no matter how unfathomable the reasons for this may be to me. For your essay on Kraus—in which (as I was able to grasp last night at the first, highly intense reading) you take up again the most magnificent, most significant elements of your thought, much more strongly and purely than could be expected in these years—does not, *as you must permit me to state, contain these reasons, or even one of them,* by any means. *I therefore must prefer to content myself with what I may call a vehement know-nothingness, not even inwardly transfigured by irony. It is a drastic know-nothingness, pure and simple, and presumably will have to remain so. This much about your letter.*

Here I shall not go into the major argument carried on between us in correspondence between March and May 1931 on the subject of Benjamin's turn to dialectical materialism. This argument was triggered by his major essay on Karl Kraus, which enraged me as much as it impressed me, as well as by his letters to Brecht and Rychner, copies of which he had sent me. The documents relevant here have been published in the edition of Benjamin's correspondence (*Briefe* 2, pp. 525–33). (Because the three major letters— two from me and one from him—are especially important for an understanding of our relationships and discussions, I have reprinted them as an appendix to this book.) It is not surprising that I took the initiative in these matters, both where a clear statement of his attitude toward Judaism and where his materialistic production were concerned. Being far removed from the entanglements that prevented Benjamin from taking a firm stand made it easier for me to formulate the essential points unambiguously, indeed provocatively. What I was consciously concerned with was to function as a catalyst in these necessary clarifications. That Benjamin himself did not particularly welcome such clarification I could easily grasp, but it took me some time to understand that at bottom that clarification was not possible for him. His later work proved that he was incapable of making a decision between metaphysics and materialism (as he conceived of the latter). Benjamin's attitude toward dialectical materialism as a heuristic principle rather than as a dogma (his position from 1931 on) left the way clear for the continuing development of a metaphysical, intellectual wellspring that had little, and frequently enough nothing, to do with the categories of materialism. In keeping with this there was also his enduring attachment to Jewish categories, which may be discerned in his writings to the end.

How much these Jewish interests continued to affect our relationship is probably documented best by my detailed reply to Benjamin's letter of June 20, 1931, not long after the above-mentioned exchange of letters. This letter illustrates the climate of our relationship, a climate that by then could be expressed only in correspondence, at an especially important point. Benjamin had informed me in strict confidence of the cautious resumption of closer relations between Dora and him. He also had asked me for some "hints" on my thoughts about Kafka (in connection with his projected review of Kafka's posthumously published volume *Beim Bau der Chinesischen Mauer* [The Great Wall of China]), and finally he wanted to hear my opinion of the very tempestuous Zionist Congress in Basel in the summer of 1931. The original of this letter was preserved among his papers, for owing to its particular interest he had removed it from our correspondence and placed it among his notes on Kafka. I wrote on August 1, 1931:

Dear Walter:

Your last letter, in which to my joy I found at least some biographical information about you, lies before me, and I implore you to realize that in this regard you can never do too much of a good thing for me. The well-known obscurity and problematic nature of metaphysics and its sister sciences (like politics and ethics) can be complemented most agreeably by the brightness of your autobiography. Take this avowal to heart, and write me how and where you are living. Your confidential communication about a reconciliation between you and Dora, be it ever so embryonic, moves me greatly. I am sure you understand that

I would regard it as one of the most joyous events of my own life if at least some more friendly light were brought into the terrible, chaotic darkness in which your relationship sank at the end. No one who witnessed your happier years can believe that all this was necessary. There never could have been so much darkness around the two of you for your life to have been drawn so helplessly into this degrading game of bitterness. In those years this was the only thing that made me regret I was not in Germany; I believe I would have been capable of bringing about your separation, if it was necessary, under less catastrophic circumstances.

You were the first to tell me of Rowohlt's bankruptcy. **Die litera-rische Welt** *does not arrive here any more, and I see only a few of the more or less gloomy products of German reaction. I would be surprised if you could not place your essays with several publishing houses. I assume that you will dedicate the first volume of your collected critical reflections to the memory of Gundolf. In any case, however, you ought to style your projected Kafka review so that it has a place in the book, for it really is morally unthinkable for you to publish a book of criticism that does not include Kafka. Since you ask me for a "hint" in this regard, I can only say that I do not own the posthumous volume as yet and am acquainted with only two items of the greatest perfection from it. I have of course already had "individ-ual thoughts" about Kafka, although these do not concern Kafka's position in the continuum of German literature (in which he has no position of any sort, something that he himself did not have the least doubt about; as you probably know, he was a Zionist), but his position in the continuum of Jewish literature. I advise you to begin any inquiry into Kafka with the Book of Job, or at least with a discussion of the possibility of divine judgment, which I regard as the sole subject of Kafka's production [worthy of] being treated in a work of literature. These, you see, are in my opinion also the vantage points from which one can describe Kafka's linguistic world, which with its affinity to the language of the Last Judgment probably represents the prosaic in its most canonical form. The ideas I expressed many years ago in my theses on justice (which you know) would in their relationship to language serve me as a guide in my reflections on Kafka. It would be an enigma to me how you as a critic would go about saying something about this man's world without placing the* **Lehre** *[teaching], called*

Gesetz *[law]* in Kafka's work, at the center. *I suppose this is what the moral reflection—if it were possible (and this is the hypothesis of presumptuousness!)—of a halakhist who attempted a* linguistic *paraphrase of a divine judgment would have to be like. Here, for once, a world is expressed in which redemption cannot be anticipated—go and explain this to the goyim! I believe that at this point your critique will become just as esoteric as its subject; the light of revelation never burned as unmercifully as it does here. This is the theological secret of perfect prose. The overwhelming statement that the Last Judgment is, rather, a martial law was made, unless I am mistaken, by Kafka himself.*

The package with Brecht's Versuche *that you promised has not arrived yet. If you manage to get hold of another copy of the new volume of the Proust translation, I hope you will present it to me. For my part, last week I sent you a German essay of rather intricate content, as well as a book review. A lot of my stuff, almost ten galleys, is about to appear in periodicals, but those things are slow to come out. A rather extensive Hebrew essay, almost book-length, on the history of a* terminus technicus *in the Kabbalah, has been appearing slowly but surely for the past six months in a quarterly published by the university. It is my serious intention to write more in German because no historian of religion is capable of reading Hebrew. Conversely, my Jerusalem magicians can enjoy my revelations solely in Hebrew.*

Unfortunately, the only way I can respond to the modest inquiry presented at the end of your letter as to how the last Zionist Congress should be assessed is by detailing the very disagreeable situation in which it left us. To tell the truth, the development of the last two years, culminating in the decisions of this congress, made evident the radical split between my conception of Zionism, which I heard characterized as a religious-mystical quest for a regeneration of Judaism (a characterization I agree with), and empirical Zionism, whose point of departure is an impossible and provocative distortion of an alleged political "solution to the Jewish Question." Now, Zionism as a movement certainly always has been far more than the empirical form of its organization, but surely in all these years there was the chance for people like me to pursue our cause—which, God knows, originally had nothing to do with Englishmen or Arabs—within this organization. Or, rather, it was a matter of indifference to us (at least from 1920 on), because the legitimacy of the real historical event of Zionism in any case was assured. But because in recent years the purely reactionary forces in Zionism have asserted themselves in their way, both politically and morally, and this congress even reached decisions that directly affect this aspect of the matter, the crisis in our relationship to this cause has become acute for me and many others. I do not believe that there is such a thing as a "solution to the Jewish Question" in the sense of a normalization of the Jews, and I certainly do not think that this question can be solved in Palestine in such a sense. I have always realized that Palestine is necessary, and that was enough, no matter what was expected of the event here; no Zionist program bound our hands here. This time things have changed. Because of the demand —originated and presented by the small Jerusalem circle to which I belong—for a clear-cut orientation of Zionism, an orientation that ought to be demonstrated concretely on the Arab question but that of course derived from an entirely different point of view, one not related to foreign policy, and owing to the fantastic agitation organized against our position since 1929 (a campaign I assume you don't even know about), a resolution about the "ultimate aim" of Zionism now has been passed that is openly directed against us and in accordance with which we would, strictly speaking, automatically no longer appear as "Zionists" in the sense of the organization. To be sure, like it or not, the foreign policy represented by us ("us" being a scant twenty men, "deracinated intellectuals," as we are called here, who nevertheless have exerted extraordinary influence) will be pursued here, though unfortunately too late and under suppression of our authorship. Since it is not matched by any inner attitude, which ultimately will be the only decisive factor, this foreign policy will remain an empty shell. Yes, a fantastically reactionary resolution was passed against Magnes and the teachers of the university who, to put it succinctly, are carrying the banner of Ahad Ha'am. The resolution, to be sure, was passed against the most determined opposition, for it went too far for the Socialists, with whom we are in a serious conflict, because we are reproaching them with a reactionary policy toward the Arabs; this has caused people to be damned angry at us. The resolution was intended to shut us up, but it has no real significance—except possibly the fact that every German anti-Semite will be able to justify himself with it very successfully if he wants to demand that the universities be *"cleansed" of troublesome theoreticians. (The Zionist Congress is anything but an authoritative body as far as the university is concerned.)*

Although the forces that are about to accomplish the wrecking of Zionism certainly can be identified, who knows whether you will understand me when I say that Zionism has triumphed itself to death. It has anticipated its victories in the intellectual realm and thereby has lost the power to win them in the physical realm. It fulfilled a function, you see, and with an enormous effort that it certainly had not intended. We were victorious too early. *Our existence, our sad immortality, which Zionism had come along to stabilize in an unshakable way, once again has been assured temporally—for the next two generations, but at a most horrendous price. For even before the connection was reestablished and secured in the life of the country and the language, we lost our forces in a field on which we never intended to fight. When Zionism prevailed in Berlin—which means in a vacuum, from the point of view of our task—it no longer could be victorious in Jerusalem. History's claim to us has been satisfied long since, but we never realized it. It turned out that the historical task of Zionism simply was quite different from the one it posed itself. For years the despair of the victor has been the real demonism of Zionism; this is perhaps the most important world-historical example of the mysterious laws according to which propaganda (the substance of our defeat) works. The mountains of articles in which the intelligensia documented our victory in the visible realm before it had been decided in the invisible realm—that is, the regeneration of language—are the true Wailing Wall of the new Zion. Now it is no longer a matter of saving us—consolation for an unjust victory could, after all, lie only in oblivion—but of jumping into the abyss that yawns between our victory and reality.*

In the empty passion of a vocation become public we ourselves have invoked the forces of destruction. Our catastrophe started where the vocation did not maintain itself in its profanation, where community was not developed in its legitimate concealment, but where instead the betrayal of the secret values that lured us here became transformed into a positive side of the demonic propaganda. By becoming visible our cause was destroyed. The encounter with Sleeping Beauty took place in the presence of too many paying spectators for it to have ended with

*an embrace. Zionism disregarded the night and shifted the procreation
that ought to have meant everything to it to a world market where there
was too much sunlight and the covetousness of the living degenerated
into a prostitution of the last remnants of our youth. That was not the
place we had come to find nor the light that could enflame us. Between
London and Moscow we strayed into the desert of Araby on our way
to Zion, and our own hubris blocked the path that leads to our people.
Thus all we have left is the productivity of one who is going down and
knows it. It is this productivity in which I have buried myself for years,
for, after all, where should the miracle of immortality be concealed if
not here? But this brings us back to Kafka!*

*Accept my most cordial regards and pardon my brevity on such
a boundless subject. If you cannot or will not reply, send me at least
a picture postcard with your photo and autograph.*

Yours,

Gerhard

The second part of my letter contained, in incisive German
formulation, ideas that I was presenting at that time in greater
detail in a Hebrew essay. As Benjamin's answer shows, this letter
moved him greatly. He thought that "by way of these questions we
would reach a surprising understanding of the other questions, only
seemingly alien to them, that have been open between us for some
time" (*Briefe* 2, p. 540). This hope, to be sure, was not fulfilled,
nor could it have been in view of my rejection of the class-struggle
theory as a key to an understanding of history. Later Hitler also
did his share to render this key obsolete, though not in some
important aspects. But Benjamin paid me a great compliment: "I,
at any rate, regard these lines of yours as a kind of historical
document." His reaction to my statements about Kafka was also
surprisingly positive, and he wrote me that he had been thinking
along lines that closely paralleled my own ideas.

In fact, Benjamin's lecture on Kafka had come into being
shortly before that time, although it was not published in its entirety until 1955. It originated in the extended reflections that
Benjamin had been making with recourse to his Bachofen studies.
Although here he reverted to the Jewish categories of Aggadah and

Halakhah, on which I also had based myself in part, in conversations with Brecht in Le Lavandou at the beginning of June he was surprised by Brecht's "extremely positive attitude toward Kafka's work" (*Briefe* 2, p. 539). To be sure, according to Benjamin's notes on a conversation of June 6, 1931, Brecht regarded Kafka as "the only truly Bolshevist writer." To the extent that the discussion of Kafka came within Benjamin's purview, these were the poles between which it took place before the existentialist and psychoanalytic interpretations of Kafka (which neither of us found to our taste) came to the fore.

In the meantime Benjamin's essay on Kraus had appeared in print. On a microscopically written card from Le Lavandou dated June 8 he informed me that he very belatedly had sent me a copy. In May I had drawn his attention to a very reserved, not to say uncomprehending, remark by Kraus (in the *Fackel* of May 1931, p. 52).* He wrote me about it:

You now have delved into this matter possibly more deeply than I— for I have not yet received the issue of Die Fackel, *which you were first to give me the news about. . . . I have to reserve judgment on what Kraus writes until I have read it, for I don't know to what extent it is in keeping with the remarks that Kraus made at a reading about eight weeks ago, which I of course have detailed information on, although I was not present. However this may be, in a word, Kraus's reaction could not reasonably have been expected to be different from what it was; I only hope that my reaction also will be within the realm of what reasonably may be predicted—namely, that I shall never write on him again.*

I have been away from Berlin for four weeks now. At first I was at Juan-les-Pins with acquaintances, then briefly in Sanary and Marseilles. Right now, and probably until my return at the end of the month, I am at Le Lavandou. The time is not lost, as I can pursue my activities on various levels here, starting with my work on Kafka, above all on the extraordinary posthumous volume, and down to my collabo-

---

Die Fackel was the only nonscholarly German periodical to which I had subscribed since 1923.

*ration with [Wilhelm] Speyer, which two years ago thoroughly aston-
ished Escha. Not only Speyer is here, but also Brecht, with a whole
retinue of friends and new projects. At the moment we are doing
preliminary work on a new play. I shall see to it that the new volume
of* Versuche, *which contains a magnificent verse narrative for children, is sent you immediately upon publication. I am well aware that
your last letter is still unanswered [a reference to my published letter
of May 6]; it is important for me to tie the continuation of our debate
more closely to Brecht's production, which for the time being I am
using ideologically as testimony for myself.*

Brecht's work in reality meant nothing to the continuation of our
debate. Benjamin spoke of it again on a number of occasions, but
he was not able to make me understand in any comprehensible
sense the tension between the two conflicting "ideological" faces
that he at that time and even later showed to Brecht and to me. For
a long time I could have only a vague notion of what we now know
from Brecht's complaints in his *Arbeitsjournal* [Working diary]
about Benjamin's "mysticism in spite of an antimystical attitude"
and his perennial "Judaisms": namely, that what attracted me so
much in Benjamin's thought and tied me so closely to him was
precisely the element that Brecht was bound to find annoying about
him. I did not get an idea of the paradox of Brecht's production,
of which only a few plays in the first volumes of *Versuche* had
moved me, until I went to Berlin on my European trip of 1932 and
attended a performance of *The Threepenny Opera*, which had then
been playing to full houses for two years. I was astonished when
I saw that a middle-class audience that had lost all sense of its own
situation was here cheering a play in which it was gibed and spat
at with a vengeance. Three months before Hitler's assumption of
power, for anyone who watched such a spectacle with detachment
this was a true prelude of what was to come. I hardly could be under
any illusions about the fact that a major part of this audience was
Jewish.

   An aspect of Benjamin's own output, accessible in an entirely
different manner and particularly moving, opened up to me after
the fall of 1931 with the first of the letters that began to appear
in the *Frankfurter Zeitung* at that time—letters that he had

unearthed and provided with magnificent, brief introductions.* Here I found the author again as he was familiar to me: undisguised and, despite all his profundity, of an urbanity and simplicity of expression that bespoke a mature intellect in all its sovereignty. I wrote him a rapturous letter, which as his reply indicates, pleased him very much (*Briefe* 2, pp. 541–43).

Benjamin's encounter with Surrealism probably prepared the ground for his experiments with hashish, which he began shortly after our separation and his return to Berlin and which he wrote me about several times in those years. As late as 1932 a book on this subject was among his projects that remained unfinished. Naturally he did not want to content himself with the notes and descriptions that have been preserved but wished to probe the philosophical relevance of such perceptions from an altered state of consciousness, which he regarded as more than mere hallucination. This was still wholly in keeping with his conception of the scope of genuine experience that I have discussed earlier. Of his notes on this subject he sent me only a printed one, but he repeatedly requested my strictest discretion about the experiments he made with two physicians, Dr. Fritz Fränkel and Dr. Ernst Joël. In these experiments he derived special inspiration from the presence of Ernst Bloch and a lady friend who later took her life. Benjamin was extremely cautious in the use of the drug, and when I questioned him in Paris in 1938, he told me that he had completely stopped using it several years before.

The unrest that kept impelling him to travel all through those years reached a particular apex with his divorce from Dora. This unrest seemingly gave way to an outer harmony and occasionally an "inward serenity," which he sometimes mentioned in his letters to me when, in late fall of 1930, he moved to Prinzregentenstrasse no. 66 in Berlin-Wilmersdorf. He took over this apartment from the painter Eva Boy (the pseudonym of Eva Hommel, later the wife of the painter van Hoboken), who told me about Benjamin more than thirty years later in Ascona. For over a year this was a furnished apartment, but then he managed on his own hook, vividly describing this situation in a letter as "inhabiting an apartment of my

---

* The reference here is to *Deutsche Menschen*. See p. 63—Trans.

own." It was a two-room studio apartment opposite that of his cousin Egon Wissing, and one had to climb a narrow staircase to reach it. Benjamin had a large study with room for the two thousand volumes to which his library had in the meantime grown, as well as for *Angelus Novus*. It was the last time that Benjamin had all his possessions together in one place. In reality he spent almost half the period during which he occupied this apartment in traveling. In the same letter in which he told me about his new circumstances (*Briefe* 2, pp. 544–47), he asked me "as soon as possible and most urgently" for my opinion of Otto Heller's *Untergang des Judentums* [The decline of Judaism], a totally worthless book promoted by the Communist party. I offered my judgment, which was as detailed as it was devastating, by return mail. Compared to the meretricious, ignorant twaddle of this tome, even the most rough-and-ready, vulgar brew of Zionism was bound to appear as the voice of truth and, above all, as an honest diagnosis of the situation of the Jews, regardless of all the crises that I had spoken about a few months earlier in the letter above.

In the same letter I also informed Benjamin that I would come to Europe for an extended period in the middle of March 1932 to search for manuscripts and that I counted on meeting him there. Over the five years that had passed since my first European trip so much had been stored up that could not be expressed adequately, if at all, in letters, and the years had brought so many disappointments, crises, and turning points in his life that a heart-to-heart talk between us was imperative. This much was clear to me.

What I could not have known was something more critical than that. As evidenced by Benjamin's diary entries made at Juan-les-Pins early in May 1931, two weeks after his reply to my attack on his materialistic position, he recognized an increasing readiness to take his own life. This was probably due less to my attack than to his general "battle fatigue on the economic front" and his feeling that basically he had lived his life in the fulfillment of his greatest desires. He regarded the "three great love experiences" of his life —evidently those with Dora, Jula, and Asja—as concluded. "In my life I have become acquainted with three different women and three different men within me. To write the story of my life would be to present the rise and fall of these three men as well as a compromise among them." He even composed a "diary from the seventh of August nineteen hundred and thirty-one to the day of death," which begins with these words:

This diary does not promise to be very long. Today came Kippenberg's negative response, which gives my plan all the relevance that only hopelessness can give it. Today I told I. that I would have to find a "way equally convenient but a bit less definitive." The prospects for it have become very slight. But if there is anything that can heighten the determination, and indeed the serenity, with which I am contemplating my plan, it is intelligent use of the last days or weeks, a use that is worthy of a human being. The days and weeks just past left much to be desired in this regard. Incapable of undertaking anything, I lay on the sofa and read; at the end of a page I was often so absent-minded that I forgot to turn it, usually being absorbed in my plan and wondering whether it was ineluctable and whether it was better to carry it out here in the studio or at the hotel.

It is understandable that these intentions, which stirred within him for another year and pressed for their release, were among the things he excluded from his letters to me, even though he discussed them in confidential conversations with I., one of his lady friends at the time (presumably Inge Buchholz).

His letters from that period betray an inner tranquillity and composure in the face of outward difficulties. I was not able to discern the real reason for this, but it is clearly evident from the above diary entries: Benjamin was at peace with himself and had finished with his life. He had experienced an unusual satisfaction that summer: Adorno, who had achieved *Habilitation* as a *Privatdozent* at the University of Frankfurt, carried forward Benjamin's ideas both in his thesis and in his inaugural lecture, which meant that at least in aesthetics Benjamin had found a kind of disciple. Apart from brief visits to Frankfurt, which Ernst Schoen facilitated by obtaining radio assignments for him, Benjamin carried on a cordial though not tension-free correspondence with Adorno. In those pre-Hitler years Benjamin's closest relationship was with Gustav Glück, the youthful director of the foreign department of the Reichskreditgesellschaft [Reich loan association]. Both Adorno and Glück were younger than Benjamin. Glück, a native Viennese from the circle around Karl Kraus whom Benjamin had met through Brecht, was a man of extraordinarily noble character and profound culture, but (and this was somewhat uncommon in those circles) he had no literary ambitions and was completely free of vanity. Although I did not establish close contact with Glück until much later, his personality is indelibly engraved on my mind. In a letter from that period Benjamin informed me that Glück had served as the model ("to be understood *cum grano salis*") for "Der destruktive Charakter" ["The Destructive Character," in *Reflections,* pp. 301–3], one of his most powerful short prose pieces.

Shortly before my departure for Rome, Benjamin wrote me on February 28, 1932:

Oh, dear Gerhard, today I noticed to my horror that you are planning to leave on the twelfth and that your letter has been lying here for almost two months. Perhaps your departure will be delayed a bit. I am now dictating these lines to make sure they are put on paper. . . . As almost always in such cases, it would take too long or be too short to say why I did not write. And the long and the short of it is that in recent weeks I have been at my wits' end with all this writing, or with the difficulties I unfortunately must face in connection with this writing. Not everything I could say about it is suitable for dictation, but I hope we shall speak with each other in the course of the year. My only consolation in this activity in ten directions is that I learn more and more to reserve my pen and my hand for the few important subjects and babble the ongoing stuff for the radio and the newspapers into the machine. That the introductions to the letters are among the written things will, I hope, be confirmed for you by the new letters. . . . If anything but 25- or 50-pfennig articles were salable in this country, the book that is about to be formed by these letters of course would have found a publisher long ago. But as things stand, I negotiate with this firm and that, not under any illusions. Sometimes it seems to me as though something else is coming into being behind my back—in the form of some notes I have been making for the past few weeks on appropriate (or, rather, usually inappropriate) occasions concerning the history of my relationship to Berlin.

If this letter still reaches you in Palestine, please send me immedi-

ately a copy of your letter to Mrs. [Edith] Rosenzweig. By way of exchange you can schnorr *me out of the last two volumes of Brecht when you visit me. For the rest, I have now staked my entire existence on the fame or afterfame of Brecht, because after two years of intrigues I recently managed to gain possession of a copy of the first printing of his* Hauspostille *[Manual of piety], which consisted of only 25 copies and was never commercially available.*

What are the two major studies, about which you give no details out of supercilious modesty and modest superciliousness? And may I hope to receive a proof copy of your Kabbalah article for the Encyclopedia? *

Here the Goethe centennial is starting up, and as the only person besides at most two or three others who knows something about the subject, I of course have no share in it. But couldn't you let me give a blast on the Palestinian tuba in celebration of the day?

Plans I cannot make. If I had any money, I would bolt before another day goes by, but I don't know when [and] if this will happen.

Write quickly, and don't cut me in Europe.

> *Most cordially yours*
> *Walter*

This letter, which was not available to me when I edited his *Berliner Chronik,* thus indicates that preliminary drafts for these notes made on Ibiza, whose existence I considered only hypothetically in my afterword (p. 125–26), actually came into being in Berlin in January and February of 1932.

Benjamin's apprehensions about the Goethe centennial, however, proved unfounded. "The commercial boom of the Goethe centennial" (*Briefe* 2, p. 547) brought him a chance to earn money as well. This enabled him to decide rather abruptly to follow his old acquaintance Felix Noeggerath to Ibiza (Noeggerath had discovered the island, which was still "inside information" at that time).

On April 7 or 8, Benjamin left Hamburg on a freighter and made friends with its captain and other officers. After eleven days he arrived in Barcelona, and from there he took the mail steamer

---

**The Encyclopaedia Judaica.* Benjamin received an offprint.

to Ibiza. He remained there for almost exactly three months, living without any modern conveniences yet in an atmosphere he found appealing, on an inconceivably small amount of money—less than two marks a day! To his friends he wrote long letters about the island and his doings there. Despite the press of work that kept him busy, these often very beautiful letters seem to betoken a well-rested man who only gently hinted at the utter loneliness in which he was going to celebrate his fortieth birthday and at the gnawing meditations about himself and his life, about which he wrote me in his reply to my detailed letter of congratulations. I did not learn until months later how complicated his situation really was.

I had arrived in Rome in the meantime and was studying the kabbalistic manuscripts in the Vatican. We started discussions about possible prospects of a reunion. The eventual failure of all these plans made my heart heavy and gave me much food for thought that year.

To be sure, from the very beginning a shadow was cast over Benjamin's sojourn on Ibiza by the fact that, while still in Berlin, Noeggerath and he had become the victims of a confidence man who had rented to the former a house on Ibiza that did not belong to him and had rented Benjamin's Berlin apartment as well. Not only did the man not pay the rent, which greatly exacerbated Benjamin's situation, but he also stole some things from the apartment. The swindler disappeared quickly enough when the police went looking for him, but for several weeks Benjamin was tormented by the idea that

through a chain of unfortunate circumstances the person in question might have got his fingers on the closet—a locked one, actually— containing my manuscripts. Since he is not just a confidence man but probably somewhat dissolute generally I am profoundly disquieted, particularly because of the papers relating to my work on the Arcades; these, after all, represent three or four years of study and thought and contain the most important directives for me, if not for others. I hope that no second incident parallel to the Agnon case [Agnon's library had been destroyed by a fire in his house] will have occurred in your circle of friends. This much is evident: poverty is an evil, and some of the practical arrangements prompted by it are the devil's work. If my Berlin affairs were in order, I could consider leisurely staying here for a long time or coming back here. I shall not so easily find another place where I can live under tolerable circumstances in the most magnificent scenery for barely 70 or 80 marks a month—and perhaps soon even more cheaply, for in a few days I am moving in with the Noeggeraths, who have fixed up for themselves a dilapidated little farmhouse twenty minutes from town [San Antonio], right by the woods and the sea. . . . On the one hand, my funds are very low; on the other, common sense bids me honor the inaugural festivities of the Third Reich with my absence. No one seems to be sure when these will take place, however. Incidentally, I shall include here a pertinent remark that I made recently and that, as I learned later, already has made its way to Germany. Perhaps it will be better still if you hear it directly from me rather than secondhand: The Third Reich is a train that does not leave until everyone is on board.

In my first letters from Rome I had told Benjamin for the first time about Salman Schocken, one of the most memorable figures of German Jewry. As the owner of a large chain of department stores in cities in central Germany, a highly cultured, self-educated person and a man passionately interested in Jewish intellectuality, Schocken was considering publishing plans that later assumed a different form under Hitler but plans that were very fruitful for the Jews in Germany. He was interested in my work, and I planned to meet him in Germany that fall and draw his attention to Benjamin as one of the most important authors such a publishing house should secure for itself. In the letter cited above, dated the beginning of May, Benjamin wrote: "If you saw any possibility of interesting Schocken, whom you mentioned, in this book [the collection of letters for which he was unable to find a publisher] or in my work generally, this of course would be of great importance. I may regard it as certain that you will bring more honor upon yourself with this initiative than with your first one. And how much I am in your debt!"

In those days he read with great enthusiasm Trotsky's autobiography and his history of the February Revolution. At the same time he also wrote:

I am now completing a series of Geschichten aus Ibiza *[Tales from Ibiza], a collection that may not be worth anything but at least will be free from all travel impressions and travel syntheses. Then I am concerning myself with recent short shadows; perhaps you will remember that I once published a few installments of* Einbahnstrasse *under that title. . . . Naturally I am using this period to read some things that hardly have been accessible to me for lack of time. For the second time I read the exceedingly admirable* Chartreuse de Parme. *Now I am doing* Der Stechlin, *by Fontane; reading this book at the Mediterranean amounts to a refinement of this author's solid comfort. Though I find it a lot of fun, I believe I understand how some people cannot stand it; in fact, sometimes I almost share in the indignation of imaginary readers.*

In May I suggested to Benjamin that we meet in July at Parma. There I would be busy for several weeks in a library that, in order not to overburden itself with work, closed its doors at four in the afternoon. Thus we would have not only plenty of afternoons and evenings at our disposal but would be able to celebrate his fortieth birthday together as well. Benjamin, however, evaded the issue without my being able to judge whether the financial reasons were really the decisive ones. He wrote:

To get back to the most urgent question: as far as I am concerned, the later the meeting the easier it will be for me to contemplate it. Weeks spent together in Parma would be extremely enticing, but how am I to finance them? I live here—without comforts in the usual sense but not without amenities—on one mark fifty per day, this being my "room-and-board price" at the Noeggeraths'. For a meeting, either the end of August or the beginning of September in Berlin would be a certain possibility; a much more concrete and infinitely more promising possibility would be the end—or possibly even the middle—of July at the Italian-French border, let us say at Mentone. How would it be if you subjected yorself to the slightly circuitous route via the Lötschberg rather than the Brenner and accordingly had a direct connection to Berlin from Ventimiglia? This probably could be combined with Munich as well. For you this would be a travel diversion that, so it

*seems to me, you well could take upon yourself in view of the value
of our meeting.*

But Mentone did not materialize either; something always seemed
to interfere. I could not have known that at the decisive moment
there had been a sudden crisis in his life. He postponed our reunion
until a meeting in Berlin, "no matter how great my inclination to
keep away from there, come what may. How much greater would
have been the chances of our being together down here, and how
much we shall be unable to discuss. To say nothing of the fact that
my Catholica would have been safe from you in Mentone." I had
written Benjamin that I had started a Catholic theology section in
my library. He wrote me that in his library there were some things
"that I would be reluctant to expose to your eloquent desires"
(*Briefe* 2, p. 553). "The University of Muri," so he wrote on June
25, "will now have to see how it copes with the matter [of his
impending birthday]. Confidentially speaking, I hope it will prove
somewhat more unyielding than the gazettes and my friends, who
will have no trouble acceding to my wishes not to make any fuss
about this day." He indicated that he was planning to spend that
day in Nice with "a rather odd fellow" whom he had already met
a number of times on his peregrinations and traversals, "and whom
I shall invite for a festive glass of wine unless I prefer to be alone."
At that time I vainly tried to guess who this allusion referred to.
Even today I cannot say for sure whether that odd fellow was not
perhaps Death and the glass of festive wine the cup of hemlock that
Benjamin wanted to drink—provided he was toying with the resumption of his death plans even then. But his letters contained no
other indication of this. He did reveal to me in a somewhat cheerful
vein in the same letter "that last year I came close to a book on
Goethe that the Insel Verlag would have commissioned from me if
. . . [ellipsis in the original]. I fear I have lost the outline, but I
still would have enough to tell about it to arouse the astonishment
of the Murian faculty, particularly the professors of Kabbalah and
medieval Jewish philosophy. Incidentally, are you, as a kabbalist,
acquainted with the novel *The Cabala* by the American Thornton
Wilder? I recently read it for the second time and must say that

it deserves to be read by you on account of its last six pages (it has 280)."

As Benjamin's letters and cards to me show, his plans for July kept changing, probably influenced only in part by Wilhelm Speyer's proposal of a collaboration in August at Poveromo (near Marina di Massa). Numerous and conflicting things were astir in him at that time. He worked with great intensity, read a lot, and made notes that were by no means intended for immediate publication. In view of his fortieth birthday he wrote, as a memoir of Jula Cohn, the autobiographical essay "In der Sonne" [In the sun].* A downright mystical passage in it contains a strange echo of Buber's preface to his book *Daniel: Gespräche von der Verwirklichung* [Daniel: dialogues on realization]; Benjamin had been very critical on reading that book many years previously, but evidently Buber's sentence about his encounter with the trunk of an ash tree unconsciously stuck in his memory. The poetic character of this passage has been pointed out by D. Thierkopf,† who regards this as a unique phenomenon in Benjamin's work. Such poetic prose occurs in a number of heightened passages, however, particularly in the book on German tragic drama. I especially noticed this years ago because at one point Benjamin argues expressly against such prose.

While I was in Milan, still hoping for a meeting with him, Benjamin spent his fortieth birthday on Ibiza after canceling plans made earlier. Shortly before that he had made the acquaintance of Jean Selz and his wife and had taken a liking to them. How all these external and internal occurrences added up to his decision to take his life in Nice (in the Hôtel du Petit Parc)—whether he had considered and prepared for it over a long period of time or whether he impulsively had resumed the suicide plans of the past year— will remain as much of a puzzle in his life as his sudden cancellation of this plan after he had made all the arrangements for it. As far as I know, he never discussed this with anyone. It was a climax of his life, a fever crisis that erupted suddenly and just as suddenly

---

*Now in Walter Benjamin, *Gesammelte Schriften* [Collected writings; 4 vol. in 9], ed. Rolf Tiedmann and Hermann Schweppenhäuser (Frankfurt/M: Suhrkamp Verlag, 1972–77), 4, pp. 417–20 and n., p. 1004.

†In *Text und Kritik* 31–32 (1971): 15, 18.

subsided. In the light of this information, which I could not have had at the time, the long letter Benjamin wrote me from Nice on July 26, in which he reacted to my birthday letter with ponderous sentences (*Briefe* 2, pp. 555–56), assumes a doubly enigmatic and even uncanny character. Veiled allusions to what was going on inside him were coupled in the last paragraph with regards that I was supposed to give Ernst Schoen in Frankfurt and a recommendation, in the indirect formulation characteristic of him, to seek there the acquaintance of Adorno, who "gave a seminar on my book on German tragic drama during the past semester." The profoundly pessimistic tenor of the preceding decisive paragraph is in keeping with the gloomy tone of his statements. Benjamin said that the chances for the fulfillment of my birthday wishes were the slightest imaginable. "It behooves both of us to face up to this state of affairs." Benjamin wrote he was doing so "with a seriousness approaching hopelessness." He spoke of the disintegration that constantly threatened his thinking and of the "small victories" in some of his writings that were balanced by the "great defeats." From this it was only a step to the farewell letter to Egon Wissing he wrote the following day, along with his will, in which he gave the hopelessness of his situation as the reason for his decision to die in that hotel room.

I include here that part of Benjamin's will (its first paragraph) that concerns our relationship; it was written with full confidence in me. I found this will in 1966 in the Central Archives of the German Democratic Republic at Potsdam and quote it according to the photocopy in the estate of Benjamin's son Stefan:

All the manuscripts in my estate—both my own writings and those of others—shall go to Dr. Gerhard Scholem, Abyssinian Road, Jerusalem. My entire estate contains in addition to my own writings primarily the works of the brothers Fritz and Wolf Heinle. It would be in accordance with my wishes if their writings could be preserved in the university library in Jerusalem or in the Prussian State Library. These comprise not only the Heinles' manuscripts but also my edited handwritten copies of their works. As regards my own works, it would be in accordance with my wishes if the university library in Jerusalem provided space for some of them. Should Dr. Gerhard Scholem publish

*a posthumous selection of my writings or of works that have appeared
in my lifetime, it would be in accordance with my wishes if he sent
a certain portion of the net profits from that edition—about 40–60%
after deducting his expenses—to my son Stefan.*

In the enclosed farewell letter to his cousin and neighbor Egon
Wissing, to whom he entrusted the execution of his will, he declared that his plan to take his life because of "profound weari-
ness" was not yet "beyond all doubt" but "probable." He again
instructed Wissing to give me the manuscripts in his estate as my
"property." "In any case, I give Gerhard Scholem all the rights
that may be required for the possible publication of my writings."
He went on: "I think it would be nice if the manuscript department
of the library of the University of Jerusalem accepted the posthumous papers of two non-Jews from the hands of two Jews—Scholem's and mine." Enclosed with the will and the farewell letter were
three separate brief, heartfelt notes to Ernst Schoen, Franz Hessel,
and Jula Radt. To Jula he wrote: "You know that I once loved you
very much. And even on the point of death, life has no greater gifts
than the ones that the moments of suffering because of you have
bestowed upon it. That is why this greeting shall suffice. Yours,
Walter."

Benjamin kept these documents and instructions among his
papers; he did not destroy them when his will to live gained the
upper hand at the eleventh hour. Shortly afterward he alluded to
these provisions in one of his letters to me.

Given Benjamin's slight interest in current political events, it
is not so hard to understand that these decisions do not appear to
have been affected by the cold coup d'état of July 20, exactly a week
earlier, in which Chancellor von Papen had deposed the Prussian
government. This gave Benjamin's situation the full material
weight of incipient poverty. In the course of the ensuing months
the leftist directors of radio stations in Berlin and Frankfurt who
had radio work to give, and who had repeatedly provided Benjamin
with well-paid assignments, lost their positions. A few weeks later,
however, I heard from Ernst Schoen in Frankfurt and from Dora
in Berlin that Walter had been on Ibiza with a woman. That was
the very attractive and vivacious German-Russian Olga Parem,
called Ola by her friends, whom Benjamin had met in 1928

through Hessel and with whom he was close friends for four years. (She also played a part in the divorce suit and gave me a very lively account of her interrogation by the judge. She tried to give testimony favorable to Walter in order to save for him his collection of children's books he was so attached to, which was claimed—successfully, it turned out—by Dora.) Ola was very fond of Benjamin because of his intellect and his charm. "He had an enchanting laugh; when he laughed, a whole world opened up," she told me. She visited him on Ibiza and also stayed at Noeggerath's place. According to her, Benjamin was in love with many women in those years and had a "very beautiful lady friend" in Barcelona, the divorced wife of a Berlin physician. I don't know for certain but believe it is possible that a contributing factor to his decision, which he did not act on at the last moment, was his disappointment at Ola Parem's rejection of his marriage proposal, which he had made to her unexpectedly around the middle of June. She told me he took this so badly that he never again asked about her when he saw her eventual husband, Philipp Schey; Schey was in the Brecht circle and associated with Benjamin in Paris for a long time later.

Our reunion did not materialize, for from the beginning of August Benjamin stayed with Wilhelm Speyer in Poveromo for three months. From there he wrote me with unusual frequency, as though he wanted to make up for the breakdown of our plans for a meeting. Four weeks after that crisis in Nice he wrote on a small picture postcard: "Unfortunately it appears as though this European trip of yours is making you a witness to the most severe crisis that has ever befallen me. If at least you were an eyewitness! But I am sitting here without seeing any of my attempts to afford the most necessary things—at least to pay a bill—succeed, completely deprived by the events at the Berlin radio station of the income that I used to be able to count on, and with the gloomiest thoughts. . . . Think over once more everything that concerns me. It is necessary." These were unmistakable warning signals in the face of which I was helpless. I urgently begged him at least to come to Berlin in October. On September 26 he wrote me there:

Dear Gerhard,

You can imagine how depressing the prospect is for me of not seeing you at all. Unfortunately we have to reckon with this possibil-

ity. The state of affairs is quite simple: I cannot finance the trip from my own resources; rather, I am dependent on Speyer, who will take me along in his car when he goes back . . . hardly before the end of October. This is connected with a play on which we are collaborating; * *also, people generally have high hopes for October here. . . . I am utilizing this situation, which despite all the misery is still relatively estimable, to permit myself the enormous luxury of concentrating, for the first time since who knows when, on one single project. The work I am doing with Speyer entails only consultative duties for me and is a fascinating rest from my own work. It is, incidentally, my only relaxation, for I write all day and sometimes even into the night. But if you imagined an extensive manuscript you would be mistaken. It is not only a short manuscript but also one in small sections: a form repeatedly prompted by the materially endangered, precarious nature of my production as well as by considerations of its commercial exploitability. In this case, to be sure, this form seems absolutely necessary to me because of the subject. It is, in short, a series of notes I shall title* Berliner Kindheit um 1900 *[A Berlin childhood around 1900]. I shall treat you to the motto:* "O braungebackne Siegessäule / Mit Winterzucker aus den Kindertagen" *[O Victory Column baked brown / With winter sugar from childhood days]. Someday I hope to be able to tell you the origin of this verse.† This work is largely finished by now and could influence my material situation very favorably in a short time if my relationship with the* Frankfurter Zeitung *had not been disrupted a few months ago as a result of a wholly inexplicable constellation I have not yet been able to investigate. For the rest, however, I hope that these childhood memories (you probably will have noticed that, far from being in the form of a chronicle, they constitute individual expeditions into the depths of memory) can be published in book form, possibly by Rowohlt. . . . Above all, let me know the exact date of your departure from Berlin. Write me how you found Stefan. Finally, a request to keep the facts contained in this letter confidential. In particular, for the time being I would not want anyone in Berlin to learn about the new book.*

*It was a detective play.

†As I later discovered, he had jotted it down in a kind of Surrealist poem when a hashish-induced intoxication was wearing off.

Thus there were only three months, albeit critical ones, between his *Berliner Chronik* from Ibiza and the new *Berliner Kindheit*, which was no longer purely autobiographical but was guided by a poetically philosophical conception, a work that brought a new note into Benjamin's creativity.

At the middle of October I had to return to Jerusalem. Benjamin did not arrive in Berlin until mid-November. In the meantime I had seen Ernst Schoen and his wife, whom Benjamin did not regard particularly kindly, in Frankfurt several times; they told me a great deal about Walter's visits there. A strange reluctance kept me from an encounter with Adorno, which was due at that time and which he probably expected. I wrote Walter about this. He replied that my reserved remarks about Adorno could not keep him from drawing my attention to Adorno's recently published first work on Kierkegaard. "For the rest, the case of the author is so complicated that it cannot be presented in a letter. If I tell you that Adorno already is conducting a second-semester seminar about my book on German tragic drama as a continuation of the first one without indicating this in the catalogue, you have a thumbnail sketch that may be serviceable for the time being. Independently of that, you definitely ought to take cognizance of his book." In Berlin I met Dora, whom I found greatly changed, and through the good offices of a mutual friend I also met Walter's relative Günther Stern (later Günther Anders) and his first wife, Hannah Arendt, for whom Benjamin already seemed to represent a weighty intellectual authority—surely a rarity in those days.

On October 25, Benjamin wrote me at Jerusalem in a review of his situation, which was another variation on the above information, that his writings were "at present the object of a boycott that could not be organized better if I were a little Jewish clothes-dealer in Neu-Stettin." The *Frankfurter Zeitung,* so he wrote, had failed to acknowledge or print all his letters and manuscripts. "The letter the editors of *Die literarische Welt* wrote to inform me that they did not care to receive contributions from me at this time I shall leave to the manuscript section of the Jerusalem library, and if the dispositions of the German fatherland prevail, the library will receive this letter quite soon." This was a dark allusion to the provisions of his will, written two months previously. In the same letter he commended two books to my attention: "It is [Arthur] Rosenberg's *Geschichte des Bolschewismus* [History of Bolshevism], a book published by Rowohlt to which I owe much revealing information. The second book is a little study on the philosophy of language that provides an uncommon amount of food for thought, although its complete lack of a theoretical foundation gives one pause. It was written by Rudolf Leonhard, until now a rather insignificant writer, and is called *Das Wort* [The word]. It is an onomatopoetic theory of words exemplified by illustrations." The recommendation of Rosenberg's book came too late, for I had already met the author, a close friend of my brother Werner and a teacher of ancient history at the University of Berlin. We had exchanged our latest writings: his book on Bolshevism and my lengthy article "Kabbalah"; he very much liked the sections about the dialectics of Isaac Luria, one of the greatest masters of the Kabbalah. Rosenberg sent me a presentation copy of his book with the words "From Luria to Lenin!"

Under the prevailing circumstances, Benjamin's last letter of that year, followed by the manuscript of "Berlin Childhood" and a request for my reaction, could not be anything but profoundly pessimistic.

You need only to remember the fact that the "intellectuals" among our "coreligionists" are the first ones to offer the oppressors hecatombs from their own circles just to be spared themselves—to know how anyone can fare who deals with such intellectuals, be it in their capacity as editors or owners of the press. . . . It [the "worst"] could certainly not be countered by a shift of my activity to the French sphere. Despite all the contact I have with the matter of that linguistic life, the position from which I approach things is far too advanced still to fall within the purview of a public readership. I reflected about this problem in Italy, and not for the first time. The result was always the same.

A month later his pessimism had given way to a more optimistic view, althogh one only moderately so. He informed me that he had established a relationship with Horkheimer's *Zeitschrift für Sozialforschung* [Journal for social research]. If one also considers that at that time he not only became absorbed in two Jewish

publications of mine but also, in connection with the preparation
of a radio play about spiritism that never materialized, looked into
the literature of this "spider-thin esoteric science," one probably
gets an idea of the polarization of his horizon two weeks before
Hitler's seizure of power. Benjamin added to this information that
he had "quite insidiously and for my private amusement fashioned
myself a theory about these things [spiritism] that I plan to develop
for you over a bottle of Burgundy some evening in the distant
future." As to the now-finished series of his "innumerable" radio
talks, the texts of which I had requested for my archive and which
have been preserved in East Berlin, he wrote deprecatingly in his
last letter from Germany that they held "no interest other than the
past economic one."

It was really a great misfortune that we were not able to have
a heart-to-heart talk in those days. From what I knew of Benjamin
I had to assume that inner inhibitions and insecurities probably
played a larger part in our failure to meet in 1932 than did the
external reasons that were given their shape or even triggered by
them. Our physical separation in the long years until 1938 undoubtedly had a dual impact. In one sense it heightened the intensity of written communication that stayed alive over long periods
of time. I was far away; what he told me stayed with me, and in
his letters in which he often informed me about his inner and outer
situations there vibrates a feeling of trust. But in a different sense
the fact of his new development did intensify a feeling of remote-
ness. There were many things that Benjamin, being the way he was,
could not express in letters—and this became increasingly true as
the years advanced. This meant that we sought no conflict but also
that the things we avoided were magnified by silence. Thus too
many of the things that ought to have achieved a thorough clarification in a discussion between two friends remained in abeyance. The
ensuing five years suffered from this. Something had remained
mute that had not been designed to be so, and like everything thus
unspoken, it was dangerous.

The Years of Emigration
(1933 –1940)

If I give but a relatively brief account of this long period, during which I met Benjamin only once (for a few days in February 1938 in Paris), this is due to a special state of affairs. For these years there are available not only Benjamin's letters to me, the majority of them unpublished, but also all my letters to him. (I had no way of knowing about the latter when the selected correspondence was published.) Most of Benjamin's personal papers and in particular the letters to him from the period before 1933 were lost. If, as is very probable, they fell into the hands of the Gestapo in Berlin, they were presumably destroyed, along with the Gestapo's files, in accordance with a decree dated February 1945, which I learned about from the deputy director of the Central Archives of the German Democratic Republic. That those of Benjamin's papers that fell into the hands of the Gestapo in Paris in 1940 were preserved is the result of an accident caused by unusual circumstances. I inspected those papers, consisting mostly of correspondence addressed to Benjamin, in the above-mentioned archives at Potsdam in October 1966. Having been graciously granted admittance to them, I found there my own letters from those years. At that time I was assured I would be sent photocopies of these and other letters, but I did not receive any in 1967, evidently upon instructions from those higher up. What benefits the appropriate authorities expect by denying access to documents to which I hold the copyright is no more comprehensible to me than the fact that no reason was ever given. If this material became accessible, I could give a complete book-length documentation of our relationship in those years. But as long as this primary source is blocked —which means that many allusions in Benjamin's letters remain inexplicable—I cannot bring myself to go into details that can be made comprehensible only by reference to these letters. Since I have kept drafts or copies of only few of those letters or portions thereof, I shall content myself with presenting a survey of those years, which is given more concrete shape only by a report on my visit in Paris from vivid memory and on the efforts that followed it.*

Benjamin remained in Germany under the new regime only until the middle of March. My friend Kitty Marx [Steinschneider], who visited him at my instigation at the beginning of March before her departure for Palestine, was impressed by the striking composure with which he seemed to face the situation. This serenity, to be sure, found stronger expression in the outward attitude he displayed to other people than in his letters, which often enough bear witness to the unrest that quite understandably agitated him. For example, just a few days before Kitty's visit he wrote me: "The small amount of composure that people in my circles muster toward the new regime is used up quickly, and we realize that the air is hardly fit for breathing" (*Briefe* 2, p. 562). But even letters expressing such an attitude are remarkably free of the panic that gripped so many in those days. Perhaps this is due to the fact that Benjamin had come face to face with death in July 1932 and that consequently such prospects no longer frightened him. In point of fact, in his letters to me in those years there was only one unmistakable reference to the idea that under certain circumstances he would put

*This correspondence was restored to the author by the East German state archive in November 1977 on the occasion of his eightieth birthday and has since been published under the title *Walter Benjamin—Gershom Scholem: Briefwechsel 1933–1940* (Frankfurt/M.: Suhrkamp Verlag, 1980).—Trans.

an end to his life and that this would be determined not by "inner" factors but by purely financial ones. At any rate, that is how it read.

Benjamin left Germany on or about March 18, 1933. After a stay of more than two weeks in Paris he again went to Ibiza, where he remained for almost half a year. In those days he wrote me an unusual number of letters, and long ones. Alfred and Grete Cohn, friends of his youth, were in Barcelona at that time. Life on the island still drew him under its spell, although the atmosphere in the Noeggeraths' home, where he stayed at first, had changed, bringing about a looser relationship that came close to a dissolution of the marriage. Mr. and Mrs. Jean Selz, with whom he worked on a French version of *Berliner Kindheit*, and possibly also the projected visit of Inge Buchholz lent a somewhat brighter coloration to his life.

Benjamin did a great deal of work. His prose sketch "Agesilaus Santander," of which I have given a detailed account elsewhere ["Walter Benjamin and His Angel," in *On Jews and Judaism in Crisis*, pp. 198–236], furnishes eloquent testimony to his inner situation in those months when he had ample occasion for retrospection. His major efforts were devoted to that first essay on the social position of French writers, which had been commissioned by the Institut für Sozialforschung [Institute of Social Research]; this occupied him during the first half of the year. Even though Benjamin closely involved himself in the work of the Institute during the coming years and took the tensions arising from this involvement in stride, the very first intimate revelation he made to me on the subject is not without a note of reserve. In his first letter from Ibiza he wrote: "The very fact that I have to write the essay, which in any case constitutes pure fakery, virtually without any source material, gives it a certain magical aspect that will be displayed boldly in Geneva [the seat of the Institute] but hidden from you." As happened with a number of subsequent literary assignments from the Institute whose subjects he originally found none too congenial, he was not as displeased with the completed essay as might have been expected from his initial complaints. The essay had been wrested from the most difficult circumstances. "Something unchallengeable could not be produced here. I believe, however, that readers nevertheless will derive from this an insight into connections that never before have been made so clearly recognizable." When his essay appeared a year later, it caused a written argument between us that was moderate in tone but rather vehement on both sides as far as the substance was concerned.

In the meantime Benjamin's friends in Eretz Yisrael had begun to consider how they could manage to get him there for an extended period. Benjamin's reaction to this news and also to invitations (Kitty Steinschneider, for example, invited him to Rehovot, where she and her husband were living at the time) was always basically very positive, but in each instance he always had reasons for holding back or for a temporary postponement of plans. There was a similar situation in 1935, but unfortunately no concrete steps were taken.

When Benjamin returned to Paris in October 1933, he found himself in extremely difficult economic circumstances. In his attempts to improve them he was bound to become all too clearly aware of their occasionally utterly humiliating aspects. It must not be forgotten that in this situation the offer of the Institute to guarantee him a minimal living in return for his work was bound to constitute something like a lifesaver for him and that orientation suitable to the projects suggested by the Institute was a vital necessity. It is unimaginable what would have become of Benjamin in Paris without the help of Friedrich Pollock and Max Horkheimer, which undoubtedly was spurred by Adorno's understanding of Benjamin's situation and productivity.

Here, too, Benjamin displayed in a most extraordinary manner that power of intellectual concentration I have mentioned in my discussion of ealier crisis situations. The fact that at this very time in addition to his work for the Institute he returned to his meditations on Kafka, which were certainly not in line with that work, proves what a central position these reflections had in his mind. No matter how much his ideas were to be integrated into a new system of coordinates, as he put it, he still cared greatly about sequences of ideas for which this system could have no significance. Nowhere was this shown more clearly than in his thoughts on the philosophy of language in the widest sense and those reflections on Kafka in which his "Janus face," as he liked to call it, assumed sharp contours. One side of it was offered to Brecht, the other to me; he certainly did not conceal this fact from me. He urged me to tell him my ideas about Kafka, which were, after all, diametrically opposed to those of Brecht, whose spoken views Benjamin took down. In May 1934, Benjamin wrote me: "Your particular views of Kafka emanating from Jewish insights [would be] of the greatest importance to me in this undertaking—not to say virtually indispensable." It was no different with the philosophy of language, though here he was able to reveal his thoughts more easily in the direction of the sociology of language. When Benjamin resumed work on his study of the Paris Arcades, a project in which to his initial surprise the Institute showed a positive interest from 1934–35 on, the linguistic-philosophical tendencies greatly receded before the historico-philosophical ones.

Even though in his letters Benjamin expressed himself on his projects and their progress frequently and in detail, one important aspect of a personal nature remained concealed from me, an aspect that he well may have deliberately avoided going into, although, as I realized only on my Paris visit, it played a considerable part in his work. This aspect was the tension—or let us call it the lack of sympathy—between Brecht and the group around the Institute, something that must have troubled Benjamin a great deal. As Benjamin's contacts with both sides grew closer in the period of emigration—in his Paris years he enjoyed Brecht's hospitality in Svendborg during the summer months on three occasions—the dialectical situation in which he found himself must have been far more taxing for him than I could suspect. The only thing that struck my attention was that though he often wrote me about Brecht and his literary works, which he kept urging me to become acquainted with, despite all the information he gave me about his relationship to and work with the Institute he never sought to induce me to read, much less study, the *Zeitschrift für Sozialforschung*, or in particular to give him my reaction to the long essays by Horkheimer that appeared in its pages. Thus, although I saw the journal occasionally in the university library in Jerusalem, I believe I commented on its contents in my letters only infrequently.

From October 1933 on, Benjamin's sojourn in Paris was interrupted not only by the visits to Brecht but also on three occasions by the prolonged hospitality offered him by Dora, who had in the meantime opened a pension at San Remo. Once, in the winter of 1934–35, he spent four months in this "asylum in San Remo," and he was there for several weeks in September 1936 and July 1937. In exile he also established closer relations with his sister Dora, with whom there had been much friction after the death of their mother. In Paris, between 1935 and early 1938 (when he moved into a large room of his own at 10 rue Dombasle) there were a number of periods when he lived in the small apartment that Dora occupied at 7 Villa Robert Lindet. Dora, who had been a social worker and remained unmarried, became seriously ill in 1935 with Bekhterev's [spinal cord] disease. She died of the disease in Zurich in the spring of 1946, having successfully escaped to Switzerland during the war. I visited her there in the Paracelsus Clinic three days before her death.

In the first two years of his emigration Benjamin wrote with unusual frequency; then the correspondence slowed down, and as with his correspondence with others, there sometimes were pauses of several months that were followed again by detailed letters. In the six months between October 1935 (when I decided to separate from my wife) and April 1936 (when I informed him of my divorce) there was an almost complete hiatus in our correspondence. This profoundly disquieted him, for I did not have enough strength during those months to inform him of the causes of the interruption. During this period he wrote me only once, on March 29, 1936; it was a melancholy letter, in which he also referred to his own silence.

Dear Gerhard,

No matter which of the gods may have responsibility for the correspondence of earthlings, it seems that the threads of ours have slipped from his hands only to fall into the clutches of some devil of silence.

I must admit, though, that to the extent that my own interior serves this devil as an arena, his activity is by no means a mystery to me. The manifold and disappointing fluctuations of the date of our reunion carry much weight in this regard. And they burden me still more when they cause me to wonder whether you are imbued with the importance, indeed the overdue nature, of this reunion as much as I am. The period in which we have been expecting it constitutes a river of increasing inclination that our written messages find it harder and harder to struggle against. By this I mean not only our letters but also communications like my latest offprint, "Probleme der Sprachsoziologie" [Problems of the sociology of language], and perhaps it was no accident that it brought me no signal from you. If in such a context I realize the risk that I can spare my latest work still less than many previous projects (because it is more important), the risk of entering the zone of our correspondence (and thus of its latent periods as well), I cannot always suppress my uneasiness. For the rest, my occupation with this work, which completely absorbed me in January and February, is a cause that brings a bright touch to the tableau of my silence.

It will first appear in French, maybe soon, maybe not until the end of the year; the Zeitschrift für Sozialforschung, *which is going to publish it, prefers the translation to the original. The title of the latter is "Das Kunstwerk im Zeitalter seiner technischen Reproduzierbarkeit" ["The Work of Art in the Age of Mechanical Reproduction," in* Illuminations, *pp. 219–44]. At the moment I see no chance of publishing the original text.*

More about this work—that is, its text—another time. Today I would like to address to you only the suspenseful question about your occupation with Oskar Goldberg's Maimonides book. This would give me at the same time a first impression of the book itself, and I hope I can count on receiving your reaction very soon.

Today I do not want to expatiate again on the outward facts of my existence here. The big book has been put aside in favor of the new project, which is closely connected with it methodologically, although not at all as far as its substance is concerned. Before I take it up again I shall have to write a brief study on Nikolai Leskov, which I am obligated to produce. Once again I have put the Fuchs on the back burner. Incidentally, I hope you have read Leskov, one of the greatest storytellers. . . .

The audible relief with which Benjamin then received my explanation of the events that had led to my silence is discernible in his next letters. It was as if a load had been taken off his mind. I do not remember whether I wrote him about Goldberg's book, one of the most outrageous polemics against Maimonides as the real corrupter of Judaism—that is, Judaism as Goldberg thought it should be. Maybe a response to this is in the East Berlin archives. In any case, I recommended to him Leo Strauss's recently published important book *Philosophie und Gesetz: Beiträge zum Verständnis Maimunis* [Philosophy and law: toward an understanding of Maimonides]. Benjamin even considered writing a review of this book, which was a searching though problematical analysis of the central role of political philosophy for Maimonides' view of Judaism. In such a review he could have put at opposite ends the two poles of a "political philosophy" of Judaism, both of which aroused his interest and were bound to strike related chords in his own thinking: the liquidation of that magical element in a rational esotericism and on the other side the nurturing of a strictly magical, mythical view.

Prior to taking up the far-reaching subjects of his work that are touched upon in these pages, Benjamin had in 1934 shown that "Janus face" in two works that came into being at approximately the same time. For while he was working on the long Kafka essay that I had been instrumental in getting commissioned, and while we were carrying on a lively dialogue about it by mail, he wrote the lecture "Der Autor als Produzent" ["The Author as Producer," in *Reflections*, pp. 220–39], which he gave on April 27, 1934, at the Institut pour l'Étude du Fascisme (INFA), a Communist front organization. The lecture really constituted in a visible tour de force an apex of his materialistic efforts. The text figures in his letters and conversations, but I never got to see it. When I importuned him in 1938 in Paris, he said, "I think I had better not let you read it." When I did read this essay, I began to understand. From that period, incidentally, dates Benjamin's acquaintance with Arthur Koestler, who at that time was the honorary treasurer of INFA, and who later, in 1938, lived in the same building that housed almost exclusively emigrants.

I received the French text of the essay on the work of art in June 1936. Benjamin wrote: "I don't know whether you will find it accessible. If indeed you do, despite the presumably very reserved reaction expected of you, I would be extraordinarily interested in the impression it makes on you. In the meantime I have finished another, not quite so voluminous manuscript . . . which you would probably find far more agreeable, and not only from a linguistic point of view." That was the Leskov essay, "Der Erzähler" ["The Storyteller," in *Illuminations,* pp. 83–109]. In one of my letters I emphatically had drawn his attention to the books of Lev Shestov and advised him to seek his acquaintance. He shirked this assignment for a rather long time. Perhaps he brought himself to do it only in connection with his essay on Leskov. The above reference to "Der Erzähler" was followed by this sentence: "Tomorrow finally I shall make Shestov's acquaintance."

My reticence in response to the essay on the work of art was unmistakable. Benjamin's reaction was touchy: "I don't mind . . . admitting to you that the far-reaching impermeability that my latest work seems to be pitting against your understanding (taking the word not only in its technical sense) has made my heart heavy. If, as it seems, the essay no longer contained anything that referred you back to areas of thought in which both of us used to feel at home, I prefer to think, at least for the time being, that this is due not so much to the fact that I have drawn a very new map of the provinces of one of these areas but because the legend on this map was in French." In the same letter, dated October 18, 1936, Benjamin rightly expected that I would receive his forthcoming book *Deutsche Menschen* [German people] more favorably. He explained to me that "the title of the book, *Deutsche Menschen,* [is] explainable only by my interest in camouflaging this collection, which could perhaps do some good in Germany." As a matter of fact, I wrote Benjamin very enthusiastically about this book.

Meanwhile, his letters between 1934 and 1937 repeatedly contain complaints about an assignment given him by the Institut für Sozialforschung, an essay on the collector Eduard Fuchs that he had undertaken *nolens volens,* although he was more satisfied with the final result than he had expected of this bread-and-butter work.

When he sent me *Deutsche Menschen* in January 1937, he inscribed it as follows: "May you, Gerhard, find a chamber in this ark—which I built when the Fascist flood started to rise—for the memories of your youth." This motif was lent a specifically Jewish note in his inscription in his sister's copy: "This ark, built after a Jewish model, for Dora—from Walter. November 1936." We owe the information about this dedication to Johannes E. Seiffert, who acquired this copy in a secondhand bookstore in Zurich.* The "Jewish model," however, is not the Midrash in a newly discovered profound sense, as Seyffert interprets, but, much more simply, the rescue from the Fascist flood via the Word. The author has captured in a book—has constructed like an ark—that which can withstand the Flood. Just as the Jews took refuge from the persecutions in the Writ, the canonical book, Benjamin's own book constitutes a saving element fashioned after the Jewish prototype. When in the spring of 1936 the protracted Arab riots began to erupt, I wrote him very pessimistically about this situation. In those days, before the Royal Commission under Lord Peel proposed the partition of Palestine, I saw no practicable way out. Walter agreed with me and wrote on June 25:

Your letter of June 6 for the first time goes into the political situation in Palestine, which has been very much on my mind with reference to you as well as because of its very existence. Of course, I lack the data to form an independent judgment (which in concrete politicis *is not my strong suit in any case). I am all the more eager to obtain detailed and, if possible, direct reports. To the extent that I have managed to do so, I must concede that I have not encountered anything designed to refute your pessimism. I have been impressed particularly with the presumable effect of the negotiations currently taking place here on the Syrian question. . . . And furthermore, it would be very alarming if the Arab movement really were as popular in the Orient as people here say it is.*

I fear that the psychic reactions of the Jews may be hardly less harmful than the material actions of the Arabs. And if you, being right there, see no way out, it is of course far less possible for me to see one.

To be sure, Benjamin was no more hopeful about the European situation than the Palestinian one. At that time he began his efforts, which were to extend over a number of years, to acquire French citizenship. Despite some highly placed advocates like Alexis

*Jahrbuch des Instituts für Deutsche Geschichte (University of Tel Aviv) I (1972): 160.

Léger, André Gide, and Jean Giraudoux, men he had known since the twenties, these steps were not successful. Giraudoux, who earlier had helped him with the problems involving residence permits, had been appointed minister of information on the eve of World War II, but he also had become an out-and-out anti-Semite, as evidenced by his book *Pleins pouvoirs* [Full powers, 1939], in which there is no dearth of downright Streicherian tones.

Both of us were aware of the problems that years of separation posed for a correspondence. Given the progressive inner isolation in which Benjamin found himself in Paris, despite all outward connections, he was particularly sensitive to such things. A case in point is his letter of May 6, 1934 (published in *Briefe* 2, pp. 603–6), which I had to regard as a warning signal. The intensity of our correspondence in the first two years of Benjamin's emigration, however, guaranteed an easier overcoming of such difficulties. As this intensity diminished in the ensuing years, we repeatedly brought up the urgency of a reunion and a frank discussion. When further plans to visit Palestine did not come to fruition, Benjamin's remarks became more doleful and more urgent. On February 11, 1937, he wrote:

Dear Gerhard,

Although I am not an impatient man I do know hours when I feel rather uncertain whether we shall ever see each other again. A cosmopolis like Paris has become a very fragile thing, and if what I hear about Palestine is true, a wind blows there in which even Jerusalem may start swaying like a reed. (About England it is my opinion that for the past few years its policy has been determined exclusively by the certainty that the Commonwealth will cease to exist forty-eight hours after the outbreak of a war.) To get back to our reunion, at times I picture it—if only to be able to cling to its image—as the reunion in a storm of leaves from trees that stood far apart.

In the same letter he wrote me about the very disquieting turn which the development of his son Stefan had taken and which greatly occupied him and Dora. "As you can see, my thoughts, no matter whether they revolve in small or large circles, are gloomy ones. My work at present is not designed to make them any brighter." This refers to the "production of the text" of the essay on Fuchs, which was so repugnant to him. Two months later the successful completion of this work had brought him a somewhat more hopeful prospect for the immediate future, "and I do not need to tell you that I would be glad to see our reunion dipped in such brighter hues, no matter whether its background was the towers of Jerusalem or the gray-blue facades of the boulevards" (*Briefe* 2, p. 729).

In the summer of 1937 I received an invitation to give some lectures in New York, beginning in late February 1938, on the results of my studies in Jewish mysticism. Thus we were finally able to make concrete plans for a reunion. What I had in mind was to meet him very briefly in Paris on my way to New York and then spend a longer period with him in the summer of 1938. This plan elicited vigorous opposition from him because "there is no guarantee that the meeting planned for the summer can take place if you set it for Paris. At the moment I don't know where I am going to be in the summer." At that time, in late November 1937, he wavered between San Remo (with Dora) and Denmark (with Brecht). I later managed to gain five days in Paris between the end of my lectures in Jerusalem and the passage to America, before which I also had to meet my mother in Zurich; our meeting took place in mid-February. Benjamin suggested that I stay at his sister's apartment, but when I arrived she was too ill to have company, so I checked into a hotel. On the trip through Italy and Switzerland I had caught a cold and had to take strong medicine if I did not want to spend these days in bed. My ability to express my views in detail thus was somewhat impaired, although this did not prevent lively and even stormy discussions.

I had not seen Benjamin in eleven years. His appearance had changed somewhat. He had grown stockier, his bearing was more careless, and his mustache had become much bushier. His hair was streaked heavily with gray. We carried on intensive discussions about his work and his basic outlook, and of course we talked about subjects that had not been taken up in our letters. Thus his essay on the philosophy of language, "Das mimetische Vermögen" ["On the Mimetic Faculty," in *Reflections*, pp. 333–36], which he considered important, was the subject of his repeated complaints that I had not reacted to it; this became clear and significant to me only in this conversation. The focus of our discussions, however, was of course Benjamin's Marxist orientation. In 1927 this question, which he tended to evade at that time as not yet ripe for discussion, could be treated without personal tensions, but in 1938 the situation was different. Years laden with a heavy cargo of political events had intervened, and both of us could not help contemplating our reunion with some tension. If Benjamin wrote to Kitty Steinschneider after my departure that our "overdue philosophical discussion came off in good fashion," that was a friend's extenuation, for the discussion had taken place in an emotionally rather charged atmosphere and even had included two or three downright dramatic moments relating to Benjamin's own feelings, his relationship to the Institut für Sozialforschung and to Brecht, as well as to the trials in Russia, which greatly excited the entire world at the time. Characteristically enough, none of these dramatic moments concerned the Zionist cause.

On the first day, when I was still hardly able to talk much, Benjamin read to me various notes and spoke with great warmth about Fritz Lieb and his association with him over the past three years. It became very plain to me in Paris that Benjamin's relations to his fellow Marxists were marked by something like constant embarrassment, which of course was connected with his attachment to theological categories. This was true of Brecht as much as it was of the circle around the Institute. Benjamin's painstaking alertness and his emphasis on the identity of views could not conceal the fact that something had to be excluded. Brecht was visibly disturbed by the theological element in Benjamin. Benjamin was not unaware of the fact, nor did he conceal it from me. Horkheimer and other associates of the Institute had absolutely no use for it at the time, and only Adorno still responded to it on a wholly secularized plane. Adorno himself had no real theological interest, but he noticed that it held a central significance for Benjamin. So it came about that in the circle of Marxists with whom he associated, Benjamin could form a genuine friendship with only one person, namely Fritz Lieb, an altogether uncommon figure. For Lieb, one of Karl Barth's most original pupils, really was a trained theologian (at that time a *Privatdozent* for theology at the University of Basel) and a true

Socialist of Communist persuasion. He was the only person to whom Benjamin's theological dimension in his later years was directly comprehensible and unabashedly significant. Lieb was able to meet Benjamin on the level of the latter's own concerns. If memory serves, he was the only person in the years of Benjamin's emigration whom Benjamin addressed with the familiar *du* after only a few encounters; this never became his practice with the circle around the Institute or with Brecht. Lieb, whom I met only in the last years of his life, radiated something from the world of faith that the others did not possess.

When we were able to take up our discussions, Benjamin's essay on the work of art immediately assumed a position in the foreground. I analyzed for him my understanding of it, what I found magnificent and also what I found highly questionable. I attacked his use of the concept of aura, which he had employed in an entirely different sense for many years and was now placing in what I considered a pseudo-Marxist context. In my view, his new definition of this phenomenon constituted, logically speaking, a subreption that permitted him to sneak metaphysical insights into a framework unsuited to them. But I particularly criticized the second part, whose completely forced, unacceptable philosophy of film as the revolutionary art form of the proletariat seemed to me to have no discernible connection with the first part. Benjamin emphatically defended his orientation. He said that his Marxism still was not dogmatic but heuristic and experimental in nature, and that his transposition into Marxist perspectives of the metaphysical and even theological ideas he had developed in the years we had spent together was in fact meritorious, because in that sphere they could become more active, at least in our time, than in the sphere originally suited to them. His reply to my critique of the second part of his study is cited elsewhere.* Benjamin said, "The philosophical bond between the two parts of my study that you miss will be supplied by the revolution more effectively than by me." Someone who did not believe in *that* revolution hardly could make any response to this statement.

*In my essay on Walter Benjamin in *Judaica II* (Frankfurt: Suhrkamp Verlag, 1970), pp. 214–15.

A different though also rather impassioned turn was taken by our conversation about Brecht and my reservations concerning several books that Benjamin had recommended especially to me, reservations that I had expressed by prolonged silence in my letters. For example, I regarded Brecht's *Dreigroschenroman* [Threepenny novel] as an altogether inferior product, whereas Walter had sent me a copy of his enthusiastic critique of this work. Benjamin said, "I don't understand you. You were the one who so highly commended Scheerbart to me some years ago. You could not praise him enough, and I am sure you were right in doing so. And now that I commend Brecht to your attention, who is completing what Scheerbart started so well—namely the writing of a totally unmagical language, a language cleansed of all magic—you show no interest!"

I told him that this was not true at all; after all, I had read wonderful magical poems by Brecht. "Yes, those were early works, in the *Hauspostille*, but even though he may not have known anything by Scheerbart he later did follow in his footsteps, and the *Revolutionäre Theaterbibliothek* [Revolutionary theatrical library], which you esteem so highly, is surely a prelude to the prose of Brecht's plays. You were delighted with the prose in *Lesabéndio*, and now you get worked up about the *Versuche* and the *Dreigroschenroman.*" I replied, "But in Scheerbart there was an element that is lacking in Brecht." "Which is?" "The delight in infinity, of which there is nothing in Brecht, where everything boils down to only the revolutionary manipulation in the finite." (This delight was an element that had particularly impressed me in my mathematical years.) Then Benjamin said, "What matters is not infinity but the elimination of magic." We remained at odds, but Benjamin's championship of Brecht did impress me; because I was not ready to believe in Marxism, however, Benjamin's enthusiasm and theoretical support of the "epic theater" remained quite alien to me. In those days he read to me some wonderful poems by Brecht that, so he told me, were still unpublished. I vividly remember the way he recited Brecht's "Sonett über die Gedichte Dantes auf die Beatrice" [Sonnet on Dante's poems about Beatrice], speaking the privately circulated obscene version of the second line with perfect nonchalance, as though it contained the most commonly used word, but looking me full in the face while doing so. He promised to copy the poem for me later, and he did keep that promise, though not without revealing to me that the copy differed from the spoken text as he assumed I remembered it. Benjamin told me that Brecht had written many obscene poems, and he counted several of these among his best.

That conversation made me realize fully the polarization in Benjamin's view of language. For that abolition of the magic of language, which conformed to a materialistic view of language, was certainly in unmistakable conflict with all his earlier reflections on language, reflections under theological, mystical inspirations that he still maintained and even developed in the other texts he read to me in those days, as well as in his essay on the mimetic faculty. That I never heard him make an atheistic statement was surely no cause for surprise to me, especially after a number of letters from the thirties, but it did surprise me that he still could speak quite unmetaphorically of "God's words," in distinction to human words, as the foundation of all linguistic theory. The distinction between the word and the name, which twenty years earlier (in 1916) he had made the basis of his essay on language and had developed further in the preface to his book on tragic drama, was still alive in him; his essay on the mimetic faculty still lacks even the slightest hint of a materialistic view of language. On the contrary, matter appeared here only in a purely magical connection. Benjamin evidently was torn between his predilection for a mystical theory of language and the equally strongly perceived need to struggle against it in the context of a Marxist view of the world. I mentioned this to him, and he admitted this contradiction quite candidly. He said it was simply a matter of a task that he had not yet mastered but for which he had high hopes. His "Janus face" still bore the liveliest expression.

When our conversation turned to Benjamin's work under the auspices of the Institute and his attitude toward the Institute generally, we discussed the question of his readiness to come to Palestine, a readiness he had expressed in quite a few of his letters of those years. Benjamin emphasized that he owed to the Institute the chance to function within a framework, albeit a very modest one, and to pursue his thoughts, although he really did not find some of the assignments he received from it to his liking. He said he felt in profound sympathy with the orientation of the Institute but that he did not mind telling me that there had been repeated reservations and potential conflicts. Benjamin presented to me some of the arguments that since have been documented in detail in the apparatus of the *Gesammelte Schriften* [Collected writings], edited by Rolf Tiedemann and Hermann Schweppenhäuser; in Benjamin's oral presentation, however, there was a stronger tone of continuing criticism and even bitterness, which was definitely not in keeping with the conciliatory vein of his letters to Horkheimer. A sting had remained in his heart. Benjamin said that what mattered to him was that the Institute was giving him a chance to complete and publish under its auspices his study of the Arcades, with which he had been involved for so many years; he had to regard this as his magnum opus, although he realized the limits of this cooperation. He hoped that I would meet the people of the Institute, particularly Horkheimer and Adorno, in New York, where I planned to spend almost half a year. Benjamin expressed himself about his relationship with Adorno, whom he greatly commended to me, in especially positive terms; he spoke about his relationship with Horkheimer with greater reserve. As I knew neither man, I was not able to appreciate the evident nuances in this presentation, nor did I (as always in our conversations) see any reason to go into profoundly personal matters unless he broached them himself. Thus I was able to form an opinion about this subtlety only when I was in New York, and I intended to bring it up for discussion during our proposed meeting that summer. I reminded him of our correspondence about the book by Franz Borkenau (*Briefe* 2, pp. 625–35), which the Institute had launched very pretentiously in 1934 and which I had regarded as more philosophical *chutzpah* than a stringent Marxist analysis, and I asked him whether the work of the Institute still was proceeding along these lines. I told him that Horkheimer's programmatic essays about what was now being circulated under the code word "critical theory" (for the word Marxism, which, as Benjamin explained to me, was now taboo for political reasons) had failed to enlighten me in this regard. (Only in New York did I learn from Adorno that they had realized in the meantime the flimsiness of this bulky concoction.)

During our discussion of this situation and the specific conditions and possible limitations of Benjamin's work, I brought up the subjects that, although important for Benjamin, were bound to be unmanageable or indigestible from the standpoint of the Institute —such as Benjamin's continuing and passionate interest in Kafka's works. Here Benjamin made an unexpected revelation. He said that he would feel greatly liberated if he were able to be completely independent of the Institute for a protracted period (he mentioned at least two years). He said that this was out of the question in Europe, but if I saw a way of procuring for him an assignment that would guarantee him this independence, he would not hesitate to sever his ties with the Institute for a prolonged period or permanently. Considering the major Kafka edition that was being published by Schocken Verlag, did I see any possibility of suggesting or procuring such an assignment, a book about Kafka? He said he was ready at any time to come to Palestine for the entire period required for such a work. A week earlier I had met with Schocken in Zurich, and we had had a long conversation about the orientation of his publishing house and the lively interest that he took in my own work. He had just published a Hebrew book by me about an important manuscript in his collection, a book I had dedicated to him on the occasion of his sixtieth birthday, and he seemed to be disposed to listen to recommendations from me. My conversation with Benjamin had convinced me that he was under greater pressure than I had assumed, and I proposed that Max Brod's Kafka biography, which was then about to appear, serve as the occasion for approaching Schocken. Benjamin readily agreed to this. A short time previously Benjamin had mentioned to Adorno, who had just moved to New York, the necessity of defending values in Europe, but no such thing came up in his conversation with me.

In our conversations about the Institute we touched upon its position—for the uninitiated an impenetrable one—toward communism as then manifested in the perspective of the Moscow trials, and also spoke about the attitude of the group around the Institute toward the Communist party. From Benjamin's rather mysterious formulations I could get no clear sense of the real situation and was not sure who was a Communist and who was not, who was a Trotskyite and who a Stalinist. Benjamin's own attitude astonished me and led me to surmise that it reflected the stance of those at the Institute. He expressed himself very tortuously and would not commit himself in any way, so our conversation was not at all gratifying. I expected him to say something about Asja Lacis, but since he did not mention her name I avoided bringing it up. I had no idea, of course, that she was herself among the victims of the great purge, and to this day I do not know whether she already had been arrested by then or whether Benjamin knew about it. But I can still picture Benjamin's reaction when I let myself be carried away during our stormy discussion of these matters to ask him a very delicate question about the membership of a certain man in the Communist party. Although it was his usual custom to pace up and down rapidly in the room, he suddenly stared at me for a long time with a kind of uncanny resoluteness, only to blurt out an emphatic "Yes" that permitted no further reaction. Afterward I was quite surprised when it turned out in New York that unlike Brecht the Institute group—especially the Jews among them, who constituted the overwhelming majority—consisted with few exceptions of passionate anti-Stalinists. The *Zeitschrift für Sozialforschung* systematically avoided dealing with the problems arising from the Russian experiences and conditions—and in this it was not much different from Brecht himself.

On another occasion we had a discussion about anti-Semitism. When I came to Paris, the windows of the bookstores were quite often decorated with Céline's book *Bagatelles pour un massacre,* which had recently appeared. That was a wild anti-Semitic polemic of more than 600 pages that I, ever an attentive reader of anti-Semitic literature, acquired immediately, though my knowledge of French hardly sufficed to understand much more than half of the author's extravagantly vulgar vocabulary. The book caused quite a stir. That Céline's nihilism had now found a natural object in the Jews was bound to give one food for thought. Benjamin had not yet read the book, but he was under no illusions about the dimensions of anti-Semitism in France. He told me that those of Céline's admirers who were influential on the literary scene got around taking a clear stand on the book with this explanation: *"Ce n'est qu' une blague"*—meaning that it really was nothing but a joke. I tried to show him how frivolous such a recourse to an irresponsible phrase was. Benjamin said his own experience had convinced him that latent anti-Semitism was very widespread even among the leftist intelligentsia and that only very few non-Jews—he named Fritz Lieb and Adrienne Monnier—were, so to speak, constitutionally free from it. He cited a few examples that I am ashamed to repeat, although they are engraved indelibly in my memory. Perhaps it was due to such experiences, which certainly were easy to have in those years, that Benjamin, who himself on two occasions had considered marrying non-Jews, resolutely came out against mixed marriages between Jews and non-Jews at a discussion among French leftists that his good friend Gisèle Freund told me about. She said this had come as a great surprise to her and had greatly perplexed all those present.

Despite such reflections and experiences, Benjamin's great liking for France was unchanged. In contrast to this, I was not the only one to notice an unmistakable coolness and even antipathy to England and America. Benjamin told me at the time that he no longer was capable of adapting. Presumably this emotionally weighted vacillation was at least partly responsible for the failure of various attempts to get Benjamin to England or America in time. In 1946 his former wife, Dora, told me that in 1939 she had tried in vain to persuade him to go to England with her, where she was about to start a new life after the passage of anti-Semitic laws in Italy. She said that he also had cited to her the same reasons that militated against such transplantings.

One afternoon or evening we spent with Hannah Arendt and her husband-to-be, Heinrich Blücher; Benjamin was on very good terms with both during his Paris years. Hannah's position as director of the Paris office of the Youth Aliyah, which sent children to Palestine, had taken her to Jerusalem once or twice, and we had formed a closer relationship there. This Paris meeting among the four of us was very animated. Blücher and Arendt took an impassioned stand against the Moscow trials, and I asked myself with redoubled anxiety what was really behind Walter's noncommittal stance in this matter. To be sure, both were far removed from Marxism, which surely had played a big role in Blücher's past, but Benjamin seemed to attach fairly great weight to Blücher's political and military analyses. In those days I learned that Hannah Arendt had worked on what was from a Jewish perspective a rather delicate subject—namely, Rahel Varnhagen—and was putting the final touches on a monograph about her. The failure of the Jewish emancipation shed an entirely new light on figures like Varnhagen, and Benjamin, who was more familiar with her from his occupation with Goethe than I was, seemed to be very interested in this work.

In April, Walter wrote me in New York (where I was studying the Jewish Theological Seminary's kabbalistic manuscripts after the completion of my series of lectures) that he had now received Max Brod's Kafka biography. He furnished a devastating critique of it in a magnificent sentence (*Briefe* 2, p. 748). I thereupon invited him to write me a detailed letter about this book and his own view of Kafka, which I might be able to present to Schocken in an effort to induce him to commission a book from Benjamin in the spirit of our Paris conversation. This is how that wonderful letter of June 12, 1938, came into being (*Briefe* 2, pp. 756–64); enclosed with it was another letter bearing the same date. In the meantime I informed Benjamin that I had made the acquaintance of Teddie and Gretel Adorno at the home of Paul and Hannah Tillich and that we had formed an unexpectedly close relationship at a subsequent long meeting at Adorno's home. (Adorno's letter to Benjamin about this appeared in the *Neue Zürcher Zeitung*, December 3, 1967.) The accompanying letter reads as follows:

Dear Gerhard,

In order to make the enclosed letter presentable, I thought it was advisable not to burden it with personal matters.

This does not mean that it is not intended primarily for you personally by way of thanking you for your suggestion. For the rest, I cannot judge whether you will consider it expedient to let Schocken read it tel quel. *In any case, I believe I have gone into the Kafka complex as deeply as I possibly can at the moment. For the time being, everything henceforth will have to take a back seat to my Baudelaire study.*

I have seen with pleasure that many things go well as soon as I turn my back. What complaints I have received de part et d'autre *in the past about you and Adorno! And now it turns out that it was a false alarm. No one is more pleased about it than I am.*

One of these days I shall write to Adorno and mention the Kafka letter to him. You can, of course, share it with him. Nevertheless, I ask you to mention the publishing prospects that may flow from this letter only with extreme caution, as though they were your own and not known to me. But your assessment of the situation may make you decide that it will be better not to mention it at all. One reason why this matter should be considered carefully is that the semiofficial character of my letter would not escape Adorno.

You may perhaps explain to him that you induced me to contribute the letter to your archive of my esoteric writings. I fear this explanation may come extremely close to the truth.

In any case, with this document I have acquired the right to receive soon a very detailed report of your peregrinations through Jewish New York. I beg you not to be too laconic in this report, especially since after your last letter of May 6 and my own dispositions the chances of our meeting still remain uncertain. . . .

Most cordially yours,
Walter

P.S. Don't forget to give me your impressions and any news about the Institute.

In point of fact, I read the Kafka letter to the Adornos; understandably enough, it made a profound impression upon them, although they did not fully understand the background detailed here. The good spirit that prevailed in the meetings between Adorno and me was due not so much to the cordiality of the reception as to my considerable surprise at Adorno's appreciation of the continuing theological element in Benjamin. I had expected a Marxist who would insist on the liquidation of what were in my opinion the most valuable furnishings in Benjamin's intellectual household. Instead I encountered here a man who definitely had an open mind and even a positive attitude toward these traits, although he viewed them from his own dialectical perspective. My relationship with Horkheimer, with whom we once spent a long time in a restaurant, was quite different. There was a dual difficulty: I did not at all appreciate Horkheimer's essays in the *Zeitschrift für Sozialforschung,* and, perhaps under the influence of my Paris conversations with Benjamin, personal contact with him did not inspire any confidence in me. It was my distinct impression that Horkheimer —that is, his Institute—recognized Benjamin's intellectual potential but could not achieve any real contact with the man. Even much later, many years after Benjamin's death, several encounters with Horkheimer only confirmed this impression in me.

Adorno and Horkheimer urged me to pay a visit to the Institute. Since this was in keeping with Benjamin's desires, I agreed after prolonged hesitation and in July went there for a rather lengthy visit. On that occasion I had exhaustive discussions about Benjamin with several associates, including Leo Löwenthal, who was known to me from my Frankfurt period in 1923. I also made the acquaintance of Herbert Marcuse, at that time the Hegelian of the Institute. The impressions I received in these so varied encounters and conversations are contained in my report to Benjamin (of November 8, 1938), where I also shared with him my opinion of his position and prospects in the Institute, an evaluation in which positive and negative aspects commingled. Benjamin's reply (*Briefe* 2, p. 803) clearly reveals his agreement with my judgment.

Although Benjamin in June had still counted on the possibility of returning to Paris in August and meeting with my wife, Fania, and me, he informed me in July that this plan was frustrated by the exigencies of his work (the first draft of his essay on Baudelaire). He actually remained in Denmark until the middle of October. The controversies surrounding the text he produced and sent me in early 1939 with a request for my reaction have played a considerable part in the literature on Benjamin, and some of them were quite unfair. In this context I shall say only that to my mind the accusations that have been made against Adorno and his critique are ludicrous.

As I had had such high hopes for our reunion, its cancellation constituted a great disappointment. For my days in Paris, Benjamin initially suggested that I stay with his sister, or, if that could not be arranged, that I go to the Hôtel Littré, not far from the rue de Rennes, where he was well known. How great was my surprise when it turned out that we had landed in a hotbed of French fascism, where the concierge and quite a few of the guests gave us strange looks and the only available newspaper was the *Action*

Française. It has remained a mystery to me how Benjamin could have steered us there. We got together with Hannah Arendt on several occasions, and I remember a long conversation about Benjamin, his genius, and his unfortunate situation in connection with his position toward the Institute. Hannah Arendt had a profound aversion to the circle around the Institute, particularly Horkheimer and Adorno (the feeling was mutual). She indulged in gloomy speculations about the Institute's conduct toward Benjamin, which far exceeded my own reservations and which she did not conceal from Benjamin.

After my return to Jerusalem, Benjamin impatiently expected not only a lengthy report about America and the Institute (he spiritedly complained as early as the end of September 1938 that he had not received one) but also about the results of my intervention with Schocken. But Schocken had not yet arrived in the country, and I was not able to speak with him about my proposal to commission a book on Kafka from Benjamin until the end of the year and the beginning of 1939. It turned out, however, that Schocken, whom I gave various of Benjamin's writings to read— among them the unpublished article on Goethe, the complete text of the long essay on Kafka (only half of which had appeared in print), and the letter to me about Kafka—had absolutely no appreciation of Benjamin. This came as a surprise to me, as I had expected a man like Schocken to have a particular appreciation of such an intellect. In two or three long discussions I tried to explain to him what I saw in Benjamin and how I imagined the solution of the obvious conflict in his production. Schocken, however, made fun of these writings and gave me a lecture in which he declined to support Benjamin, concluding that Benjamin was something like a bogeyman of my own invention. I could not very well report these sad conversations between Schocken and me to Benjamin if I did not wish to enrage him, so I had to limit myself to telling him the result. Before I was able to do so, however, Benjamin's situation had come to a head in a dual sense. In November 1938 the *Zeitschrift für Sozialförschung* had declined to publish the study of Baudelaire he had written that summer, and when in February 1939 he offered to send me the manuscript for my reaction, he wrote me that he had to resume work on the study without delay;

this shaped up as a revision of the rejected chapters or a resumption with entirely new motifs. In addition to Adorno's very detailed critique, which he had before him, he expected my reaction to benefit his future work. He thought that my critique "might be related [to Adorno's] in important points." But another factor was added to the delicate situation in which this rejection had placed him. On March 14 he wrote me the following letter; I need not detail how much it upset me, especially within the context of my unsuccessful efforts with Schocken.

Dear Gerhard,

While you still have sundry cargo of ideas from my last letter lying at anchor and waiting to be unloaded, this new boat is setting out to sea freighted far beyond the load line with much heavier cargo —my heavy heart.

Horkheimer informs me that the Institute is in the greatest difficulty. Without stating a definite date, he prepares me for the end of the subvention that has been my sole subsistence since 1934. Your eyes did not deceive you, and your obedient servant never assumed for a moment that they did. To be sure, I did not foresee any catastrophe. As their letter indicates, these people did not live on the interest, as one would assume in the case of a foundation, but on the capital. The major portion of this is said to be still available but immovable, and the rest is supposed to be almost used up.

If you can accomplish anything with Schocken, it should be done without delay. The documentation you need to bring up the Kafka plan is in your hands. I would, of course, have to accept any other assignment he may be able to give me within the range of my possibilities.

There is no time to lose. What kept me plugging along in earlier years was the hope of someday getting a halfway decent position at the Institute. What I mean by halfway decent is my minimal subsistence of 2,400 francs. To sink below this level again would be hard for me to bear à la longue. For this the charms exerted on me by this world are too weak and the prizes of posterity too uncertain.

The important thing is to survive an interim period. At some future time these people probably will distribute some money. It would be desirable still to be around on that occasion.

Do not give these things more publicity than may be necessary to help me. If I can manage to show Horkheimer and Pollock that they are not the only ones who look after me, there is a chance they will exert themselves in my behalf.

This is all for today. Don't keep me waiting for an answer, provisional though it may be.

Most cordially yours
Walter

P.S. I had just signed this letter when yours of March 2 came. In the minimal inventory of my chances I had regarded Schocken as one of the more likely ones. Perhaps you will think of something to replace it. I was pleased to notice that without knowing my present prospects you have kept my visit to Palestine in mind. The way things seem to shape up now, the question of whether it will be possible to assure me sustenance in Palestine for a number of months becomes important. (I don't imagine that this can be financed from your own funds.) As things stand, among the various danger zones into which the earth is divided for the Jews, France currently is the most dangerous for me, because here I am completely isolated economically.

In a later letter I shall go into your comments on "Baudelaire." At a first reading most of them seemed very much worth considering to me.

In response to this letter, which left nothing to be desired in the way of gravity, I made an attempt among a small circle of people in Jerusalem to raise the sum that might make possible Benjamin's aforementioned sojourn. The situation at that time hardly could have been more unfavorable. The only dependable person who was ready to contribute an appropriate amount of money was the painter Anna Ticho, whom I had introduced to Benjamin in Paris a year earlier; he had made a great impression on her. Thus I could not promise him anything really definitive. His (partially published) answer of April 8 left no doubt that he regarded his situation as desperate and considered suicide if his economic position deteriorated markedly. I had no way of knowing specifically what was going on between him and the Institute. Benjamin did not believe it would be possible for him to move to the United States.

"Such a move would be possible only on the basis of an invitation, and such an invitation would be possible only at the instigation of the Institute. You probably know that the quota is filled for the next four or five years. I regard it as very questionable whether the Institute, even if that were in its power, would want to suggest such an invitation at this time. For it cannot be assumed that this invitation would solve my financial problems, and to see such problems raised in its immediate vicinity presumably would be particularly annoying to the Institute." Benjamin did not conceal from me that the situation that had arisen made it difficult for him to do "work oriented toward the Institute" (*Briefe* 2, p. 810). He once more wrote about a possible trip to Palestine and what steps were conceivable in this direction. "If a stay in Palestine becomes economically possible, I can count on financing the trip from here." That was the atmosphere in which the new version—Benjamin called it an *Umformulierung* [reformulation]—of the Baudelaire essay came into being during the ensuing months. Benjamin fell silent for many months. Hannah Arendt, who also had made efforts in his behalf after that ominous news, wrote me in late May: "I am very worried about Benji. I tried to procure something for him here and failed miserably. Yet I am more than ever convinced of the importance of securing him a living for his further work. To my mind, his production has changed down even to stylistic details. Everything comes out much more definitely, much less hesitantly. It often seems to me as though he is only now getting to the things that are decisive for him. It would be horrid if he were impeded in this."

It turned out that the situation was not as desperate as Benjamin had viewed it and that the behavior of the Institute toward him was far more positive than he and others had feared. His stipend was not discontinued, and with brief interruptions he remained in Paris all summer and finished his Baudelaire essay, forgoing an invitation to Sweden. About a week after the outbreak of the war I wrote him a very worried letter to Paris; I did not hear from him until November 25, following his discharge from the camp. He wrote me that he had lost a great deal of weight but felt fine. The revised version of his study of Baudelaire, he said, had met with great acclaim in New York. His (published) letter of January 11, 1940, contained only veiled allusions to the shock that the Hitler-Stalin Pact had given him; he spoke of "activities of the zeitgeist that have provided the desert landscape of these days with markings unmistakable for old Bedouins like us" (*Briefe* 2, p. 846). But Grete Cohn-Radt later told me that when he returned from the camp at the end of 1939 he had informed her that he was actually relieved to be finished with Russia for good now, for he had never been comfortable with this relationship. This confirms a report by Soma Morgenstern, to whom Benjamin read his theses on the philosophy of history, written in early 1940, as an answer to this pact. The sentence following the veiled statement in the last letter that reached me must refer to the passionate discussions on Russia and Marxism that we had had in Paris two years earlier: "Even though it is sad we cannot converse with each other, I do feel that the circumstances [i.e., our physical separation] by no means deprive me of such fiery disputations as used to take place between us from time to time. Today there no longer is any reason for them. And perhaps it is even proper to have a small ocean between us when the moment comes to fall into each other's arms *spiritualiter.*" When he wrote this, he was mulling over the projected "Thesen" and must have assumed that they eliminated any reason for the differences of opinion that had been the subject of such fiery disputations between us.

In the spring of 1940 he sent me a copy of the "Thesen," but like the letter that presumably accompanied the manuscript, this never reached me. Hannah Arendt, who told me this, assuming I had received these things, wrote me that because of his wholly unorthodox latest "Thesen" Benjamin had been "rather afraid of the opinion and reaction of the Institute from the beginning." The Institute did not receive different versions of the text from Hannah Arendt and Martin Domke until 1941; the latter was published in 1942, in the Institute's mimeographed memorial publication for Benjamin. It is certain, however, that in his correspondence with the Adornos and Horkheimer regarding the "Thesen," which he was going to send them in May (he never got a chance to do so), Benjamin particularly emphasized the continuity of this study with the ones he had done previously for the Institute. This was as much a fact as the far-reaching, daring new ideas that were to place historical materialism under the protection of theology.

In early January 1940 there appeared the voluminous double issue of the *Zeitschrift für Sozialforschung,* which he had urged me to peruse in his letter of January 11, 1940—not only because of the two major essays of his that it contained (the offprints he sent me later would have sufficed for that), but because he wanted to hear my opinion of Horkheimer's essay "Die Juden und Europa" [The Jews and Europe]. That was an unpleasant matter. The extent of Benjamin's accommodation to the Institute, even in the case of a subject that by no means placed him under any pressure, hardly could be better documented than by our antithetical reactions to this essay. I was not aware of this at the time because, as already mentioned, the letter that must have contained his response never reached me. The extant correspondence with Horkheimer and Adorno reveals that Benjamin expressed his complete approval to both of them; I, however, who knew somewhat more about the subject, rejected the essay with the greatest vehemence. I still possess the first draft of that part of my long letter of February 1940, in which I threw open for discussion various questions that had been raised by this issue and especially its important article on Jochmann. I assume that this draft differed only slightly from the letter I actually sent. The subject was explosive enough to warrant a clear stand. This is what I wrote:

You wish to learn my opinion of Horkheimer's essay "Die Juden und Europa." After repeated readings I do not find it difficult to give it an easily understood formulation: this is an entirely useless product about which, astonishingly enough, nothing beneficial and new can be discovered. The author has neither any knowledge of nor any interest in the Jewish problem. It is obvious that at bottom no such problem exists for him. Thus it is only out of propriety that he deigns to express himself on this subject in passing. A comparison with Marx's essay "Zur Judenfrage" [On the Jewish question], of which exactly the same thing is true, readily suggests itself, and more than that: I am in all modesty of the opinion that the author wanted to rewrite Marx's essay (which evidently appears very profound to him) mutatis mutan-

dis: *for the situation that exists 100 years after Marx (years that not exactly have shown the wisdom of that—repulsive—essay in the best light, no matter how fashionable it once was to quote from it).*

The man explains nothing—except for a banality that for years one has been able to read in every Jewish provincial paper for the little man: in the totalitarian state the Jews are being deprived of the old economic foundations of their existence. This is true and not new. But on the subject itself the author has nothing whatever to say. Nor does he deal with the subject that he announces—"The Jews and Europe"—with a single sentence (he almost tries to show it has nothing to do with Europe but that fascism is already lurking everywhere), although to my mind this is a real problem—the elimination of the Jews from Europe—whose meaning and significance he does not see and presumably is incapable of seeing. He does not ask for the Jews: *what will they be like when they are deprived of this soil, after terrible demoralizations and strategies of annihilation (he does not even care about this, for the Jews interest him not* as Jews *but only from the standpoint of the fate of the economic category that they represent for him—as "agents of circulation," p. 131). Nor does he ask* for Europe: *what would a Europe actually look like after the elimination of the Jews? Though there would be all sorts of questionable things in this. It is in keeping with this spirit that he has no* answer *of any kind to give to the Jews, for whom he does not even* ask—*except for the facile final phrase with the horrible allegorization of monotheism, which obviously has nothing to say to the* unallegorizable *Jew and* his *concerns within mankind. How this man would poke fun at others who employed such a mode of thinking as "answers"!! (In the foreign-language summaries the whole, somewhat ludicrous helplessness of this final recommendation becomes even more apparent!).* . . . *The man makes it easy for himself, in an underhanded way.* "Politically *speaking, pogroms are aimed more at the onlookers—to see whether someone will make a move," etc. Well, with such wisdom dialectics is prostituted, and all I can say is that anyone who has such an idea on the* meaning *of pogroms has no right to offer anything on the subject. The* style *of Horkheimer's writings has always been repugnant to me because of a certain brash impudence of instrumentation, and in this essay that impudence has unfortunately now found its way home in the most exact sense of the word. This* Jew *is the last person who has the stuff for an unsentimental analysis (one that covers the subject itself and not its most decayed emblems) of "The Jews and Europe," the genuine question that concerns us, you and me, equally and decisively. As words addressed to the Jews in the Second World War, the essay leaves one* "ratlos wie Geisterrede" *[disconsolate like spectral speech], to quote Benjamin.*

Many years later I learned from Adorno that the title that had so enraged me because of its unrelatedness to the article's contents was not by Horkheimer but by Adorno! In fairness it must be added that later, after the murder of millions of Jews, Horkheimer decisively changed his Jewish position.

This was probably the last direct communication between Benjamin and me. I awaited his response with great suspense, and to this day I have no idea what it was like. Only in 1941 and 1942 did I learn from letters from Adorno and Hannah Arendt how Benjamin fared in those months before and after his flight from Paris. After all I have told here it is evident that Walter repeatedly reckoned with the possibility of his suicide and prepared for it. He was convinced that another world war would mean a gas war and bring with it the end of all civilization. Thus what finally happened after he crossed the Spanish border was not a surprising irrational act but something he had prepared inwardly. Despite all the astonishing patience he displayed in the years after 1933, combined with a high degree of tenacity, he was not tough enough for the events of 1940. As late as September, he mentioned his intention of committing suicide to Hannah Arendt on several occasions. The only authentic information about the events connected with his death is found in a detailed report written on October 11, 1940, by Frau Gurland, who crossed the border together with him, to Arkadi Gurland, a member of Horkheimer's Institute. I received a copy of this letter from Adorno in 1941.

From Frau Gurland's letter of October 11, 1940:

. . . In the meantime you must have heard about our terrible experience with Benjamin. He, José, and I left Marseilles together in order to share the trip. In M. I became rather good friends with him, and he found me suitable as a traveling companion. On the road through the

*Pyrenees we met Birmann, her sister Frau Lipmann, and the Freund
woman from* Das Tagebuch. *For all of us these 12 hours were an
absolutely horrible ordeal. We were totally unfamiliar with the road;
some of it we had to climb on all fours. In the evening we arrived at
Port Bou and went to the police station to request our entry stamps.
For an hour, four women and the three of us sat before the officials
crying, begging, and despairing as we showed them our perfectly good
papers. We were all* sans nationalité, *and we were told that a few days
earlier a decree had been issued that prohibited people without nation-
ality from traveling through Spain. They permitted us to spend a night
in the hotel,* soi-disant *under guard, and we were introduced to three
policemen who were supposed to escort us to the French border in the
morning. The only document I had was the American one; for José and
Benjamin this meant that they would be sent to a camp. So all of us
went to our rooms in utter despair. At 7 in the morning Frau Lipmann
called me down because Benjamin had asked for me. He told me that
he had taken large quantities of morphine at 10 the preceding evening
and that I should try to present the matter as illness; he gave me a
letter addressed to me and Adorno TH. W . . . [sic] Then he lost
consciousness. I sent for a doctor, who diagnosed a cerebral apoplexy;
when I urgently requested that Benjamin be taken to a hospital, i.e.,
to Figueras, he refused to take any responsibility, since Benjamin was
already moribund. I now spent the day with the police, the* maire, *and
the* juge, *who examined all the papers and found a letter to the
Dominicans in Spain. I had to fetch the* curé, *and we prayed together
on our knees for an hour. I endured horrible fear for José and myself
until the death certificate was made out the next morning.*

*As previously arranged, the gendarmes called for the four women
on the morning of Benjamin's death. They left José and me in the hotel
because I had come with Benjamin. Thus I was there without a* visa
d'entrée *and without customs control; the latter took place in the hotel
later. You know Birmann and can judge our situation when I tell you
that when she and the others arrived at the border up there, they refused
to go on and said they agreed to be returned to the detention camp in
Figueras. Meanwhile I had gone to the police station with a certificate
from the doctor, and the chief was very impressed by Benjamin's
illness. So the four women received their stamps. (Money also changed
hands, and quite a bit of it.) I received my stamp the next day. I had*

to leave all my papers and money with the juge *and asked him to send everything to the American consulate in Barcelona, which Birmann had telephoned. (The people there refused to do anything for us, despite a lot of explanations.) I bought a grave for five years, etc. I really can't describe the situation to you any more exactly. In any case, it was such that I had to destroy the letter to Adorno and me after I had read it. It contained five lines saying that he, Benjamin, could not go on, did not see any way out, and that he [Adorno] should get a report from me, likewise his son.*

I learned about Benjamin's death, on September 26 or 27, on November 8 in a brief letter—dated October 21, 1940—from Hannah Arendt, who was then still in the south of France. When she arrived at Port Bou months later, she sought Benjamin's grave in vain. "It was not to be found; his name was not written anywhere." Yet Frau Gurland had, according to her report, bought a grave for him in September for five years. Hannah Arendt described the place: "The cemetery faces a small bay directly overlooking the Mediterranean; it is carved in stone in terraces; the coffins are also pushed into such stone walls. It is by far one of the most fantastic and most beautiful spots I have seen in my life."

Many years later, in the cemetery that Hannah Arendt had seen, a grave with Benjamin's name scrawled on the wooden enclosure was being shown to visitors. The photographs before me clearly indicate that this grave, which is completely isolated and utterly separate from the actual burial places, is an invention of the cemetery attendants, who in consideration of the number of inquiries wanted to assure themselves of a tip. Visitors who were there have told me that they had the same impression. Certainly the spot is beautiful, but the grave is apocryphal.

APPENDIX

Correspondence from the Spring of 1931
concerning historical materialism

(GERHARD SCHOLEM TO WALTER BENJAMIN)

Jericho, March 30, 1931

Dear Walter,

I am staying in Jericho for a week, occupied with loafing and the like in preparation for next week's visit of my mother and brother in Jerusalem; tomorrow morning I am taking a little trip to the Dead Sea, where I have never been in all these years. In the midst of my idleness the copies of your letters to [Bertolt] Brecht and [Max] Rychner arrived; these have to take the place of an "original letter," then. Your letter to Brecht confirms my long-harbored expectation that the periodical you wrote me about cannot amount to anything, although in ignorance of the details I could not say much about it. I would like to make some comments about the other letter, however, for I feel it is, so to speak, addressed to me as well. I am very sorry not to be acquainted with Rychner's essay, which perhaps contains real insights. But what can be said about your letter is presumably independent of it—the question dic cur hic? ["Say why you are here"—a

· 227 ·

medieval proverb] is, in any case, well formulated. I beg you to consider my remark in the same spirit of benevolence, as an abbreviation you had a right to expect of the reader of that letter.

Since my first acquaintance with more or less extensive samples from your pen of those reflections on literary matters in the spirit of dialectical materialism, I have realized ever more clearly and distinctly that with this production you are engaging in a singularly intensive kind of self-deception. In particular, your admirable essay on Karl Kraus (which unfortunately I do not have with me here) documents this for me most significantly. The expectation expressed by you that a reader who evidently is a man of insight, like Herr Rychner, will know how to read "between the lines" of this essay a justification for your sympathies for dialectical materialism in any sense at all seems altogether illusory to me. Rather, the very opposite will be the case, and this is what I mean: it seems to me it is clear to any objective reader of your writings that though in recent years you have tried— frantically, if you will pardon the expression—to present your insights, some of them very far-reaching, in a phraseology that is as close as can be to the Communist kind, there is (and this is what seems to me to matter) an astonishing incompatibility and unconnectedness between your real and your pretended modes of thought. You gain your insights not through strict application of a materialistic method but quite independently of it (at best) or (at worst, as in some writings of the last two years) by playing with the ambiguities and dissonances of this method. As you very aptly write to Herr Rychner, your original and solid insights grow out of what we succinctly can call the metaphysics of language, and this is exactly what could make you, once you attain undisguised clarity, a very important figure in the history of critical thought, the legitimate bearer of the most fruitful and most genuine ongoing traditions of a Hamann and a Humboldt. Your ostensible efforts, however, to put these results within a framework in which they suddenly appear as sham results of materialistic reflections introduce a completely alien formal element that any intelligent reader can easily detach, which stamps your output of this period as the work of an adventurer, a purveyor of ambiguities, and a card-sharper. You will understand that I use such demonstrative expressions only with the greatest reluctance. But when I think, for example, of the downright fantastic discrepancy in as magnificent and central a work as the Kraus essay between the true method and the method presented by the terminology, when I consider how suddenly every-thing becomes lame because the insights of the metaphysician about the language of the bourgeois—*in fact, even about the language of capitalism—in an artificial and therefore all too transparent manner* are identified with those of materialism about the economic dialec-tics of society *(so much so that they seem to derive from each other!), then I am dismayed to have to tell you that this self-deception is possible only because you will it, and more than that: that it can endure only if it is not put to the materialistic test. I maintain that I am absolutely certain about what would happen to your writings if you were ever of a mind to publish them* within *the Communist party, and this prospect is quite dismal. I almost believe that you desire this in-between state, yet you ought to welcome any means of ending it. That your dialectic is not that of the materialist to which you strive to approximate it would become evident with unambiguous clarity and explosiveness the moment your fellow dialecticians unmasked you as a typical counterrevolutionary and bourgeois—something that would be inevitable. As long as you write for bourgeois and about bourgeois, a* real *materialist will not care (I should say, will not give a hoot) whether you wish to surrender to the illusion that you are of one mind with him. On the contrary; from a dialectical point of view it would be in his interest to foster your illusion, because even he would recog-nize that in* that *area your dynamite could be stronger than his. (If you will excuse the parallel, this is comparable to the way in which the materialists in Germany have encouraged certain psychoanalytic Bolshevists à la Erich Fromm, who in Moscow promptly would be sent to Siberia.) In their own camp the materialists cannot use you, because there the purely abstract identification of your spheres is bound to collapse at the first steps toward the center. But since you yourself are interested in a certain* in suspenso *state of your illegitimate relation-ship—from another vantage point, as it were—you get along with one another quite well. The only question is—to say this too in a fitting manner—how long the morality of your insights, one of your most precious possessions, can remain sound in such a dubious relationship. For even though you may see it that way, it is* not true that you ask *yourself how far it is experimentally possible to go with a materialist's orientation, since it is evident that you never and in no instance have assumed this stance in your creative process, and I believe I may say as an old theologian that you are quite incapable of assuming it successfully. And given a certain robust capacity for decision-making that I believe I can assume in you in this specific case, it is conceivable that your insights (which, as you so truthfully say, were gained in the theological process) can be applied after a fashion to the materialistic terminology with some unavoidable shifts that do not correspond to what is depicted*—dialectica dialecticam amat *[dialectics love dialectics]. Thus you could get along with one another for a very long time —that is, for exactly as long as circumstances permit you to remain in your ambiguity, which can be very long under the prevailing historical circumstances. I deny completely that there has been anything that, as you claim in your letter to Rychner, has led you to apply materialistic thought, to which your production really makes no genuine contribution; I also fully understand that you have arrived at the self-deception that the introduction into metaphysics of a certain slant and terminology—in which there is reference to classes and capitalism but hardly their opposite—make your reflections materialistic. Of course, the sure means of proving the truth of my view—namely, membership in the KPD [German Communist Party]—I can recommend to you only ironically. For as regards the extent to which a strict observance of the real materialistic research methods removes one from the ideal stance of the metaphysical-dialectical scholarship (to vary your formulation)—as a friend I am not easily capable of advising you to make such an investigation, which could lead only to a* capitis diminutio *[execution of your life, i.e., loss of spiritual existence]. I am more inclined to assume that one day this relationship will come to an end just as suddenly as it started. If I am wrong about this, the high price of this error will, I fear, have to be paid by you—which would be paradoxical but quite in keeping with the situation that then would arise: you would not be the last but perhaps the* most incomprehensible *victim of the confusion between religion and politics, the true relationship of which you could have been expected to bring out more clearly than anyone else. But, as the ancient Spanish Jews used to say, what time can accomplish, reason can too.*

About other matters another time. I await letters from you always; perhaps this one will start your fountain pen rotating polemically!

With most cordial regards,
Yours,
Gerhard

(WALTER BENJAMIN TO GERHARD SCHOLEM)

Berlin-Wilmersdorf, April 17, 1931

Dear Gerhard:

It is just as impossible for me to answer your long letter as early as today as it is to delay acknowledging receipt of it any longer. I admire the generosity implicit in the fact that you wrote it by hand; this tells me that you did not even assure yourself of a copy of this document. It will be preserved here all the more carefully; please do not take this to mean "concealed" or "buried." Rather, the fact of the matter is that I have a certain chance of doing justice to the task this letter poses for me only if I prepare a response methodically, and the first step in this direction is to go over what you have written with a few people close to me. There is primarily Gustav Glück, whom you do not know as yet—not a writer but a ranking bank official—and perhaps also Ernst Bloch. Incidentally, it could broaden my base, which is narrow enough to begin with, if you could take a look at Brecht's Versuche *series. Kiepenheuer, its publisher, is coming to see me in a few days; I shall try to wangle a set for you. Incidentally, weeks ago I sent you the very important essay on opera from the* Versuche, *but you did not react to it. I refer to these things because your letter, though not intended to go beyond* ad hominem *arguments, breaks through my own position to hit projectile-like the center of the position that a small but extremely important avant garde occupies here at present. Much of what has led me increasingly to declare my solidarity with Brecht's production is expressed in your letter; this means, however, much in that production with which you are not yet acquainted.*

From the tone of these lines you will notice that your logical expectation that your letter will provoke a polemical statement from me cannot materialize. Nor can your letter elicit any expansive or emotional reaction on my part, the reason being that my situation is much too precarious for me to be able to afford this sort of thing. After all, I would not dream of claiming that my situation is infallible or even correct in a different sense—that of being necessarily, symptomatically, productively false. (Such sentences do not accomplish much, but since from such a distance you have recognized so clearly the great outlines of what is going on here, I must try to give you an idea also of smaller things, of the reflexive overtones, so to speak.) In particular you should not think that I am under the slightest illusions concerning the fate of my writings in the Party or the duration of a possible membership in the Party. It would be shortsighted not to regard this situation as capable of change, albeit under no lesser condition than a German Bolshevik revolution. It is not as though a victorious Party would revise its position toward my present writings in the least, but it would make it possible for me to write differently. This means that I am determined to stand by my case under all circumstances, but this case is not the same under every circumstance; it is, rather, a corresponding one. It is not given to me to respond to false circumstances correctly, i.e., with the "correct thing." Nor is this desirable for as long as one exists, and is minded to exist, as an individual.

Something else that must be formulated just as provisionally is this: there is the question of vicinity. Where is my production plant located? It is located (and on this, too, I do not harbor the slightest illusions) in Berlin W. [West], W.W. [West West], if you like. The most sophisticated civilization and the most "modern" culture are not only part of my private comfort; some of them are the very means of my production. This means that it is not in my power to shift my production plant to Berlin O. [East] or N. [North]. (It would be in my power to move to Berlin East or North, but I would have to do something different there from what I am doing here. I admit that such a step could be demanded for moral reasons. But for the time being I shall not accede to such a demand; I shall say that I, especially I and a great many others whose position is like mine, are being given an extremely hard time. *) But do you really want to impede me with my little writing factory located right in the middle of Berlin West quite simply because of my imperious need to distinguish myself from a neighborhood that for certain reasons I must accept—do you want to prevent me from hanging a red flag out of my window, saying that it is only a little piece of cloth? If someone produces "counterrevolutionary" writings, as you quite correctly characterize mine from the Party's point of view, should he also expressly place them at the

---

*Meaning, by the political instances, the Communist party.

disposal of the counterrevolution? Should he not, rather, denature them, like ethyl alcohol, and make them definitely and reliably unusable for the counterrevolution at the risk that no one will be able to use them? Can one ever be too clearly distinguished from the pronouncements and the language of people whom one learns more and more to avoid in life? Is not this clear distinction, if anything, understated in my writings, and should it be increased in a direction other than the Communist one?

If I were in Palestine, it is entirely possible that things would be quite different. Your position on the Arab question* proves that you have quite different methods there of unambiguous differentiation from the bourgeoisie. Here there are no such methods. Here there is not even this method. For with a certain justification you could call what I call unambiguous the height of ambiguity. All right, I am going to extremes. A castaway who drifts on a wreck by climbing to the top of an already crumbling mast. But from there he has a chance to give a signal leading to his rescue.

Please think all this over carefully. Make me a counterproposal, if you can.

For today, and so as not to keep you waiting, I shall close with my most cordial regards.

Yours,
Walter

(GERHARD SCHOLEM TO WALTER BENJAMIN)

Jerusalem, May 6, 1931

Dear Walter:
Your brief letter embarrasses me a bit because at the end it asks me to take a stand that I cannot take on what you present in it. You describe your situation once more. Well, that was not exactly what I wanted to bring up. I disputed neither the special nature of your situation in a bourgeois world nor one's (obvious) right to take the side of the revolution in historical decisions nor the existence of the sad

*As a member of Brith Shalom.

phenomenon of vicinity or weakness or whatever you want to call it. And you rightly say that your letter is as yet no answer to the matter I am bringing up: namely, not that you are fighting but that you are fighting in a disguise, that in your writings you are to an ever-increasing extent making out a materialistic draft that you simply are incapable of cashing, incapable precisely because of the most genuine, most substantial elements of what you have or are. I do not deny that it is possible to write like Lenin; I simply attack the fiction that one is doing so while one does something entirely different. I maintain that although one can live in this tension of ambiguity (this is, in fact, the cause of my concern), one is ruined by it (to use a very blunt expression for once)—because (and this is a point that matters most to me in your case) the morality of one's insights is bound to become corrupted in such an existence, and this morality simply is essential to life and in no case can be neutralized. You write that my letter concerns not only you but many others with whom you are inclined to discuss it. Well, I can only welcome this, and it is evident to me as well that it concerns Ernst Bloch; perhaps you can already gather this from what I wrote you about his book [Spuren]. . . . You write that I should make you a counterproposal. This could read only as follows: stand by your genius, which at present you are so futilely trying to deny. Self-deception can lead too easily to suicide, and the honor of revolutionary orthodoxy would, God knows, be too high a price for yours. You are endangered more by your desire for community, even if it be the apocalyptic community of the revolution, than by the horror of loneliness that speaks from so many of your writings. To be sure, I am willing to stake more on that horror than on the metaphors you use to cheat yourself out of your vocation.

Most cordially yours,
Gerhard

INDEX

Benjamin, Georg (brother), 14

Benjamin, Stefan (son), 51, 66, 68–70, 73–75, 77, 94, 187–88, 190, 204

Benjamin, Walter, and *Angelus Novus* (periodical), 91, 102–4, 106–9, 112–13, 115; and *Angelus Novus* (Klee watercolor), 100, 102, 108, 111, 178; appearance and manner of, 4–5, 8–9; in Berlin, 3–6, 9, 12, 16, 19, 26, 36, 87, 107, 111, 127, 150, 160, 182, 191; as book collector, 37, 66, 71, 92, 114–15, 189; bourgeois world, views on, 53–55; on Capri, 122–24, 155; and Communism (Marxism), 45, 53, 116–18, 122–25, 128, 134–35, 146, 152, 158, 163–64, 206–7, 209–13, 228–34; death of, 225–26; dreams of, 61–62; experience, concept of, 29, 59–60, 178; and Expressionism, 65–66, 134; family of, 10, 14, 85, 87, 89, 114, 121, 127; *Habilitation*, efforts to attain, 56, 85, 87, 92, 111, 113, 115–16, 121, 126, 129; and Hebrew study, 58, 89–90, 135, 137–39, 143, 149–51, 153, 156, 158, 160, 161; in Heidelberg, 101–2, 111; home of, 6; in Ibiza, 182, 184, 186, 188, 196; and Institut für Sozialforschung, 196, 197–98, 202, 206, 207, 209–12, 215–17, 218–20, 221, 222; language study and linguistic work of, 33, 38–39, 89–90, 92, 106–7, 125, 137, 143, 149, 155, 197–98, 205, 208–9; marital life of, 55, 76–77, 93–95, 99, 114, 121, 127, 157–58, 162; materialism, views on, 124, 168–69, 209, 228–30, 234; military service of, 11–12, 17–18, 26, 34, 36, 46; in Munich, 19–20, 25–26, 32–33, 35, 38, 48, 95, 100, 105; myth, concept of, 31–32, 61; Palestine, views on, 28–29, 116–17, 203–4; in Paris, 37, 51, 67, 126–27, 130–43, 196–99, 204, 213, 219–20, 224; Paris Arcades, projected study on, 135, 151, 153, 155, 167, 182, 198; personal traits of, 23–24,

42, 53–55, 67, 147, 159, 193, 197; political views and activity of, 23–24, 78, 80, 84, 125, 139–40, 164, 188, 203, 213; and religion, 54–56, 72, 88–89, 91, 137–38, 149; in Russia, 37, 123, 127–28, 138, 152; suicide intent of, 178–79, 186–88, 196, 219, 224; and Surrealism, 134–35, 177, 190n; in Switzerland, 15, 17, 21, 39, 42–45, 52–85, 87; will of, 187–88, 191; women, relations with, 55, 94–95, 115, 120, 123, 132–33, 141, 153, 178, 188–89; in the Youth Movement, 3–5, 10, 12–13, 17–18, 20–21, 42, 51, 56, 64, 82, 94, 100; and Zionism, 3–8, 11, 24, 28–29, 138

WORKS:

"Agesilaus Santander," 115, 196

"Analogie und Verwandtschaft" (Analogy and relationship), 85

"Die Aufgabe des Kritikers" (The task of the critic), 167

"Die Aufgabe des Übersetzers" ("The Task of the Translator"), 100, 121, 143

"Der Autor als Produzent" ("The Author as Producer"), 201

Berliner Chronik ("A Berlin Chronicle"), 4, 12, 17, 181, 191

Berliner Kindheit um 1900 (A Berlin childhood around 1900), 190–92, 196

"Zum Bilde Prousts" ("The Image of Proust"), 146

Briefe (Letters), 23, 26, 30, 49–50, 87, 89, 91, 93, 108, 117, 120, 123–25, 150, 152–53, 156, 158–61, 165, 168, 174–75, 177–78, 181, 185, 187, 195, 204–5, 210, 214, 216, 220–21

"Der destruktive Charakter" ("The Destructive Character"), 180

Deutsche Menschen (German people), 63, 202

Einbahnstrasse ("One-Way Street"), 119, 132, 134, 140, 154, 184